# A Seedling of Hope

# A Seedling of Hope

*Optimism in the 21st century
from Prophet Mohammed's legacy*

Dr. R. J. Bagha

ISBN 978-1-7771966-0-8

# DEDICATION:

Dedicated to my cat and pet bunnies.

That should bring my family down a notch and a deserved "tut tut" from you. It is the family, y'know, that encouraged me to keep writing and the reason why you have to suffer this book. This is also true: one of the bunnies cut the wire to my keyboard putting a stop to my ramblings. I looked at the two I have. Both pretended to look innocent. Were they faking to look innocent? I gave up: they always look innocent. The cat often sat on the keyboard and, fortunately for you, the finished product is half of what it would have been. If you want to thank them, let me know.

To my wife with much love for her patience and her insight into the animal world that form significant portions of the book.

To my sister Sabira with much love. Her fortitude in times of adversity, her love for the poor, and her faith in her Creator are lessons penned in this book.

To my parents and in-laws for their unwavering support. To Ghalib and Anver, my uncles, for teaching me to appreciate God's bounties, the Good which is easy to see, the "Bad" for its important lessons in teaching me humility.

**To all animal lovers and environmentalists. You represent the best of humankind and I salute you.**

# CONTENTS

# PREFACE

The light was fast disappearing in the winter cold, as I made my way to the Memorial Park in Sudbury, Ontario. It was January 31, 2017. My shoes sank into the deep snow and I could feel the cold bite above the ankles. Minus 9 degrees, but it felt chillier. As I neared the gathering, the sight of candles glowing in the disappearing light warmed my heart and I forgot the cold.

The winter was not about to deter people, and they did not have to be Muslims to feel the pain; the vigil itself had been organized by non-Muslims to honor those who had died in the mass shooting at a Quebec mosque earlier that week. Six unarmed people were simply attending prayers at a local mosque and were shot at point-blank range; the children affected would never have to wait again for their fathers to come home. They will have wished that last hug had been a longer one.

Those present at the vigil came from *all faiths, including Christians, Jews, Muslims, as well as others.* I am sure there must also have been people who did not have a belief in God, but still they came.

My name was called out. I had not known that I was going to be one of the speakers, but someone obviously knew I would be there, or knew that I was the president of a mosque in Sudbury and may have assumed I would be there. As I quickly made my way to the podium, I saw the police chief, smiling kindly. I do not remember what I said, my mind in a blur trying to concoct an impromptu speech.

But I do remember saying one thing, and I must have repeated it several times: *"**I** **feel** **like** **hugging** **each** **one** **of** **you**"*. These compassionate Canadians warmed and filled my heart to overflowing. *They did not need to be Muslims to feel the pain of others. And there are people like that all over the world.*

Yet, why did other people feel the need to hurt others? What was missing? Was it because of mental disturbance? Was it because of ignorance of the other? Was it fear?

A typical scenario may just be happening if you slip in undetected and peep in through the key hole into a rectangular or oval room in many parts of the world: The honchos in the top jobs are scratching their heads as they sit sipping drinks. They cannot understand why people are not happy with the government. The head honcho, a rich man, stands up. *The people elected an avaricious corporate person to weed out corporate greed.* It all made sense, somehow, but no one could explain how. An absent-minded professor finally figured out how this made sense, but then he promptly forgot his convoluted theory, and so it remains a ***mystery*** to this day. The honcho billionaire traces the line on the opinion poll chart with his finger for emphasis. The line goes up and down a bit and then starts to decline steadily. His finger almost reaches the bottom of the chart and then he pauses. He does not like what he sees. He suddenly flips the chart upside down, and then retraces his finger on the same line going up, then exclaims with confidence, "Now that is what I call good news. It's going up, y'see! It is going up. It's a fact. It's not fake news, as you can see. Let me take a picture…"

"But the words are now all upside down," one of the men ventures hesitatingly. "Won't people notice?"

"If you don't shut up, I will fire you. I have done that many times, y'know. Firing, I mean. *And concocting true things*. Don't you trust me?"

"Sorry," responds the man meekly. "I guess we can always say *'conspiracy theories'* if things don't work out'"

"The elections are drawing near," the leader continues, glaring at the man who interrupted him. Then he rambles on, leaving no room for anyone to interject. "And don't interrupt me when I am speaking. The people are well fed, especially with cheap beef burgers, factory-farmed chickens, and bananas and have plenty of opportunity to buy cheap oil-guzzling toys and plastics galore. It sounds fishy when they say fish are loaded with plastics. Maybe they are right about the fish though, as I've always wondered why fish taste so bland nowadays. News outlets are spewing fake news without verifying with me. Some, however, are now starting to demand protection for the environment and advocating for animal rights. They are all going bananas. They are well fed and fed up; can't win. If we ask them to tighten their belts and change the way we all live, we can say goodbye to comfy leather chairs, the White House, and Parliament. The others who tried it are already practicing *'Adios,' 'Au Revoir,'* and *'Cheerio'* in government buildings elsewhere. But *we* must stay in office. Denying that climate change is happening is not working any more. I tried it. The guys have become smarter. They read, unlike some of us. *I tweet clever gems that arouse climactic emotions* and make them wonder how I was able to get such remarkable information. I do not need to read what I tweet. It saves time. For me."

"Scientists are still insisting that the number, the intensity, and the scale of fires worldwide has something to do with climate change," the same man who had ventured to speak earlier tries again, sweating as if he is on the front lines battling the flames. The others stare at him in disbelief. He must have another vocation to run to or wants to retire early. "What do we say?"

"Say nothing," replies the leader slowly, turning to glare at the pesky questioner who quickly drops his head and pretends to have some important detail he must jot down. "Use diversion tactics to take their minds off climate change and such petty issues. Talk about the wall. Any chance we can talk to North Korea again? Can you dig some *dirt* on the new Muslim politician? A Muslim taxi driver must have done something bad. Maybe he decided to get stuck in traffic for no good reason and made a passenger late for his plane? Surely these chaps are up to no good?"

A non-Muslim physician, an *infectious disease specialist*, is sitting in the back of the cab. He is on the way to the airport and it is getting late. He left his house late, and now they are stuck in traffic. He decides he really can't change the circumstances and tries to relax, but it is difficult. The driver, a Muslim, apologizes that the air-conditioner stopped working. It stopped working this day of all days when it is so hot. The acrid smoke from all the other vehicles drifts in through the open windows. The cabbie hesitatingly tries to make conversation to ease the strain. He talks about Islam and peace hoping that a conversation on peace might help ease the strain. He points to a book on the dashboard and says it is a holy book of Muslims known as the Quran. The passenger says he has read a bit of it and knows how chapter and verses are organized. He asks to see it. The Quran is handed over. He scans the pages.

"I read the papers, y'know," the physician says. "Not many good things in the papers about you Muslims. Yes, we have heard what Islam says about peace. Can you give me the foggiest idea what Muslims are all about?"

"I know some of us haven't really done a good job of representing Islam." He looks hurt, but understands the stereotypic question. He has had to deal with such questions all his life. "Things are slowly changing though. Hopefully, more Muslims will strive to live up to its standard one day." The cars have started to inch forward, and the cabbie leans out of the window to look how far the lines of cars stretch.

"At least we are moving now," the passenger flips some pages of the Quran. The increased smog from the cars, as they inch forward, spills in through the cab's windows. The road—searing hot in the midday sun—and the surrounding high-rises preventing the free flow of air, make the heat inside the cab unbearable. "*It is a concrete jungle, and we call this civilization.* Shade from trees would have helped. Does Islam have anything profound to say about the environment and animal rights? It says here in chapter 30, verse 41, *"Corruption doth appear on land and sea because of [the evil] which men's hands have done, that He may make them taste a part of that which they have done, in order that they may return."* What does that mean?"

"Look at the state of the earth now. We have polluted not only the land but the very air we breathe in. The earth cannot sustain the ravages we inflict upon it. We have caused more damage to the environment in these last hundred years than has ever occurred for thousands of years. We have already decimated *ninety percent* of the big fish in our oceans. The National Geographic recently reported this fact"

"Interesting," remarks the passenger. "However, most humans have only the foggiest idea about air pollution, global warming, and smog. I am willing to give you an ear, to help clear the air. Tell me more about this verse in the Quran that states, *"Then watch for the day when the sky will bring a kind of smoke, plainly visible, smothering the people. This will be a terrible penalty. [They will say] 'Our Lord, remove the penalty from us, for we really do believe.'"* (Quran 44:10–12)

"You know pollution is becoming a very serious issue now. Not only here, but also in France, Australia, China, and India. Sometimes governments have to stop cars and industries and implement temporary stop-gap measures. Most big cities are now forced to take drastic actions and warn their citizens of the health hazards when smog becomes unbearable." The cabbie picks a napkin from the box on the dashboard and wipes his forehead. He offers the box to the passenger who gladly accepts it. "It will need only one major episode like a meteorite strike, or nuclear war, or a major volcanic eruption to shift the balance over and we could have a catastrophe on our hands. We need to stop wasting food and resources. We have become a civilization of "throw-away". *We need to stop ravaging the earth.* We are consumed with materialism. We cannot continue to stay distracted with cell phones, movies, barbeques, and fast motor cars."

"I am starting to like you," says the physician. "I like people who think the way you do. This new virus, **Covid-19**, has taken over the media and our social lives. I was off to speak at a conference on infectious diseases, but I guess I won't make it now. Does Islam offer any insight into epidemics or pandemics or maybe plagues or the concept of quarantine?"

"Funny you should ask that. *Prophet Mohammed, more than a thousand years ago, said that if a plague were to occur in a land, then those who are within that land should not leave it. He also said that those who are outside of the land where the plague has occurred should not enter that land.*" He pauses, trying to recollect from his memory an article he had read recently. "There is an article in the Newsweek edition of March 17 on this very thing. It is written by Craig Considine, a professor at Rice University in the US. You should read what the whole article says."

"I will. It will be very interesting to me. We certainly have a world that's in a mess. A big mess. We are all culpable, Muslims and non-Muslims alike. We have been messing up with the environment. We deny animal their due rights. The Quran makes some serious predictions about the earth. These predictions seem to be almost upon us. But tell me, do Muslims—despite knowing all this—have anything to offer for the state the world is in?"

The above scenarios end with a question. Questions that a run-of-the-mill person, like me, contends with. Questions that non-Muslims want answered to shed light on a religion that advocates peace but some of whose members do the opposite. I am here to answer those questions. It will be a revelation. *It's gonna stun you.* Sit back and relax. I am the right person to answer those darn questions. You do not have to be Sherlock Holmes to figure who I am.

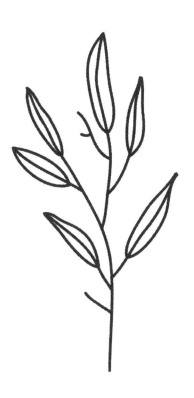

# CHAPTER 1

# FLAVORED POPCORN
# AND MUSLIMS

*"In a time of universal deceit,
telling the truth is a revolutionary act."*

—GEORGE ORWELL

I am a Muslim. *Your hair should stand on end.* You must look behind you, for I am going to change how you perceive some people around you. A quirky in-depth narrative of a Muslim engaging a non-Muslim has been missing in the literary genre, and I plan to make you read in a page-turning fashion.

*I am a destroyer.* What kind?

No, not that kind.

Rather a destroyer of preconceived ideas. Bit of introduction first before I stir emotions: I practice Podiatric Medicine in Regina with a passion for soft-tissue foot surgery. I am a humanitarian, an animal rights activist, an environmentalist, and—if the congregation is feeling emotionally braced for a lively and unconventional sermon—allowed to function as an Imam. I have recently vacated the position of the president of ICONO, a non-profit organization, responsible for establishing a mosque in Sudbury with a team of fantastic colleagues. We provide services to Muslims and non-Muslims alike. Now that the introduction is gladly out of the way, I have some interesting things to tell you. Though I am addressing non-Muslims, a number of Muslims wanted me to clear the fog for some of us as well. "Certainly, I can try. *But the fog is thicker for some who do not understand the Quran,*" I said. "*Can I bring a foghorn for such cases?*" As I waited for the answer, the people had started to run. Maybe they did not like the question, I said to myself. Nope. It was something a chap did.

This chap, a suicide bomber, detonated a powerful vest explosive strapped to the chest. More innocent people injured; the media go into frenzy. Politicians once again promise retribution, thumping their chests with such vigor that forest gorillas, miles away, probably paused from their own chest-beating to listen enviously to the awesome thuds. You also want to know—Grrr! Yes, you do! —what lunacy would make someone go absolutely bonkers and target innocent people.

Muslims earnestly hope the bomber was not someone who belongs to their community, no matter how deranged, for the event will paint all Muslims in a poor light.

When besieged with such negative rhetoric, one does not pause to think that there are 1.8 billion Muslims, about a quarter of the world's population, living in peace. Such hasty rhetoric also allows politically motivated divisive elements within society to emerge from dark closets, blinking their eyes at the light, clutching paint brushes to paint all Muslims with one color, often grayish tones and blotches aplenty due to haste.

Atrocities in which innocent people are targeted make headlines: confusion, frustration, anger, and disbelief dominate our discussions. People are bound to ask: Is this Islam? How are Muslims going to explain themselves this time? Major media outlets, quick on the opportunity, often fail to report with balance, and, wittingly or unwittingly, perpetuate further division among people.

That said, one would think that Islam has nothing to offer the "civilized" world in terms of human rights, animal rights, and the environment. Tragically, one tends to believe that one knows the religion of Islam based simply on observing some Muslims one has had contact with, or by reading about Muslims in major media outlets. After all, isn't Islam to be judged by those who profess to be Muslims?

You could be wrong. I will get into that soon enough if you hang on tight. *The answers are going to surprise you.*

## Sparks and energy

Muslims, together with members of other faiths and non-faiths, have the potential to once again kindle the world with renewed *oomph*. Sparks and energy, just what we need again. But energy and sparks of the other kind; the positive kind that brings people together and not blow them apart. There are challenges facing mankind—from human rights, animal rights, and what should be collective environmental obligations that we are not taking seriously enough—and often these are of our own making; what our hands have wrought.

*We have already deforested vast regions of the earth's surface—the planet's lungs—and we are not stopping.* We are continuing to pollute the air, spewing toxins into the atmosphere and then take stop-gap measures such as banning car use when we can no longer breathe safe air in our major cities. We have nearly decimated the fish population and we continue to bottom trawl, taking everything in, with little regard for sustainability. There are millions of species of plants and animals at risk, and we are busy fighting with each other. The Quran says, *"And the earth, He (God) has assigned it to all living creatures"* (*Quran 55:10*).

Muslims, during the initial six centuries of Prophet Mohammed's coming, did not limit the Quran merely to ritual worship, but also used it as a guide for scientific research, things that today concur accurately with exhaustive scientific research.

The early Muslims used Prophet Mohammed's directives and counsel to forge ahead establishing a vast empire, yearning to learn from the people they interacted with. They learnt and they taught. They opened up vistas of new research. Many current scientific principles were introduced, bolstered, and institutionalized by Muslims.

The formula is to understand each other. If we deprecate a people, in this case Muslims, then it becomes hard if not impossible to work constructively for the common good. *Muslims make up a whopping 23 percent of the world's population. We can use them.* If we can motivate Muslims to do their part in protecting the parts of the Earth, *we all benefit* as we live on this single planet. There are large swathes of forests—the Earth's lungs as they absorb carbon dioxide and provide oxygen—being clear-cut for palm plantations. *Many of these forests lie in Muslim countries such as Malaysia or Indonesia.* We have wildlife trade in exotic species—or their parts—being trafficked from or passing through Muslim countries. Let me give you some specific examples. The species under threat include the pangolin or the tiger populations being decimated in Muslim countries to supply markets elsewhere; deforestation in places such as Borneo (thus decimating Orangutan population to near extinction) for palm oil production to supply consumers in the West; or ivory and rhino horns from African countries passing through ports located in Muslim countries en route to consumers in such countries as China or Vietnam.

*Animals have a right to live on this planet just as humans do.* This amazing globe will no longer be amazing if we prioritize only the human species. The world is a lonely place if we place humans on a pedestal without regard for other species. The only thing that matters to most humans is that these species continue to be exploitable.

Humans, more humans, and billions more humans can get quite boring. No wonder most of us resent formal, mundane, and insincere meetings with small talk. That is because the meeting comes with a large complement of hypocritical humans. You want to trade? Give me a panda munching on a bamboo stick or a cheetah chasing its morning breakfast and I will give you my ticket to the convention with a plethora of tight-collar humans to feast your eyes upon.

*If people from different countries and organizations can come together—regardless of faith, color, ethnicity, or who wears what head cover—then we can make a huge overall difference to all who inhabit this amazing globe.*

Where do we start? We cannot start when we do not yet understand the positive potential trapped within a large segment of people— the Muslims in this case—and continue demonizing them; the loss will not be only a "Muslim-loss," but collective mankind's loss since we are all in this together, inhabiting the same planet with its finite resources of air, water, wild animal populations that are on the decline, and oceans and seas being cleared of marine life. We need Muslims to play their part in safeguarding our natural resources.

*I also want to introduce you to Prophet Mohammed briefly, for unless we know him, we cannot appreciate his concern for mankind, for animal welfare, and the environment. If we can use his counsel and instructions to motivate Muslims once again to care for the environment and give animals their due rights—knowing that Muslims will generally be more conducive to accepting messages that have religious connotations—the faster and better the results.* Yes, we need to know what Prophet Mohammed was all about, and you will be *stunned* at what I am going to tell you. Stunned, because the unsavory cookie baked by bigots is going to crumble, and you will be spared from sitting in their company as they paw the scraps. Some people, in their ignorance, blame Prophet Mohammed for disgraceful acts carried out by some Muslims. This would be like laying blame on the noble character of Jesus for a vile sexual act perpetrated by a priest upon a child under his care. If we cannot blame Jesus, then we equally cannot blame Prophet Mohammed.

*What this book will do: it will tell you some fascinating stories and anecdotes which have deep meaning for the astute observer— gems that one can extract without having to go to Aladdin's Cave and muttering some silly incantations to open a rusty door.* This narrative incorporates bits of **human absurdity** to arouse the senses and **perk the wit.** We all need that, besides coffee. We also need some answers—yes, we do! — on what Muslims are all about since we are not even sure if they are coming or going.

I want like to tell you about devilish political games being played—not that you do not already know the insidious nature of those games and who is benefiting from our silence—but present it from the Muslim perspective.

Lastly, I want to tell you about how important God is in the Muslim psyche, and why it is important for us to know so we can interact with them more effectively. You may think I know all the answers about Muslims, and you will be surprised how much I do know.

## Why, oh why...?

At the beginning of this chapter I said someone nutty detonated a suicide bomb and killed innocent people. Of course, you may assume I have the answer to why this person did what he did. I have the answer.

I do not know.

I have been unable to wrap my head around such a thing that muddles the mind. I cannot fathom why anyone would want to hurt innocent people going about their activities, minding their own business. Most Muslims I talk to are increasingly frustrated as to why anyone, from any religious faith, would target innocent people.

But I have a fair idea as to why some so-called "Muslims" would hurt innocent people. A report by both the International Centre for the Study of Radicalization (ICSR) and a detailed study by the Combating Terrorism Center (CTC) will allay much of the confusion that leaves people shaking their heads, both Muslims and non-Muslims alike. The studies report than more than half of all extremist violent terrorist acts perpetrated in Europe were carried out by so-called "Muslims" with previous criminal records seeking quick "redemption" for past wrongs, often becoming easy prey for extremist recruiters.[1] *The study of the lives of these violent extremists reveals some common patterns: these "Muslims" live outside the dictates of Islam, which enjoins regular charity, honest work ethics, and regular prayer.* Such extremists, if you were to look closely, were often involved in the consumption of strong intoxicants or drugs, gambling, lewdness, or had previous criminal records. In other words, they were not "practicing Muslims"

Since we all share space with Muslims—and since they are our neighbors, professionals, and a large part of the labor force occupying the various strata of a dynamic society with its complex intertwined sharing of goods and services—it is imperative that Muslims be taught the *basic tenets* of Islam.

*My ears just popped because someone created a vacuum by sucking all the air.*

Ah! I see why. The sudden intake of breath and a look of surprise are to be expected, and you will not be the only one registering

1 http://icsr.info/2016/10/new-icsr-report-criminal-pasts-terrorist-futures-european-jihadists-new-crime-terror-nexus/; http://www.independent.co.uk/news/uk/home-news/salman-abedi-manchester-attacker-isis-terrorist-europe-islamist-suicide-bomber-arena-explosion-a7753541.html

bewilderment, "*Really? teach Islam to Muslims?*" Please stay calm and deflate those lungs before something pops inside. I will explain.

A reasonably Quran-educated Muslim becomes a critical thinker and is able to interpret the contexts in which verses are given in the Quran. *Unfortunately, not all Muslims know the dictates by which the Quran asks them to govern themselves. Dictates of kindness, generosity, and forgiveness; steadfastness in times of adversity; charity and social responsibility—all these are too often ignored by the uneducated "Muslim" when emotionally aroused.*

Following the core principles of Islam would make it extremely difficult for Muslims to commit crimes, or fall prey to the extremist ideologies of the unscrupulous, who would find these principled Muslims very hard to convince to harm innocent others.

"Properly Islam-educated" Muslims would be able to counter and resist crude interpretative tactics (taken out of context by demagogues to achieve nefarious ends) by employing sound knowledge. These Quran-educated Muslims would create stability and generate positive energy to the whole of society.

> *Good and evil are not alike. Repel evil with what is good. Then you will find your erstwhile enemy like a close affectionate friend.* (Quran 41:34)

In this book, I will highlight and integrate matters that are of both a religious and non-religious nature to make clear our common aspirations. We all have so much in common. Even on the religious platform, we have much in common. ***Did you know that the "Ten Commandments" apply to all Muslims? Did you know that there is a whole chapter in the Quran with the title "Mary", or that Muslims love and revere Jesus, and that Allah (God) affirms in the Quran that Jesus is of "Virgin Birth" and he is "held in honor in this world and the hereafter"?***

Credit will be given where credit is due; non-Muslim countries are at the moment on the forefront of environmental advocacy and instituting laws for the welfare of animals. *But did you know that Prophet Mohammed, 1,400 years ago, established the first powerful directives for the care of animals and the planet?* More of that later, so keep those socks on.

The Islamic Empire ( and other civilizations preceding it, for we are going to be objective and give credit freely, back-and-forth) produced many scientists, philosophers, and thinkers such as Ibn Sina (Avicenna, 980–1037, Persian philosopher known for his contribution to medicine and philosophy), Ibn Rushd (Averroes, 1126–1198, known for commentaries on Aristotle's and Plato's works), Mohammed ibn Musa al-Khwarizmi (Algoritmi or Algaurizin, 780–850, who helped introduce Hindu-Arabic numerals and algebra concepts into European mathematics), and many others.[2,3]

The scientific establishment has been a bit stingy in giving credit to Muslim scientists, not realizing that we are a single humanity, occupying a single planet.

## One can always blame the ancient lamp

You may look at me and ask, with some confusion, *"Why was I kept in the dark about the various contributions Muslims made to our shared civilization?"* My answer to you is, *"Don't look at me. I had nothing to do with it. Maybe some people had some foggy ideas that giving credit to Muslims would undermine their own institutions. Maybe they childishly thought giving credit to Muslims would give some legitimacy to a religious faith they would rather see subverted.*

2  https://www.famousscientists.org/famous-muslim-arab-persian-scientists-and-their-inventions/.

3  https://en.wikipedia.org/wiki/Ziryab

*Maybe they preferred to peer at Muslims in a dim light or the ancient oil lamp did not work."*

Various caliphates (such as the Mughal in India, Ummayad in Syria and Spain, Abbasid in Iraq, and Ottoman in Turkey) of the **Islamic Empire built great cultural and economic powerhouses**, with remarkable progress in the sciences, literature, medicine, and philosophy. Like many past civilizations, they reached a peak and then slowly started to decline, with greedy despots in different regions fighting to remain in power. Thus weakened from within, the final collapse came with the advent of the Western colonialists.

Alas! Where is it today, "the tolerant and inquiring Muslim mind"? Presently much of this "Muslim mind" is numb, what with newer despots in Muslim majority countries keeping the human and physical resources of the country *"busy"* (I use this lightly) in their greed for power and a grandiose lifestyle.

Only when the inquiring mind is free from constant turmoil— free from the worry of what next will fall from the sky, or if the security at the airport will give him a hard time for growing a beard that makes him look like that guy in the "Wanted" picture stuck on the walls all over the city—does it have an opportunity to engage in the pursuit of the arts and sciences.

The only "arts" and "science" the chap can do when he wakes up today is to decide if he should *artfully* camouflage-paint a hard-hat so that he can blend in with the terrain (with military drone planes buzzing overhead in such places as Afghanistan, Yemen, Iraq, Somalia) or come up with a *scientifically* designed trampoline accurately calibrated to send explosives that are falling from the sky back to the very politicians who authorize extra-judicial killings via drones. **When Muslims were tolerant with an inquiring and open mind, they developed scientific principles that are still used to this day.**

Let us talk of hard-to-digest scientific principles from a comfortable and easy end. If a *relative* came along to discuss Einstein's theory of *relativity*, prodded me with a sharp E=mc² on the side of the belly when I've just had lunch, I will look muddled and unhappy. Even on *relatively* good days, I would have a blank expression if he brought up the theory of *relativity* and asked me to *relate* something on it. I have nothing to do with brainy chaps who confound simple folks like me with brainy things.

The other way to put this to you is: if you were to ask me to jump into the deep end of the pool when I had just came in from our Northern winter cold, and I had been taking swimming lessons last week and the swimming instructor had finally raised his hands in exasperation, I would say to you, *"Wait a bit first. Please let us take things slowly."* Then I would toddle over to the shallow end, dip my toe into the water to test the temperature, go into the water slowly, and swim gingerly to the deep end while holding onto a big rubber duck. I have only one life, and I still love to breathe air.

Therefore, the more immersive core explanations on scientific principles mentioned in the Quran will be dealt with in a later chapter. *If you are the scientific type, too bad. You just have to wait patiently.* I am still trying to figure out how to explain tough subjects without drowning first.

For now, this way here, please. Dip into the shallow end of the pool. Let me introduce you to the state of affairs in Muslim countries. Let me tell you about the insidious power of the dollar and the bizarre connection it has with the oil. This powerful dollar-oil combo is often at the heart of fueling—*fueling?*—conflicts around the world.

But first let me share a little on some everyday contributions we use today that were introduced or bolstered by Muslims in history so that you do not give dark suspicious glances at every person sporting a beard. *Here we go...*

## Hot place, here I come!

Winter was cold and tickets to a hot place were cheap. You probably did not know that when choosing a hot place, you do not go to the Middle East. Too late; better make the best of it. It is hot, yes. Extremely hot. Now you were wishing you were home crunching ice and sitting in an igloo. You have been walking in the desert to observe a little history of the place but all you have seen so far are camels and miles and miles of sand.

The sun is getting to you and you are now starting to talk to yourself. It can happen to the best of us. *"The author wanted to talk about Muslim contributions to science, human rights, and the arts—in history. In history? Why did he say "history"? What of the present-day Muslims?"* you ask yourself, a tad too loudly.

"Many of the present-day Muslims, especially those in some Arab countries are presently relaxing in their air-conditioned homes busy drinking coffee and eating dates as they give directions to poorly paid maids from Bangladesh and the Philippines on what type of make-up to put on their camels for the upcoming beauty contest." The voice seems to come from the heavens and you nearly jump out of your skin. You look up.

It is not a voice from heaven. The voice is piped down by an exhausted maid from the Philippines standing on a ladder applying mascara to the eyelashes of an unhappy camel.

"Why are you up there on that wobbly ladder? It seems you do not want to be up there. Come down. It is not safe. If you don't like your employer, why don't you go home?" you ask.

"I can't. I have not been paid in months and I can't go home even if I borrowed some money from someone else," the maid discloses sadly. "I am held virtually a prisoner what with my passport held as ransom by my boss. That is what their government tacitly allows them to do. My boss is making sure I am overworked while he sits drinking coffee in his air-conditioned tent pitched in the desert. Many present-day Muslims are perfecting the *art* of *not* practicing what they preach. They do not have any time for science as they have tons of money."

"How about Muslims in poor South Asian countries, such as Afghanistan? Are they making any new discoveries in science or the arts?" you query, steadying the ladder as it is wobbling. The camel is not taking kindly to this affront. It does not fancy its eyelashes being subjected to thick layers of paint.

"Not at the moment. They are busy scanning the skies for drones sent in by the U.S.," replies the maid. Even though she is overworked, she maintains her civility. You admire her resilience and you wish she could be accorded the same worker rights as are accorded to all foreign domestic workers in most Western countries. She looks down from her precarious perch. She has a kind face. She is flushed and sweating. "They do not therefore have time to start thinking of inventions and optics and embryology and academia that the author of this book is soon going to subject you to. Please be patient. Relax, drink some water and breathe, for you are beginning to go red. You may suffer heatstroke in this confounded heat."

"Thanks for your concern. I think *you* should come down from the ladder and get into the shade," you empathize, concerned for her health. "I read something about the rights of workers in Islam. It said somewhere that the Prophet of Islam counseled people to pay the wages of workers even before their sweat dries. He advised people to allow their workers to sit with the owners at meal times and eat with them, to share their meals. He, himself—I mean the Prophet— used to help his wives with household chores though he was busy administering a vast nation."

"I know," the maid nods, and as she does, the ladder starts to wobble again. You quickly hold it steady. The maid smiles in thanks. "There is much beauty in what the Prophet advised and practiced physically to educate his companions. His companions applied his teachings well, and Islam spread like wildfire. The first and second generations of Muslims also applied his instructions properly after he died. Islam was indeed a breath of fresh air in a dark world at that time. Then a slow decay set in over the centuries within the Muslim world, soon to be overtaken by the Industrial Revolution in the West culminating with the West colonizing many countries—both Muslim and non-Muslim nations were subdued for resource theft—essentially under the barrel of the gun. This clinched the fall of the vast Muslim empire."

"You seem to know your history well."

"A little," she humbly replies. "Progress through Science and the Arts seems to have been bogged down in many of the Arab states. Maybe it is the oil that has created a huge bog. Science and the arts appear to have been drowned in this bog. *Most Arabs are honest and generous people, it is the rich oligarchs who are the problem,* as if the very oil they produce is not able to lubricate their affairs. *The only country that is meeting the 21st century with Islamic and Arab confidence is Qatar, if you look at the rest.* The others think development is to build tall buildings with foreign labor. That is the extent of many of the Arab oligarch's foresight. If all the foreign workers were to leave, these guys here would not even know how to boil coffee. Let me get back to work. My boss is not a tolerant person."

"I understand," you respond. "I hope that a few good Muslim minds will once again breathe new life into a beautiful religion. These Muslim chaps need to read the Quran and follow the examples of their Prophet to reignite the true legacy of Islam. I can see sparks here and there, especially from the Muslims in the West. Islam may yet spring forth with a renewed renaissance."

"I hope so too," says the maid. It has become rather confusing that on the one hand Muslims say their religion is good, but some of them practice its very opposite. I hope someone can reconcile this obvious dichotomy. Maybe history will give us a brief insight as to what they were and what they left behind. It is time for some iced coffee. Please help yourself from the little Thermos I have under that tree."

## Kahve, coffee, and cough drops

Did Muslims in history contribute to major scientific advances, and do they have any important scientific findings in their Book? But let us not start with deep and complex things. Do you remember me saying something about deep ends of the swimming pool and shallow ends? Okay, good. Let us start at the shallow and easy end:

Fred and Ibrahim, two friends, meet up. Fred worked in the banking sector as a cashier in one of the local banks before it was shut down and the operations moved to a bigger bank at the City Centre. Having lost his job, he took up taxi driving, loving his new career as he could take a break anytime he wanted. Ibrahim also worked as a taxi driver, having taken up the new job when he was laid off as a history teacher in a public school. The small elementary school he worked at closed down and the students were made to move to a bigger school which housed both elementary and high school. It appeared to be the trend now: smaller enterprises being absorbed into mega-projects in a bid to save money.

Fred, who cares not a hoot about complex scientific findings in religious texts, is listening to Ibrahim. Ibrahim has been talking about scientific achievements by Muslims in history. Fred shrugs his shoulders, "Who cares? I am just going to eat a three-course meal that I paid for with a good old cheque, have coffee after, take a shower with my sweet-smelling soap, brush my teeth, and go to sleep. You guys can bicker about Muslim inventions and the origins of things because I have nothing to do with it!"

Ibrahim is not offended by Fred's remark, knowing that his friend has an abrupt straightforward way of talking. Ibrahim continues. "Not so fast, my friend. I think you should skip much of your plan if you are really averse to accepting anything that Muslims have done. The things you plan to do before you jump into bed have some sort of origin with Muslims: the three-course meal, cheque, coffee, soap, and toothbrush, or brushing on a regular basis."

"You are pulling my leg!" retorts Fred, raising his leg and jokingly tugging at his own trouser leg for emphasis, nearly falling backwards. Bring Fred to a party and he will soon have a bevy of enthusiastic listeners surrounding him, amused at his antics, entranced with his vivid imagination and eccentric intelligence.

"I mean it," asserts Ibrahim, undeterred. "Now let us see. Did you know that the three-course meal that you are going to eat—soup first, main course second, and dessert third—was introduced centuries ago by a Muslim person called Ziryab in Muslim Cordoba, Spain? This man Ziryab also created a new type of deodorant to get rid of bad odors and also promoted morning and evening baths, emphasizing the maintenance of personal hygiene. Ziryab is also thought to have invented the early toothpaste, which he popularized throughout Islamic Iberia. The exact ingredients of this toothpaste are not currently known, but it was reported to have been both medicinal and pleasant to taste."[4]

Fred is not to be put off. "I thought colonialist taught the world how to dine when they invaded the nether regions with *disciplined hordes sent to gently maraud and plunder only a few here and a few there, stealing only tiny continents.* They obviously discovered these places. It seems the natives living in these lands had no clue they were on some solid land to be discovered by foreigners. Read it in the history books. It says some colonialist adventurers *discovered* those places."

"Are you sure they were *tiny* continents? Did you say *discover?*" Ibrahim asks, amused at Fred's choice of words.

"Well, some were a little bit big like America, Australia, Canada, and New Zealand," admits Fred. "But surely a fellow called

4 https://www.independent.co.uk/news/science/how-islamic-inventors-changed-the-world-6106905.html

Vasco did lose his way and did discover America. His rusty compass must not have been working due to the salty air of the sea. He must have jumped down from his creaky ship and kissed the sand for having landed on terra firma. He must have called it *terra firma* since he was Scottish or German. Of course, he must have quickly spluttered the sand out of his mouth since kissing the sand is not very pleasant. He probably fell asleep on the shore after his tiring journey. Imagine his fright when he woke up from his nap at the shore and found himself surrounded by natives peering down at him. I think his name was Vasco-something. I am not good at history but I can tell you he must have discovered America. He probably shouted at the poor natives while brandishing his ancient rusty pistol, *'You live in America and I have discovered it for you. I have a pistol (which I hope still works), so don't argue.'*

Ibrahim is fascinated by Fred's visual explanations. "I think history is not your strong point. Vasco da Gama was Portuguese and he did not discover America. And the phrase "terra firma" has nothing to do with the Scots or the Germans. It is thought that Columbus, an Italian, is the one who discovered America, though that is under some dispute. *Regardless, you can't really discover any place for a people who are already living there.* Anyway, did you know that the cheque-system was invented by Muslims?"

"No," answers Fred.

"They called it *saqq*, a written vow to pay a set amount to avoid carrying money across dangerous places," Ibrahim continues. "A cheque or *saqq* made out in a place like Baghdad could be cashed by a Muslim doing business in faraway China.[4] There was no need to jingle coins and draw the attention of highway marauders as the chap slowly made his way to China. If caught, the robber would probably look at the piece of paper written in some mangled Arabic script, and finding nothing of value on the Arab chap and wishing he not starve, would probably give him some of his own coins, a piece of moldy bread and send him on his way."

Fred is still unconvinced about the origin of the cheque. "I thought it was our banking system that introduced cheques so that we could charge hefty interest to keep our people in check. I thought the *cheque* was to keep people in *check*. And I am sure *interest* is quite *interesting* in that it serves the interest of the bankers. Come to think of it, I think *compounded interest* must be the reason folks like me get a *compounded headache*. I know you Muslims have been directed by your religion not to have an interest system because you believe it exploits vulnerable people. That is why your banks cannot repossess houses and become richer every year, but ours do. You guys say you have to give some of your wealth to the poor. How much do you give?"

"We give 2.5 percent of any accumulated savings that has been with the person for a twelve-month period," says Ibrahim.

"Okay," Fred nods in assent. "You guys give 2.5 percent of mandatory charity every year to the less fortunate. I see a problem here. *How can you give to the poor when you do not let people stay too poor?* A guy goes out looking for the poor and comes back exhausted with blisters on his feet 'cos he can't find any. That is not very smart, is it? *Making people exhausted and giving them painful blisters.* How can you give to the poor with that kind of a system? Of course, most Muslim countries do not follow that system now, and your people are now far worse off than we are. You should have stuck to the old system of social justice that your Prophet taught you."

"I wish we had," agrees Ibrahim.

"Muslim countries wanted progress and got involved in the interest system against the command of your Prophet, but see where that has gotten you guys. Look at what the interest system has done to poor countries. They are in a vicious cycle of paying interest on compounding interest without paying a cent off the original principal."

"The interest system has been a curse for poor countries," Ibrahim admits. "It is slavery in disguise. *The only difference is that the Master and Slave are separated by greater distances.*"

"Our banks, corporations, and governments have made the interest system a big part of our economy, even if it is done on the backs of the poor in the world," Fred continues. "I do not agree with all that they do, but I am a part of the system. *We also gave ourselves the power to devalue currencies, especially if it is a foreign country.* We have installed despotic leaders in your countries who do our bidding. *Our printed paper issued by our banks is better than your printed paper even if you put multicolored hues on them.* We buy the trees from you, make paper money from them, and *sell it back to you guys* by putting *fancy symbols* on them, such as the dollar-sign or the pound-sign."

"What are you saying about printed paper? I think you are now starting to spout gibberish. Would you enlighten me?" Ibrahim is trying to keep up with Fred who is trying to make himself understood by hand gestures as if drawing a rectangular piece of paper and making a symbol of what is supposed to be a dollar sign in the air.

"I am saying that gold is no longer the gold standard," explains Fred. "It disappeared like the old genie in Aladdin's lamp as in your Arabian fairy tales. Our currency is not backed by any gold reserve in any Fort Knox where the value on our printed paper depended on the amount of gold reserves we had. Previously, any person with some dollars could come to the U.S. and exchange the paper dollar to get an equivalent amount of gold from our reserves. That meant we could only print a set number of papers and put the exact value on these papers based on our *gold reserves. Then we cleverly de-linked it.* Nixon untied that pegging of the paper-dollar to gold. We can now print papers galore and make money from thin air while you sell off all your oil, until one day you realize you have been seeing mirages just the way you do in the desert. You have been duped."

"Eh? I still do not get it." Ibrahim is trying not to scratch his turbaned head. They were talking about currencies and the chap has gone off on a tangent talking about printed paper and gold.

"You Muslim guys have been duped with the biggest hoax of the century," Fred continues. "Did you know *we own* most of the oil in your Muslim countries? We put some despots in your countries and cajoled them or twisted their arms till they uttered some expletives in Arabic that even a big man with muscles and a strong disposition would blush at, and they quickly agreed to sell oil only in U.S. dollars on the world market. ***This way we can now print dollar bills on a whim and the world has to come to us to buy dollar bills before they can buy your oil.*** Of course, it's not as simple as firing up the printer, as there are certain formulas that go into the dollar equation, the world forced into reluctant complicity. But you have to agree that ***the dollar has taken monopoly over all other currencies. The Arab oligarchs got hoodwinked*** while they were ogling at fancy ladies in our casinos. Then these autocratic oligarchs hoodwinked *you* all. We become filthy rich and you become filthier. You know how?"

"How?" Ibrahim asks.

"We become filthy rich and hand out cents to Muslim countries for every barrel of oil and your workers become filthier extracting the muck from the ground!" answers Fred. "The world has, quite aptly, given our paper the name petrodollar. We do not even have to dig on our lands for oil. We let you do the digging. In your own lands at that! We print numbers on paper and put a fancy symbol like the dollar sign before the number. Ink is cheap. *We force poor countries to sell coffee and bananas at ridiculously cheap prices in order that they can buy our printed paper before they can buy your oil which they desperately need to run their tractors to plant bananas and coffee.* If they go to an Arab country to buy oil with their local currency, they may well be told, 'La, la!' *La* means *no* in Arabic. It does not have to do with a music skit."

"I know. I do know a little Arabic," Ibrahim retorts with a huff. He does not like being thought of as a buffoon.

Fred continues, ignoring Ibrahim's discomfort. "'La, la!' they would say. 'We only sell oil in dollars on the world market. Please go buy some dollars with your devalued currency, courtesy of the World Bank and IMF, and then come buy our oil. You know what happened to Iraq, Libya, and Venezuela when they started to think of selling oil in other currencies, right? They were made to think again. See, Ibrahim? Your folks have been duped into selling oil in dollars only. *once the oil is gone up in smoke, literally, so will the protection the West has been offering their puppets in Gulf countries.*"

Fred pauses long enough for Ibrahim to interject. "Interesting about Iraq and how the Bush-Blair duo made corky stories about hidden weapons of mass destruction. *Mass lies, more like.* There must be a connection with oil and petrodollar and sinister games being played. It looks like the wealth from oil-producing countries will not be used for the citizens of the country the oil is extracted from. Most is already possessed by people *sitting far away* in other countries."

"See what I mean, Ibrahim? It is as if the oil is coming out of *our* lands!" Fred is feeling sorry for Ibrahim as he sees him wincing at the injustice, but Fred feels a duty to educate his friend, and to do it in a way that strikes a chord. "Have you tried a banana with a cup of black coffee? The bitter and sweet combination tastes really good. Our corporations get them at dirt cheap prices just by handing out small amounts of printed paper to some poor African and South American countries for their bananas and coffee. *The value you guys place on our bills is only in your heads, 'cos if you look at it, your paper and our paper are not much different after all. The real value is in the oil, but we make the world believe it's in the printed paper we call dollars.*"

"It does seem like we have been fooled," Ibrahim admits.

"Yes, you guys have been bamboozled. Our banks are smarter too. We even use banks against our own people. Our banks demand surety and they can repossess houses so that we can go on the street close by and give to the homeless poor without exhausting ourselves walking long distances. We engage in a win–win system and get cheap labor as you guys flood our streets, willing to do menial jobs that we do not like to do. The despots in your Muslim countries are doing a fine job for us. You should never read a book called *Confessions of an Economic Hit Man*, 'cos it may give you ideas."[5]

"I see the way you explain social finance is somewhat different from what most people chomping on bananas would want to think deeply about," Ibrahim remarks, marveling at the passion with which Fred makes his argument. "You do make some interesting points. I think I am going to read that book, now that you have mentioned it. I am not going to talk to you any more about banks and financial systems—systems that keep poor nations in perpetual poverty. We should leave this discussion for another day. Anyway, did you know that coffee was an Arab invention brought from Yemen to medieval Europe?[6] They called it *qahwa* and many Sufis used it to keep themselves awake for prolonged ritual worship. You should read its etymology from *qahwa* to Turkish *kahve* to today's *coffee*. I don't know why they changed the word *qahwa* to coffee, but so be it."

"I did not change the word, I swear." Fred is feeling some guilt.

"It's a small thing, really. Don't worry about it," Ibrahim tries to reassure Fred. "It is perfectly okay. I know it is hard for an Englishman to pronounce *qahwa* with its 'q.' So, please feel free to use the word coffee, because if you tried asking for *qahwa* from an Arab, and started with, 'Qa ... ka ... qaka ...,' he would probably give you a cough drop thinking you are suffering from some throat ailment. Don't worry about changing Arabic words to Latinized versions. I personally prefer the word 'coffee' to *qahwa*."

"Do you? That is good." Fred is starting to like the polite Muslim fellow even more. "I like the word coffee and also the taste of coffee"

---

5 John Perkins, *Confessions of an Economic Hit Man: The Shocking Story of How America Really Took Over the World* (London: Ebury Press, 2006)

6 https://en.wikipedia.org/wiki/Arabic_coffee

Ibrahim continues, "Did you know that the type of hard sweet-smelling toilet soap you are about to use today was a Muslim invention in which they used alkali and oils and thyme and other fragrant essential oils to make it lather and smell good? They called it *sabun*, which became *savon* and now *soap*. They used soap not only to be hygienic but also for therapeutic purposes, as some oils warded off certain ailments. You should thank al-Razi and al-Zahrawi for the soap you will use today. Both played a part in soap recipes and healing ingredients incorporated in them."

"Who?" asks Fred. "Too many Als. Al-this and al-that. Why not just say Allan or Alice? Isn't this chap Zahrawi some kind of ancient surgeon? I read something about him in university"

"Wow! Yes! You have an awesome memory!" Ibrahim is impressed. "This chap Zahrawi is also known as '*the father of modern surgery*' for his thirty-volume encyclopedia of medical practices. His medical principles and surgical tool designs were so significant that we still use many of those principles to this day, as well as almost identical tool designs in *modern surgical practice*.[7] Alkali plays an important role in the manufacture of soap. In fact, the word alkali took its origin from the Arabic word *al-qaliy*.[8] Did you know that '*Al*' in Arabic means '*The*'? In fact, many English words with an 'Al' take their origin from the Arabic language, such as algebra, alchemy, and algorithm."[9]

"Okay, okay. Stop, for heaven's sake. I was never good at chemistry and math," Fred says quickly. "I assure you I will whisper a little 'thank you' to whoever thought of putting special oils

---

7  https://www.nationalgeographic.com/pdf/1001-muslim-inventions-ed-guide.pdf; https://en.wikipedia.org/wiki/Al-Zahrawi; https://knowingthetruth. wordpress.com/tag/3-course-meal/; https://en.wikipedia.org/wiki/Muhammad_ ibn_Zakariya_al-Razi.

8  https://en.wikipedia.org/wiki/Alkali

9  https://en.wikipedia.org/wiki/List_of_English_words_of_Arabic_origin_(A-B)

in soap. I like a nice smelling soap too. If the soap has health benefits, then the better the soap, I say."

"I agree. Soap is such a good thing. Besides soap, did you know that practicing Muslims wash and rinse the exposed parts of the body like hands and face and mouth and nostrils five times a day before prayers, important *hygiene rituals* to prevent infections and something to consider in these difficult times with Covid-19 virus and other infectious disease problems upon us? In fact, now that we are facing this pandemic, Prophet Mohammed said something very interesting about such a plague"

"Oh, did he? What did he say?" Fred is interested to know what could have been said more than a thousand years ago.

"*The Prophet said that if one hears of an outbreak of plague in a region, then one should not enter it. And if the plague breaks out in a place while you are in it, not to leave that place.* If you read the article which appeared in *Newsweek* of March in this very year 2020, by Craig Considine, a professor and scholar at Rice University, on this advice given by the Prophet, you will see what I mean."

"Wow! That is amazing!" Fred exclaims. "This is the exact prescription for twenty-first century quarantine practice!"

"Didn't you say you would brush your teeth before going to sleep?" asks Ibrahim. "It is indeed a wonderful idea for keeping teeth in good order. Did you know that brushing teeth was popularized by Muslims? In fact, the Prophet instructed its *daily* use, and encouraged its use several times a day before prayers. The Muslims of the time used branches from certain trees, or roots from certain plants, which produce brush-like bristles at the end of the stick when chewed. They called it *siwak*. Some Muslims still brush their teeth with these *biodegradable* plant materials ritually five times daily, before prayers. Muslims began following this oral-hygiene practice more than a thousand years ago, following the example and direction of their Prophet who strongly recommended its daily use."

Fred interjects, his vivid imagination conjuring what it must have been like a thousand years ago, "I guess when troops were drawn up in battle formation and the ancient Persian army or the Roman army peered at their Muslim opponents apparently gnashing their teeth on some sticks—not knowing that they were simply brushing their teeth—they probably quivered with fear, their armored legs making odd clanging sounds across the battlefield. They must have felt they were done for, facing as they did a Muslim enemy prepared not only to fight with swords but 'tooth-and-nail' as well"![10]

"Ha, ha!" laughs Ibrahim. "You are not only very imaginative, but also very funny!"

"Clanging sounds made by the armor of a whole army, as their knees shook, must have made a quite a din," continues Fred, in good humor, his imagination running wild. "I am glad I was not there. If I had fallen in that armor, I would have had a hard time getting up, with my bad knees and all. I would have kept very still, hoping that nobody noticed I was still alive and peering through the armor."

To a passer-by, Fred and Ibrahim would appear to be having a verbal duel. The fact is, these *two friends* engage in this kind of a friendly tit-for-tat vocal match every time they meet. Had the passer-by lingered a bit more, he would have heard this, "I feel like it's time for some caffeine. Come with me, Fred, I will treat you to a nice cup of coffee," Ibrahim points to a coffee shop owned by a Turkish fellow. "You said you like *Mocha* bean coffee. I will get you some Turkish delights to go with the coffee. Oh, by the way, did you know that the Mocha bean actually originates from a *port city in Yemen called Mocha?*"[11]

---

10  http://www.cnn.com/2010/WORLD/meast/01/29/muslim.inventions/index.html; www.1001inventions.com

11  https://www.independent.co.uk/news/science/how-islamic-inventors-changed-the-world-6106905.html; https://en.wikipedia.org/wiki/History_of_coffee; http://www.iupui.edu/~msaiupui/quran_modernscience.htm

## Overcoming the hunkered-down worldview

Islamophobia, anti-Semitism, racism, gender-bias, preying upon the weak, and oppression in its many guises are wrong. Co-existence and peace despite our differences are right.

Right. Got that.

Muslims must engage with non-Muslims and the world they live in with positive energy, sound reason, and intelligence. An intellectual discourse obviously involves the non-Muslims according Muslims a level playing field—and vice versa, depending on who is the "host" or "home team"—with wisdom acting as the referee.

*Right. Got that too. But aren't we looking for a "winner"?*

Not exactly; the winner is not one party emerging victorious over the other. The parties on opposing sides have been trying to win something, and yet have not been able to pin down what exactly it is they are fighting for because egos and prejudices have gotten in the way. It is so obvious and it has been staring them in the face all the time. What is that thing, then?

Let us suppose **an event like the Oscars** is being hosted; but it is not really the Oscars, as the people don't have fancy hairstyles and wearing uncomfortable starchy clothes but instead are sitting in a haphazard fashion with torn shirts and bruises. The audience is made up of members of different faiths. The passionate faithful have been having a go at each other and are catching their breath before someone repeats, **"My religion is the correct one," and then someone replies, "No, it is not!" and another free-for-all battering erupts.**

The host comes onto the platform. An envelope is passed to him. The audience holds its collective breath as the host peers through a black eye to take the envelope. They want to know who the winner is after all the fights, black eyes, free-for-all brawls, and knock-out punches. They have all been searching for something, and today they are going to find out what that something is before they kill each other.

The host gingerly tears open the envelope with broken fingers, peers from one eye, and reads, "… and the winner is … **Truth**." In the audience, a big man with a tattoo and a missing tooth nudges a tiny but vicious-looking companion in the next seat with his elbow. He whispers through the gap in his incisors, "Who is that? Did he say 'truth'?" The small man (fondling a tooth in his pocket and hoping he is not discovered to have done this to the big man's jaw) whispers back, "I think that is what he said. But I do not see a person with a hat that says '*truth*' printed on it. Let us wait and see what he means."

Actually, they heard it correctly. Yes, the winner is **Truth**. It matters not who presented it accurately. Upon accepting the Truth, both parties will benefit. Truth trumps all. Sorry, I can see your reaction. *I agree, let us leave Trump out of this.* Let me rephrase it. Truth conquers all. Accept the Truth even if it comes from the mouth of babes, so a wise person would say.

Therefore, let us engage. I present my point of view, and you present yours, and we agree to disagree if all else fails. If Truth still wishes to remain enigmatic as we go through the process of unearthing its precise nature, we remain committed to hear out the other.

So, if you are ready to hear me out, then this is what I have to say: When we look at the combined number of the various Quranic references and the validity of each, then it becomes hard to refute the Quran's concurrence with established scientific fact. The Quran often makes reference to a subject, and, as if knowing that we would have questions about its abstruse nature, exhorts us to verify its pronouncements with those who have an in-depth knowledge of the matter being discussed: "So ask the People of Knowledge if you do not know" (Quran 21:7). We often find that the highest authority on the subject has the humility to acknowledge the profoundness of the particular verse referred to them, its various nuances, and can readily appreciate its alignment with the sciences.

Let us take the example of the Quran verse (21:30) that states, "*Do not the Unbelievers see that the heavens and the earth were joined together (as one unit of creation), before we clove them asunder? We made from water every living thing. Will they not then believe?"* For the chronic cynic who is ready to refute this particular verse—because it happens to be from the Quran, and everything Quranic must be opposed—the task is to look hard under every rock under every continent to undermine the verse, trying to collect dry living materials and desiccated worms, making loud noises to appease his discomfiture. The noises are generally louder if he happens to have followers who have previously looked up to him as a leader of sorts. This person will still try to delve into a subject matter that does not fall within his area of "expertise," but he does it anyway, and you will often find him lacing his arguments with mockery if he is cornered with a sound rebuttal.

*This "expert" is like the person who demands an apple, and when he is given the apple, tries to find a mark on the apple so that he can deny that it is a good apple, or end up saying with a smirk, "See that mark? Now what do you have to say about that?"*

He came with the intention of being negative and raising a ruckus. I say to him, "Look and you should indeed look, so that you are satisfied. But do it with objectivity for the apple is wholesome and good, despite your squinting efforts to find fault." If the same verse had been in his own religious book, you would not have seen him looking for a desiccated worm and checking to see if it could produce desiccated worm-babies. He would be busy holding conferences extolling the virtues of verses from his book that have scientific validity.

This chap should be challenging for a place in the Olympic long-jump final, given his ability to jump from one side to the other when verses are switched from one book to the other: all one has to do is put this chap's religious book to the other side of the gap and then watch him spring! Someone needs to pat this emotionally-charged chap on the shoulder and whisper in his red flushed ear that dialogue is not a *simplistic hunkered-down worldview*: "My religion is right, so yours must be wrong."

Dialogue and bridge-building require a more mature approach, and would go like this: "You make some interesting points. I have read the Quran briefly, but I did not really think deeply about the verse regarding the heavens and the Earth being one unit and that God, or some Powerful Force, clove it asunder, and how it may correlate with the *Big Bang Theory*. I have something very interesting to show you from my book too. Here, look at this ..."

The problem is, mature dialogue and bridge-building do not sell papers. ***Sensationalism—and fear—that sells papers***. Better if we can add an *exotic flavor* to make it sharper on the senses.

Nowadays, if we needed to more sell popcorns at the cinema, the way to do it would be to offer sharper tasting flavors than mere salted popcorn. So far, so good, it is starting to make sense. But how do we sell more papers? You can't really put *flavors on papers* and expect people to crumple it up and pop the wad into the mouth. It is a dilemma, no?

No.

***Let me introduce you to "Muslim-flavored" papers.***

## The editor and Muslim-flavored papers

As we all know, bad news, crime, and violence promotes greater public interest and results in sudden surges of newspaper sales, increased advertising revenue for the shareholders, happier fish-and-chip sellers who recycle the local paper's gossip as wrapping for your takeaways, and editors who can once again afford to put expensive jam on their toast.

Pass by the local newspaper company when recent events in the papers have not piqued your interest and peep in through the keyhole when no one is looking. If you are lucky, you may see the editor calling a staff meeting with some pink layoff slips in hand.

"Muslims have been awfully quiet for too long and paper sales have gone down, y'know." The editor is looking at the crime story writer as if he is responsible for the shrinking revenues. *There is silence in the boardroom.* Everyone is gazing at the crime story reporter. Surely it must be his fault? People are going to lose their jobs because the imbecile did not do his properly.

"Don't look at me as if I have done something criminal. I write crime, not make crime!" the crime story reporter retorts. He is determined to defend himself. "I have been going to the court house daily trying to find juicy bits but nothing seems to sell, even if it is a major crime. Give me a Muslim who stole a banana for his sick grandma and I can make it sound like he was brandishing the banana like a pistol at shopkeepers, demanding they give up buying pork, and then watch how our paper sales go up. But nothing of that sort is happening. I suggest we wait a bit before handing out those pink slips. Something is bound to happen soon."

The editor is getting impatient. His morning breakfasts since last week did not have his favorite exotic sharp-tasting passion-fruit jam on the toast. He could not afford it. Plain butter on toast made him grumpy: "Okay. I am willing to wait a few more weeks. *I know those darned Muslims have been quiet for too long.* Just keep your eyes open."

A week later, the editor calls another staff meeting with a wide grin. He motions the crime reporter to take the floor. "Someone did something awful last night. Our paper said a hard-of-hearing elderly gentleman with a hearing-aid heard something. He could not be sure as the battery in his hearing machine had died down. He heard a person shouting in some exotic language like Arabic." *There is a sudden hush in the room.* The crime reporter continues, "The elderly gentleman, who must remain anonymous for his safety, was only a mile away from the area where the crime occurred. Paper sales rocketed. Our revenues are up." There is a general sigh of relief and some applause.

The editor stands up and continues, "This thing happened in the nick of time. I was getting tired of applying only butter to my toast. No pink slips for a while. There is coffee on the table. Feel free. Try the passion-fruit jam beside the toast. You will understand why I spread jam thickly on my toast. It makes reading the morning paper more fun with some exotic-tasting foreign-sounding jam on the toast. It is like the *"Muslim-flavored"* paper. It really arouses the senses."

The crime reporter is first at the table to savor the exotic taste. "Hmm. I agree. This foreign stuff is really good! *What would we do without Muslims, eh?"*

*Give me a crime committed by a person with an exotic name. Sprinkle an ethnicity that one knows only little about. Pour into that mixture a religious background that is somewhat different from the predominant faith. If you can add a color to the batter, the better.*

Hands down: Muslims make the best exotic flavor in the papers.

Millions of regular Muslim folks going to work, schooling their children, eating stale pickles with their left-over burgers, paying bills and taxes, are certainly not going to grab your attention, and if you suddenly found your attention starting to drift as you went through this stale statement, the point is made. Do not put the book down yet, though—there is much that will **amaze** you about Islam that you did not know.

Since good news does not sell, then we have a duty to look beyond the sensational splashy headlines. No section of a people should be demonized wholesale. Sincere members of all faith communities who engage in good works should be acknowledged.

***Muslims, Jews, Christians, and all other faith and non-faith members should acknowledge each other whenever any person does deeds of goodness.*** How many of us know that a recent

*U.K. survey of charitable giving found* **Muslims** *topping the list ahead of any other major religious or non-religious group, with seven out of ten Muslims contributing to charities?* [12]

Muslims are taught that to *display* generosity in order to gain attention diminishes the purity of the deed, and so much of the goodness remains unknown to the human populace; as for the good deeds that are obvious, well, most of the media are unfortunately not too keen to print or broadcast those kinds of stories.

*But bad news, like nasty weeds, spreads and chokes fruitful dialogue and cooperation, the media acting quickly to provide shovelfuls of fertilizer.* This is especially true when crimes are committed by those thought to be Muslims, or profess to be so, regardless of whether they are practicing Muslims or not.

Just bearing a Muslim-sounding name is often enough to warrant condemnation. That is a bit unfair. Where do we begin?

Why not begin at a place that should be common but is not that common any longer?

## Common sense not so common

We are losing touch with basic human goodness and wholesome natural ethical norms. Here is an example of what I mean. To distract one of my wittier patients as I was about to perform surgery on her foot with a local anesthetic, the patient and I were discussing recent events making news in the local papers at the time. As she knows that I generally advocate for animal rights and have animal photos of my African safaris displayed in the clinic, she brought up the subject of an activist who was mentioned in the papers.

This activist was charged with criminal mischief by police and the media had picked up this juicy story. Her crime? Providing

12  http://www.thetimes.co.uk/tto/faith/article3820522.ece

drinking water in scorching heat to quench the thirst of pigs destined for slaughter crammed into a stifling metal vehicle. While the truck was briefly parked, the kind lady quickly went to give water to the thirsty pigs through vents in the side of the truck.[13] My patient made a very succinct remark that I tend to recall whenever I see things that should be obvious, yet which appear to be elusive to some. "*Common sense, it seems, is not so common after all.*"

Visibly relaxed after the surgery and while I was dressing the foot, the patient started concocting a hypothetical scenario of a lady being charged with the potential crime of giving water to thirsty pigs. I joined in. The following conversation is a gist of the scenario we made up, and which provided us with a good laugh at human absurdity.

"Sergeant, sir, we have received a complaint of a lady giving water to thirsty pigs being driven a very long distance in a huge truck. She was giving water to very thirsty pigs in this terrible heat," the confused voice of the policeman crackles over the phone. "What should I do?"

"Charge the driver."

"No, sir. It is the driver lodging the complaint," explains the cop.

"What! Really? Okay then. Charge the owner of the business for keeping pigs thirsty."

"No, sir. The driver wants me to charge the lady."

"What! You can't do that. You can't charge a lady for doing a civic duty out of compassion," retorts the sergeant.

"Sir, the driver is adamant. He wants a charge laid."

"Hmm. I don't know what to do really. He should get chickens if he wants things laid. Ha! Ha!"

"Was that supposed to be a joke, sir?" The cop is unimpressed.

"Yes."

---

13  http://www.cbc.ca/news/canada/hamilton/anita-krajnc-trial-1.3733001; http://www.theglobeandmail.com/news/national/ontario-woman-charged-after-giving-water-to-pigs-headed-to-slaughter/article27079761/

"Sorry sir. Very funny, sir. Your own, sir?"

"My very own. I like humor." The cop rolls his eyes on the other end of the line. The sergeant obviously did not get the sarcasm.

The sergeant continues, " but let's get serious. Let me think. Aah! Got it! Charge the pigs for being thirsty, locking themselves up in the truck, being pig-headed, and refusing to walk to a nearby stream to drink water in this heat!" says the sergeant smugly, feeling pleased with himself, and hangs up the phone.

The amazing thing is that in the real scenario, the driver goes scot-free, nothing really happens to the business owner, and the pigs get denied even basic compassion in their final moments so that humans can smugly prop themselves up at the top of the food chain and line their guts with pepperoni. All this while the lady gets charged with a criminal offence! We can certainly make heads roll.

When members of the human race charge a lady for kindness and then take her through the rigors of court proceedings—and for what? Providing water to thirsty animals that are going to soon meet with slaughter—one has to ask *what gives us the right to place ourselves above the animals when comparing animals and humans? Who are the animals? Are they outside the truck or inside?*

It is time someone invented a "***common-sense pill***" That person could become very rich.

My advice?

First, give a ton of *free* pills to those who kill innocent people. This includes the sole individual and also those who hide behind a façade of government writ and authorize extra-judicial murder.


## When the end does not justify the means

Killing innocents is wrong. Powerful bombs with shrapnel flying in every direction and leaving huge craters do not distinguish which woman or child to spare. Once any government starts to work outside a fair judicial process, just because people seem to be different and are living in another land, it will not be long before others start doing the same thing.

The other excuse—that civilians get in the way of bombs being thrown from the air and thus constitute mere "collateral damage"—is abhorrent, disguised to justify an evil practice in which innocent men, women, and children are disfigured, maimed, or killed.

**Collateral damage is a guise to justify the murder of civilians**, so let us call it what it is. One cannot accuse the other of moral betrayal and then employ means that defy the very essence of morality. Would the same politicians' term it "collateral damage" to their electorate if the bombs were thrown upon the innocent in their own lands? You would find their word-smiths scurrying to consult their dictionaries, trying to outdo each other in how best to condemn such atrocities. ("*Stop watching cartoons on your cell phone, dear Minister. What if someone saw you? The media is outside waiting for a speech. We must condemn such wanton and cowardly acts that occurred near us. For heaven's sake do not say 'mere collateral.' Does 'despicable murder of innocent civilians' sound okay?*")

Sane people, and we all hope to be among them, will respect each other, and whenever disagreements arise, will conduct themselves with civility and settle arguments with tact, wisdom, and peaceful dialogue. These qualities when combined with the requisites of perseverance and firmness will bring about lasting change. This is not the same as turning the other cheek. The "standing up" to what is abhorrent is an obligation for those who profess to be on a higher moral platform.

If you insult or punch the bully in a reciprocal exchange, then what is the difference between you and him? A good example to illustrate this case is an event that brought the phrase "*Is it okay to punch a Nazi?*" into mainstream vigorous moral debate—not in a university philosophy class, but rather, and surprisingly, on the internet.[14]

This happened soon after an *alt-right* activist was punched in the face during Trump's presidential inauguration, a punch that was caught on camera. The man who was punched was Richard Spencer, a white nationalist. This occurred in Washington, D.C.

When two opposing parties engage in somewhat similar abusive or violent confrontation, it detracts from the real issue at hand. The conversation now shifts from the issue being discussed to the distractive event. The public and the media now focus their attention on the event that occurred, while the more serious issue, in this case that of xenophobia and racism, is sidelined.

So far, so good. Peace-loving folks must always engage with those who are intolerant and spew vile divisive rhetoric with peaceful gestures. Offer them flowers. Omelets made from organic eggs. Or so, the alt-chaps and the neo-Nazi chaps should continue to fancifully think.

*Wrong, about the flowers.*

Where is the chap who threw the punch? His name should be sent to the *"Noble"* Peace Prize Committee, for *"noble"* gestures. I just hope the punch was a soft one for symbolism.

And who remembers the *egg-boy?*[15] He is the courageous Australian boy tackled to the ground, not by one man, but by a bunch of big men probably scared out of their wits that they were not going

14 https://www.washingtonpost.com/news/the-intersect/wp/2017/01/23/a-step-by-step-guide-to-a-meme-about-punching-a-nazi-in-the-face/?utm_term=.3b9a8fcd6ecf; http://www.irishnews.com/magazine/2017/01/23/news/we-asked-a-philosopher-if-it-s-okay-to-punch-nazis-in-the-face-901772/, and http://www.newsweek.com/richard-spencer-punch-nazi-ethicists-547277

15 https://www.washingtonpost.com/world/2019/03/25/australias-egg-boy-says-he-united-people-scientists-may-have-cracked-why/?utm_term=.178e70daf35a; https://www.nytimes.com/2019/03/25/world/australia/egg-boy-interview-christchurch.html.

to be enough. The egg boy's name should be sent to the *Nobel "Piece" Prize Committee* so they could give him a *"piece"* of pie for next time, and some eggs as well, to pop on intolerant heads.

Folks should stand up to those who insult them—with patience, fortitude, and civility, for lasting and positive effects. If all this fails, an egg (not an expensive organic egg, but one which has gone off) should be enough.

**Someone who believes he or she is a "goody-goody" person may raise a finger and ask, "Should we not all stay quiet, and stay away from all conflicts?"** I would hold the raised finger and gently turn it in the direction of the following quote:

> *The only thing necessary for the triumph of evil is for good men to do nothing.*
> —EDMUND BURKE

Fight with the pencil and the brain, not the sword. No, no. Please do not wield the sharp pencil. I only used it to denote the pen. Oh dear, some people. In verse 16:125, the Quran exhorts Muslims to always be respectful in their discourse:

> *Invite [all] to the Way of thy Lord with wisdom and beautiful preaching; and argue with them in ways that are best and most gracious: for thy Lord knoweth best, who have strayed from His Path, and who receive guidance.*

In the wake of the Trump election, there has been a rise in Islamophobia and anti-Semitism. I am not blaming Trump per se, or maybe I am but it doesn't matter; it has nevertheless given some demagogues the courage to vent their racist views.

When a mosque was burnt to the ground in Texas soon after Trump signed the anti-immigration bill targeting many Muslim majority countries, a nearby *Jewish synagogue offered the keys to their own place of worship so Muslims could continue to pray. Many Christians* also offered help with generosity and a GoFundMe campaign raised large sums to help rebuild the mosque.

*Not long afterwards, when several Jewish cemeteries were desecrated in parts of the U.S., many Muslims and Christians were quick to contribute funds to help with repairs. Muslim and non-Muslims were putting into practice, consciously or otherwise, a verse from the Quran which states, "Believers, be steadfast for the cause of God and just in bearing witness. Let not a group's hostility to you cause you to deviate from justice. Be just, for it is closer to piety. Have fear of God; God is Well Aware of what you do"* (Quran, 5:8).

If this coming-together of humanity is not beautiful, I do not know what is!

When the heinous Quebec City mosque attack took place on January 29, 2017, in which six Muslim men died and many more Muslims were injured by being shot from point-blank range by the lone gunman, Alexandre Bissonnette, a 27-year-old student from a local university, CBC Sudbury called my home as we have been known to speak for the Muslim community in Sudbury. The CBC presenter told my wife that he could not get hold of any spokesperson or imam or representative by calling the two mosques in the area and the reason for trying to get hold of me.

I made myself available, cancelled my other engagements, and awaited the CBC call. However, later my wife got a call to say that the CBC in Sudbury was finally able to get hold of an imam and so they would not be calling me. Where did they get hold of the imam? In the city of Timmins, many miles away from Sudbury. Is this an isolated incident where someone is trying to get answers on the belief-system of Muslims or what their thoughts are? I wish it were, but time and again we hear that much of Islam is unknown to people unless they are determined to make the effort to conduct independent research. Muslims need to be proactive. They must engage proactively by providing sound education on their faith knowing that there will always be more people willing to listen to peaceful dialogue than those being swayed by violent confrontation. That fateful day, many **Non-Muslims were trying to help Muslims**. Muslims must also rise up to help any segment of a population undergoing oppression, at any time, and in any part of the world. That is how we build strong societies.

> *We must take sides. Neutrality helps the oppressor, never the victim. Silence encourages the tormentor, never the tormented. Sometimes we must interfere. When human lives are endangered, when human dignity is in jeopardy, national borders and sensitivities become irrelevant. Wherever men and women are persecuted because of their race, religion, or political views, that place must—at that moment—become the center of the universe.*
>
> —ELLIE WEISEL

> *It's not our job to play judge and jury, to determine who is worthy of our kindness and who is not. We just need to be kind, unconditionally and without ulterior motive, even—or rather, especially—when we'd prefer not to be.*
>
> —JOSH RADNOR

The idea of maintaining balance and acceptance of the other despite differences appears to be on the wane. There are many people abandoning religion altogether or, when times are hard, adopting religious extremism. We see more of that in Europe with the far right and the far left, and though religion is not obvious in this shift, if you were to dig deep enough, you would find some aspects of religion at the core: rejection with passion or acceptance with passion. Abandonment of religion is therefore not a purely Muslim phenomenon; we see it in cultures all around us.

Religious extremism too is not confined to Muslims. History is replete with religious extremism across all major religions. However, Islam has been handicapped by some of the cultural baggage or regional practices that some Muslims adhere to without knowledge of their faith or scriptural sanction such as female genital mutilation and education denied to girls. Then there are those "Muslims" who commit atrocities that have been *expressly forbidden in Islam such as attacking places of worship, or harming or killing any innocent person. There is no exception to this rule, no matter the depth of grievance; the rule being so strict that one cannot retaliate in like manner even if the enemy had resorted to such acts.*

We must learn to question objectively whether a crime has been sanctioned by religion, and if it has not, then, for heaven's sake, keep religion out of the picture. Thus, a person such as *Timothy McVeigh—who was responsible for the Oklahoma City bombing that killed 168 people and injured over 600—though born a Catholic, is not representative of the teachings of the Catholic Church.*

Similarly, the tragic injustices done to the Native American people or to the indigenous races of Australia and New Zealand (not mere states taken away from them, but whole continents) cannot be blamed on the teachings of Christ (church leaders need to acknowledge historical injustices where many verses from the Bible were taken out of context and misused to advance a particular political or social agenda).

Anders Behring Breivik's terrorist act in Norway, where he was convicted of killing 77 people, is not considered a religious terrorist act. Yes, Breivik is a Christian, the media will say, "but he is not a Muslim, so let's leave religion out of the picture." Also, media will quickly point out that the same criterion of the *"separation* of perpetrator and religion" be applied in the case of Stephen Paddock, who killed about 58 people and left 500 people injured in Las Vegas. He is not a Muslim, so he is not going to attract the lurid headlines that link a particular religion to a crime committed. "See, we are sensible," the media will assert.

"Can we then, dear media, apply the same standard to a person when he happens to be a so-called Muslim?" a Muslim may ask.

"No, certainly not," the media may counter with a raised eyebrow at this Muslim's audacity (and a wink at the marketing department. A wink the Muslim would bet his beard that he saw)— sensible enough to see sensationalism, increased paper sales to a dazed public, and some extra bucks in the bank to buy camouflage glasses that should effectively hide the next wink.

*But surely Muslims must be the ones committing the worst atrocities, no?*


## Nope. Not even by the length of the turban cloth

Some of the worst atrocities in the world, such as the Holocaust, the Crusades, and the Inquisition have been committed by adherents of religions other than Islam. Compare the number of Muslim countries possessing nuclear weapons with the non-Muslim nuclear powers. While you compare, just hope that the one with the authority to press the red button is not itching, as this may annihilate millions and cause universal catastrophe that will impact you and the coming generations in ways that you cannot even begin to imagine.

The retort "I have a bigger button," in reference to North Korea is naïve and regressive. Then there are many leaders who have cleverly manipulated the police force and army to carry out their orders against taxpayers who are really the ones funding the food on their tables. These despots use the country's forces as if they are meant to serve their families and personal friends.

Bad retorts give them bad ideas. This type of message should not be coming from what is supposedly the world's greatest "democracy." Do big buttons translate to big weapons? Can one not use a small button to do the same? I am just asking. *Maybe it's an itch.*

And if a guy is itching, please give him some balm so that he will *not* itch.

Words are powerful and can have repercussions. Those in power need to use them wisely. *Because the media has been so helpful (not), many people think that it is "those Mozlems" who need to be blamed for what ails the Earth (and the stomach ache from eating too much popcorn at the cinema).*

How quickly we forget that the worst atrocities the world has ever seen were instigated or caused by adherents of ideologies or religions other than Islam: the First World War—approximately 17 million dead; not to be outdone with such paltry takings, non-Muslims unleashed the Second World War, with approximately 50 to 55 million dead; the War in Iraq , alleged to have produced approximately 12 million dead, was justified by phony allegations of the possession of nuclear weapons by the BB duo team, Bush–Blair and their entourage; the Nagasaki atomic bomb, 200,000 dead; the War in Cambodia, 3 million dead; Il Duce ("The Leader") Mussolini, 4 00,000 dead; Chairman Mao Tse Tung dishing out wanton killings instead of wontons (with a dash of soy sauce), with approximately 14 million dead; good old "Uncle Joe" Stalin, dishing out death instead of borsht, 20 million dead and millions more slowly starved to death. Yes, that was what they were called endearingly—Uncle Joe, Chairman Mao, and The Leader.

When the actions of Hitler and a long list of non-Muslim demagogues are compared to atrocities committed by Muslims, the Muslims fail by a long stretch, huffing, puffing, and limping at the end of the line.

*The Gold Cup, the Silver Cup, and the Bronze would be won by a non-Muslim.* The Muslim would be lucky to get a coal brick chucked at his turbaned head to try and catch up. Rather the coal brick than all the cups, say I.

*Keep the cups.*

Unfortunately, religion has too often been taken out of context, used and manipulated to monopolize power and subdue and terrorize people. Here then is a mind-blowing statistic that many people are not aware of: according to a FBI database, the majority of terrorist acts in the U.S. were committed by non-Muslims (1980 to 2005 statistics).[16] A 2017 report in the *Independent* states, "*Most of the designated terrorist groups in the US are right-wing extremists, not Muslim, according to a new report.*"[17]

Disappointed?

I plan to turn preconceived notions on their heads to clear some fog, as I stated earlier. It is not necessarily a "feel-good" book. I concede you will like some of it and hate me for some of it. Now is the chance to keep the book down and go sulk quietly. *But if you do, you will miss some funny bits, especially the last chapter*—the dessert— which tells you about some wacky "Muslim" despots in deserts. For now, however, we need to get pretty serious about our planet.

A radical change needs to happen to how we perceive life on Earth. Like the *Titanic*, the Earth-ship is convulsing with its last shudder before it goes down and us with it—and yet we sit smug and complacent. At least the *Titanic* had horns to warn people, and some people did escape the tragedy. In our case, there are no life rafts

16  https://www.fbi.gov/stats-services/publications/terrorism-2002-2005

17  https://www.independent.co.uk/news/world/americas/us-politics/terrorism-right-wing-america-muslims-islam-white-supremacists-study-a7805831.html

to take us to safety. *None. There is no shore. The earth is our entire lifeline. It sinks, we sink.*

We thought the extinction of the Dodo bird was a tragedy. **The UN now reports there are one million species at risk of extinction,**[18] and we are still twiddling our fingers. We cannot sustain wasteful lifestyles forever—and though we know it—we are not speaking out with enough alarm. *Our silence is deafening.*

We have an obligation to every living creature on Earth. We throw bombs. *We are killing each other, and as we do so, the explosives spew more toxins into the air. they die now, we die slowly later.* We need to restrain our politicians from carrying out things we find abhorrent. They entice us with "we are here to protect you" and "military-industrial progress," making us participants in allowing the production of lethal weapons by the billions, often at the bidding of a few perverse warmongers who in turn sell it to despots to subdue their citizens and others. They say that they are doing all these "good" things on our behalf. They lie, and they want us to be part of the lie.

Environmental degradation is going on full steam ahead; **the earth-ship is on collision course**. We need to alter our trajectory radically. Our politicians are blasé, their hands on the helm, or shrugging their shoulders as the elections are drawing ever nearer.

Animals too are undergoing great suffering due to human apathy and greed. Let us try to put ourselves into their shoes, or hoofs, or flippers. Animals, being subservient to our powerful minds and ingenuity, are unable to complain and respond to the harshness they are often made to endure. The absence of speech in animals should not equate to the absence of common sense in humans who claim superiority. Compassion would be to put ourselves in their hooves, so to speak, and show empathy.

---

18 https://www.nationalgeographic.com/environment/2019/05/ipbes-un-biodiversity-report-warns-one-million-species-at-risk/

Was Prophet Mohammed empathetic to their needs? We shall examine this to show you what kind of person he was.

There are many good books, both from Muslims and non Muslims, on animal welfare in Islam, but they are often too scholarly to engage many readers in this current fast-paced dynamic and fluid internet age. I plan to make this book an amazing, easy read, to keep you turning its pages. You will know so much about Islam you did not know before; we can use this information to forge closer ties among us and to care for this Earth-ship that is convulsing, taking in toxic water of our own making.

*We need everyone, Muslims and non-Muslims; the animal under duress cares not whether it was a Muslim or a non-Muslim who came to its aid.*

Neuroscience research indicates that on average our digitalized generation has an attention span shorter than that of the goldfish.[19] This book is an attempt at a compromise: to find a way to engage the reader in the subtleties of the harsh realities now facing the Earth, to relate historical information to current challenges and to deal with serious issues from a vantage point that we all may be able to relate to via an engaging read.

Leave the goldfish alone and do not  stare at it to prove this theory. It is circling, yes, I know. I mean, really, what else is it supposed to do? We would lose our attention span too if we kept circling all day.

---

19 http://time.com/3858309/attention-spans-goldfish/

# CHAPTER 2

# THE SCIENCE OF THINGS

*How came the bodies of animals to be contrived with so
much art, and for what ends were their several parts?*

*Was the eye contrived without skill in Opticks, and the ear
without knowledge of sounds? ... and these things being rightly
dispatch'd, does it not appear from phænomena that there is a
Being incorporeal, living, intelligent?*

—Isaac Newton, *Opticks*

Were you to quickly scan the pages of history from the beginning
of Islamic thought to the early seventeenth century CE, Muslims
appear to have been generally more welcoming to different ideas, the
adoption of other perspectives, cultures, and ways of life that did not
exactly conform to their own.

Unfortunately, stagnation has set in within the general Muslim
community, what with squabbling potentates in Muslim countries
fighting to amass more wealth and power and thereby keeping the
populations in those countries (on the whole) busy trying to keep
themselves and their families alive, or out of prison.

For instance, the Muslims of those historical times were not afraid to translate pagan Greek philosophy into Arabic, though they shunned pagan worship. The Muslims were keen to understand the world around them. They learnt from other cultures, adopted and enlarged upon ideas that were alien, yet reasonable. They bolstered, elaborated and added to the scientific knowledge existent at the time. Here are a few examples:

## Optics/Astronomy/Study of ancient texts

### Optics

For hundreds of years, it was held by scientists such as Ptolemy (85–165 CE) that we perceived objects because the eyes emitted light, as if from an interior lamp. A Muslim scientist, Ibn al- Haytham, known as "the father of optics," in his seven-volume treatise on optics, *Kitab-al-Manazir*, proposed that light traveled in a straight line, and that, contrary to the belief that light traveled from the eyes to the outside, it was actually light bouncing off objects entering the eye that made us perceive these objects.[20]

He also established the principle of conducting experiments repeatedly to test the validity of a theory, the foundations of scientific research inquiry that we use today.[21] His words are profound:

> The duty of the man who investigates the writings
> of scientists, if learning the truth is his objective,
> is to make himself an enemy of all that he reads,

---

20  https://www.britannica.com/biography/Ibn-al-Haytham#ref729295; https://explorable.com/conduct-science-experiments; https://en.unesco.org/courier/news-views-online/ibn-al-haytham-s-scientific-method; https://www.britannica.com/topic/Kitab-al-manazir

21  http://www.1001inventions.com/house-of-wisdom

and ... attack it from every angle. He should
also critically examine himself as he conducts
experiments, so that he may avoid falling into
either prejudice or leniency.

### Astronomy and the study of ancient texts

The first astronomical observatory was built in the eighth century in
Baghdad by caliph al-Mamun al-Rashid, the founder of the House
of Wisdom.[22] At this center, different sciences, such as astronomy,
mathematics, philosophy, optics, and medicine, were studied,
developed, and advanced. Translation activities into Arabic (especially
the academic works from Persian, and Greek such as Ptolemy,
Aristotle, Plato, and Euclid) were being inked and researched.

Since the telescope had not yet not been invented, observational
sextants were developed, some fairly large, to observe the movements
of stars and the orbiting planets, and the angles of the sun.[23] This
passage from the Quran is relevant:

God is the one Who created the night and the
day, the sun and the moon. Each one is travelling
in an orbit with its own motion. (Quran 21:33)

Great intellectual movements were taking place in the Islamic Empire
at a time when European thought was stagnating in the shackles of
the Dark Ages, science being seen to be in conflict with the Church.
The Dark Ages lasted for many centuries, beginning about the sixth
century CE. During the same period, Islamic thought, culture, and
scholarship were in full bloom, with an empire stretching from

22 http://www.astronomy.com/news/2017/02/muslim-contributions-to-
astronomy; http://www.electrummagazine.com/2012/11/muslim-astronomers-in-
the-islamic-golden-age/.

23 https://en.wikipedia.org/wiki/University_of_Al_Quaraouiyine

Baghdad in the north to Egypt in the south, from Moorish Spain in the west to China in the east.

## Higher academia and women in research and leadership

### Higher academia

Muslim women in the early stages of Islamic influence studied different sciences without restriction. The daughter of a wealthy merchant established what many historians, and also UNESCO and the *Guinness Book of World Records*, consider to be the first continuously-running degree-awarding university in the world, in 859 CE, in Fez, Morocco, the University of Al-Qarawiyyin.[24]

I visited this university a few years ago, while it was undergoing restoration and it confirmed to me that here indeed one can find proof that in Islam, religious worship and the study of the arts and sciences went hand in hand; religious education and what today we call "contemporary studies" were never mutually exclusive.[25] Jews, Christians, and Muslim scholars from all over the world came to study astronomy, mathematics, and philosophy at this university.

The second oldest university must have been in Europe, surely?

Nope.

The second oldest university was founded in 970–2 CE, in Egypt, known as Al-Azhar; a degree-granting university in which the modern fields of science and religious exegesis were embraced.[26] Does it matter who established what first? To set the historical record

---

24 https://whc.unesco.org/en/list/170; https://www.cnn.com/style/article/fez-al-qarawiyyin-medina-restoration-unesco/index.html

25 https://collegestats.org/2009/12/top-10-oldest-universities-in-the-world-ancient-colleges/.

26 http://www.quran-m.com/firas/en1/index.php/human/172-the-miracle-and-challenge-of-the-quran.html

straight, certainly, more to unite us than to divide us, as we continue to share knowledge and borrow from one another in our common aspirations of scientific advancement and the establishment of peace throughout the planet.

## Women in research and leadership

Scientific scholarship and leadership in Islam were not limited to the male domain; during Prophet Mohammed's time and for a few generations after his passing away, Muslims adopted and practiced this principle well. Guess who founded the university of Al-Qarawiyyin? A woman: the university was established by Fatima al-Fihri.

Prophet Mohammed's wife, Aisha, was a teacher as well, imparting education to many great Muslim scholars and thinkers of the time. These scholars came from afar seeking knowledge from her once Prophet Mohammed had passed away. The cultural restrictions placed on women in some Muslim majority countries to pursue education have absolutely nothing to do with Islam.

## Embryology

Most of what we know now of the development of the human embryo is through the utilization of sophisticated instruments and powerful microscopes since, in the early stages of development, the miniature embryo can be studied only by using such microscopes. Prior to the initial developments of the microscope by Leewanhoek (1632–1723), who was the first to observe spermatozoa under the early rudimentary compound microscopes, the scientific world of the time thought that the human child was a miniature version of the child as it grew and emerged from the womb.

Then a person—Mohammed—appeared in the deserts of Arabia reciting verses he said he had received from a Creator and went on to transform a people into one of the greatest civilized empires. The quest for knowledge and discovery became the admired norm. His recitation of the verses makes even more sense in the twenty-first century with the availability of new technology. The Quran says:

> We [Allah] created man from a quintessence of clay. We then placed him as a nutfah [drop] in a place of settlement, firmly fixed, then We made the drop into an alaqah [leech-like structure], and then We changed the alaqah into a mudghah [chewed-like substance], then We made out of that mudghah, izam [skeleton or bones], then We clothed the bones with lahm [muscles, flesh] then We caused him to grow and come in being and attain the definitive [human] form. So, blessed be God, the best to create. (Quran 23: 12–14)

Here I will introduce an authority on the subject matter. Dr. Keith Moore is the foremost authority on the development of the human embryo, and his textbooks are widely used in medical schools. He is the recipient of numerous awards and honors, including, in 1984, the J.C.B. Grant Award, which is the highest honor granted by the Canadian Association of Anatomists.

Dr. Moore has also served in many academic and administrative positions, including as President of the Canadian Association of Anatomists (1968–70). Upon learning what the Quran had to say about the developing embryo states, he admitted that he astonished by the accuracy of the statements that were recorded centuries ago, long before the science of embryology was established. One must bear in mind that at that microscopic level, it is impossible to see the developing embryo with the naked eye and one must utilize the most advanced microscopes of our age.

In his book *The Amazing Quran*, Gary Miller observed:

*I had the pleasure of interviewing Dr. Keith Moore for a television presentation, and we talked a great deal about this—it was illustrated by slides and so on. He mentioned that some of the things that the Qur'an states about the growth of the human being were not known until thirty years ago. In fact, he said that one item in particular—the Qur'an's description of the human being as a "leech-like clot" ('alaqah) at one stage—was new to him; but when he checked on it, he found that it was true, and so he added it to his book. He said, "I never thought of that before," and he went to the zoology department and asked for a picture of a leech. When he found that it looked just like the human embryo, he decided to include both pictures in one of his textbooks. Dr. Moore also wrote a book on clinical embryology, and when he presented this information in Toronto, it caused quite a stir throughout Canada. It was on the front pages of some of the newspapers across Canada, and some of the headlines were quite funny. For instance, one headline read: "Surprising thing found in ancient book!" It seems obvious from this example that people do not clearly understand what it is all about. As a matter of fact, one newspaper reporter asked Professor Moore, "Don't you think that maybe the Arabs might have known about these things—the description of the embryo, its appearance and how it changes and grows? Maybe there were not scientists, but maybe they did some crude dissections on their own—carved up people and examined these things."*

*The professor immediately pointed out to him that he (i.e., the reporter) had missed a very important point—the slides of the embryo that had been shown and had been projected in the film had come from pictures taken through a microscope"* [27] *(The microscope was discovered in the late 16th century)*

Other renowned authorities, such as Dr. E. Marshall Johnson; Dr. T. V. N. Persaud; and Dr. Joe Leigh Simpson, have also remarked on the profound nature of the references in the Quran to the development of the human child.[28]

## The origin of the universe and the molecular basis of life

*Do not the unbelievers see that the heavens and the earth were joined together [as one unit of creation], before we clove them asunder? We made from water every living thing. Will they not then believe?* (Quran 21:30)

---

27  https://d1.islamhouse.com/data/en/ih_books/single/en_The_Amazing_Quran.pdf

28  E. Marshall Johnson, Professor and Chairman of Anatomy and Developmental Biology (Thomas Jefferson University); T. V. N. Persaud, Professor of Anatomy and Professor of Pediatrics and Child Health (University of Manitoba, Canada); Joe Leigh Simpson, Professor and Chairman of the Department of Obstetrics and Gynecology (Baylor College of Medicine, U.S.A.)

How could Prophet Mohammed, a person living in the desert, have had such profound information, as described above, that we now know to be scientifically coherent in the twenty-first century?

In 2006, two physicists were awarded the Nobel Prize for the "Big Bang Theory."

### The molecular basis of life

We now know that we are composed of 57–60 percent water, knowledge of the true extent of water in our body composition assisted by the invention of the microscope and other devices. The importance of water as the basis of life is undisputed by astronomers and those looking for life in the outer planets.

"Oh. We always knew that," someone may say.

"Not so fast," a wiser person may counter. "Not only did we know about that more recently; in fact, in 2018, we discovered that we have the *largest* organ in the body known as the *interstitium*, mostly made of fluid, 'hidden' away in our bodies for all these many years, until some clever people decided to examine it closely under new and better instruments called confocal laser endomicroscopes.[29]

How could we have missed the biggest organ in the body?

Well, we have been squishing and drying tissues while preparing slides for pathologists for so long that we could not really tell that connective tissue and interstitium are separate components, and that the interstitium has a unique structure and that it functions in a specific way just as an organ would.

And we only discovered this in 2018?

Indeed, yes. Since it is mostly made of water, and we have been drying tissues to examine under microscopes for many decades, we somehow missed it. Until now, we thought that the skin was the

---

29 https://www.cnn.com/2018/03/27/health/new-organ-interstitium-study/index. html; https://news.nationalgeographic.com/2018/03/interstitium-fluid-cells-organ-found-cancer-spd/

largest organ, "Oops. Let us quickly revise our anatomy books before the public starts questioning just how smart we are."

## Ocean research

> *And it is He Who has let free the two seas [kinds of water]: this is palatable and sweet, and that is salty and bitter; and He has set a barrier and a complete partition between them.* (Quran 24:40)

Modern scientific instruments have been able to establish that there is a very distinct stratification where the two waters meet, unknown to science until very recently, and that they do not really blend into each other, but rather, there is a distinct intersection where the two meet.[30]

## Honey and healing

The Quran is an ocean of knowledge for the seeker. It makes the exhortation that we should reflect on its verses as they are signs and evidence of an ingenious Creator. Being true to this exhortation, and having a special love for bees, I felt I needed to look at a verse in the Quran making mention of bees and honey,

> *Then to eat of all the produce (of the earth), and find with skill the spacious paths of its Lord: there issues from within their bodies a drink of varying colours, wherein is healing for men: verily in this is a Sign for those who give thought.* (Quran 16:69)

---

30 Raymond C. Smith and Karen S. Baker, "Optical properties of the clearest natural waters (200–800 nm)." Applied Optics 20, no. 2 (1981):177–84; https://oceanservice.noaa.gov/education/kits/estuaries/media/supp_estuar05a_wedge.html.

An opportunity arose when I had to submit a research proposal during my studies in podiatric medicine. I decided to conduct an experiment on the antibacterial property of honey (fortunately, a masters degree in microbiology as a background to my present profession was to come in handy) to see if I could contribute to the medical information already available in which researchers were trying to help promote the healing of recalcitrant non-healing wounds; and for myself, to understand more on the depth and veracity of the verse that I found interesting.

So, I approached my professors, obtained approval, and with their help obtained penicillin-resistant ATCC (American Type Culture Collection) strains of three common wound infecting bacteria; staphylococci, streptococci, and pseudomonas. Testing these bacteria against different non-pasteurized honeys in an exhaustive research procedure using nutrient agars, Petri-plates, multi-wells with aliquots, incubation, and zones of inhibition revealed an interesting result: honey was found to exhibit inhibitory effects against these bacteria—some types of bacteria more susceptible to some types of honey—with Manuka honey exhibiting overall better results.

The following question arose from one of my professors: was it simply osmotic concentration of honey in these wells exhibiting the inhibitory effects? To test this potential supposition, we boiled the honeys in short bursts thus maintaining generally the same osmotic concentration (if anything, the osmotic properties would increase), and re-tested them again. The result: almost no demonstrable inhibitory effects were obtained when honeys were heated. There was some special antibacterial property or substance in honey that was being destroyed with boiling.

Honey in medicine has been known since ancient times. Manuka honey is more mainstream now, but at the time I was doing my experiment, there were few studies of its potency in the world, only some early studies done in Australia. Now you can even find manuka honey at your local grocery department. "Fine," someone may say "We've known about honey since ancient times, so what is new?" I would tap the chap on the shoulder and reply, "I hope you did not forget that I was testing these honeys against penicillin-resistant strains." Mine was a preliminary study, and more research is needed to test against newer antibiotic-resistant strains.

New research in how bees communicate is quite another thing! I was so intrigued by how bees communicate that I looked at the verse again. There it was; God has taught the bee how to navigate with skill the spacious paths of the Lord. We now know that bees do a special dance to inform other bees of the distance, the pathway to take, and where to find the nectar so they are not all wasting time looking here and there when one bee already has important information to relate on where to find the best nectar!

## One would think an ancient book would have ancient ideas

The Quran has many verses that a person with an objective outlook would find  truly amazing: many verses correspond to recent and important scientific inquiry. The chances of a person in the desert (Prophet Mohammed), *1,400 years ago, presenting these points with accuracy, one after another, in line with modern science,* are pretty remote: possibly few in billions.

We are talking about a person in the desert, in the purity of marked isolation, a man who could not read, and who claimed to receive revelations from The Creator of all things. He would receive the verses from Archangel Gabriel, recite the verses as received, and the scribes would write it down.

If a book without a top cover were to be discovered in the attic of a contemporary twenty-first century avant-garde scientist, there would be wonder within the social and scientific community as to how one man could accomplish studying the many branches of science and the arts within one lifetime—and they would hail it as remarkable.

Let us assume the scenario: A member of the panel composed of social scientists, human and animal rights activists, historians, technocrats, philosophers, and environmentalists who have been analyzing the book (found in the attic) gets up and verbally sums up what most of the committee has been thinking as they have sat around the table scrutinizing the finer details of the book during the past fortnight since its discovery, "*It is fairly current. It addresses social issues, human rights, the rights of each member of a family unit, how the universe was formed, time, space, inner working of the human mind in matters of compassion, greed, avarice, and how to better oneself. The scientific principles within the book would be a boon for many other researchers. The author must be brilliant. Let us see if we can find the top cover, hopefully it will shed light on who authored such a masterpiece.*"

An athletic member of the panel quickly volunteers to go look in the attic again. They scurry to the scientist's house, almost tripping over themselves in their hurry and excitement, to see who must have authored such a magnum opus. The agile member deftly clambers up the ladder and starts rummaging as the team waits below. They wring their hands anxiously and some, their nerves frayed with anticipation, jump up every time they hear the chap in the attic sneeze due to the accumulated dust. Then they hear a shout, "*Ah, yes! Found the top cover!*"

The panel cries out, almost in unison, "What does it say?" "*It says 'Quran'*" the reply comes. The athletic member holds the top cover gingerly and slowly comes down. The anxious team jostles around the ladder nearly causing the poor man to take a tumble. "*Stop, for heaven's sake!*" He holds the ladder tightly with one hand, uttering expletives about certain nincompoops having brains but no patience. He refuses to come down and waits to make sure that the entire team of intelectuals moves far away from the ladder. A frail scientist in big horn-rimmed glasses and a glistening large head packed with neurons who had been pushed against the ladder in the commotion is taking the heat, *"You there! Were you the one trying to topple me down?"* he glares from his precarious perch down at the poor scientist. The scientist moves to the end of the room closer to the door, ready to make a quick getaway if the athletic member decided to take things further. He peers closely to see who must have pushed him against his will, designing scientifically intricate plans to trip the culprit if he ever were to find who caused him such embarrassment.

The author of the Quran? Not Prophet Mohammed. He was merely delivering a message from the Creator. The Quran simply means recitation of revelation, **as received**, from the Master of the Universe.

Prophet Mohammed, more than a thousand years ago, was reciting breathtaking things on the origin of the universe, about the origin of life, and saying things about the ocean while living in the desert.

Would we phrase this as "new things in an ancient book"? Not really; **the Quran was designed to stand the test of time. It is as current today as it was in 570 ce.**

We need a dose of sincerity and humility if we are true to ourselves in wanting to know about the Book. We are all free and independent and we can always reject any idea if we do not like it. However, we first need to acknowledge that we have preconceptions. We are a product of circumstances that have molded our lives, and that our thoughts and ideas may be reflective of the millions of interactions that occur during our lives. *Why not add to the collection of experiences and read a few chapters of the Quran? Objectively, of course. It may or may not offer an insight.*

Let us try—no matter how hard it is—to be objective. If being objective on a consistent basis is difficult, at least we keep our prejudice at bay for the brief amount of time we need to hear the other person out *fully.* Let us grab our metaphorical cups labeled "objective" and hold them the right side up—for if our cups were inverted to match our mindset, then nothing, no matter how profound, is going to go in—and let our minds receive information and then we can decide if that information warrants credence and further attention.

Pretense, derision, and malice should be banished when we sit down. Let maturity and wisdom guide our dialogue. Just as I brought the Quran, bring out your books, your ideas, your challenges, your fears, the beauty of verses that deal with compassion that is in your books, and let us understand you as well. For example, there are many instances in the Bible where Jesus showed his love and compassion to the poor and the needy, and allowed us to recognize that none of us are entirely sinless, and that we should not be too quick to condemn, as when he said of the woman accused of adultery … *"He that is without sin among you, let him first cast a stone at her."* (John 8:7). The statement is beautiful and packed with great wisdom. It is not that he condoned adultery, but part of the lesson for me is that that we should look at ourselves first before accusing and condemning others too quickly.

*"If you were to look for some good in a person, you will surely find it, and if you are looking for something bad in a person, you will surely find it."* Abraham Lincoln is believed to have said part of the phrase I just quoted, though some dispute the source. It does not matter who said it first, it makes sense. The same rule applies to the Quran. *Some people will read it to find fault and some will read and keep turning pages and find much good in it.* The choice is the *approach* one takes when reading the Quran, Bible, Torah, or other religious books. We direly need to come together with the intention of knowing the other, as there is no better way to empathize and understand than to place oneself in the other person's shoes. This will unite us and encourage us to be good to each other.

The unity of humankind, the unity of God, understanding of the other while appreciating differences, and empathy: is that not the ultimate religion?

## A is for apple, but if it smells fishy, it's a fish

That is basic science if we have a sense of the olfactory. But then, we not only smell, we also see. And what we sometimes see, we do not like. We often judge a whole religion based on our observation of just a few of its adherents that we may have had personal experience of. Thus, we may unjustly blame Islam, Christianity, Judaism, and other religions based on the naïve and simplistic calculation that *if person A is bad, then religion A must be bad too. This is bad science.* All the apples in all the piles are not bad. It is a bad apple in a good pile. All religions have a few bad apples. Do all citizens of a country abide by their government's constitution and the principles of good they often invoke and want us to abide by? Look at our own penal institutions: *are they all empty?*

If we were to take the Quran as the "constitution" by which Muslims are supposed to govern themselves, and which indeed most Muslims do, we nonetheless discover that, unfortunately, a few do not adhere to its tenets.

There are bad people within any religious fold and there are evil recruiters who want them to do bad things. Recruiters can also be politicians—they know how to emotionally charge people and if any opportunities were to arise, they are quick to respond and sow discord—their ultimate agenda is as crooked as they are. Recruiters in their many forms are quite adept at picking the fruit on the fringes that is not sound. Muslims too have their share of unsavory fruit.

The greater a Quran-educated Muslim or Bible-educated Christian one is able to produce—adherents who are easily able to locate references that place emphasis on compassion and unity from their respective Books, and able to counter divisive tactics with sound knowledge—the better the chances that the pesky recruiters will sit idle twiddling their fingers and take up another activity. They can buy a one-way ticket to Mars, and we shall pitch in with a fundraising bake-sale to help send them on their way.

Someone may say, "Get rid of religion then. It seems to cause more anarchy and more wars."

*Anarchy.* That reminds me. I have several vivid memories of my late father while living in Africa, one being especially poignant. As a young teenager growing up in a small town called Mwanza, near Lake Victoria in Tanzania, Africa, I was witness to the decency of the man. We had just closed shop and were heading home when we heard a large commotion. A person zoomed by, with a mob of people running and shouting to catch the person.

He was a probably a petty thief, maybe grabbed something from a store but was discovered; the mob was in hot pursuit to exact "instant justice."

They call this "*mob justice*" in some parts of Africa, and if they end up catching the thief, it would be a miracle if he comes out alive. A short distance from where we were, he was tripped by someone and he fell. As the crowd caught up to him, they started picking big stones and rocks and started pelting him while he was on the ground begging and shouting for them to stop; bloodied, pleading and crying. My dad ran and started pulling the men away, shouting for them to stop and to let the police deal with this, but to no avail. I, on the other hand, was pushed towards the fringes by bigger, stronger men. In a final desperate act, my father threw himself on top of the thief trying to shield him from the attack, in the process getting hit with a few stones.

The crowd started to pause. Fortunately, the police soon arrived and the thief was escorted away, bloodied, but alive. A mob is not a group you reason with, and you may end up becoming a casualty, but my dad's sense of justice forced him to take drastic action.

We walked home in silence. We never talked about this. This man, my dad, respected the law. He despised anarchy, people taking the law in their own hands. Even more so, he was a kind man and he shunned all types of violence. He was not a very religious man, but he observed the religious dictates of good.

Religion is here to stay. Like it or not. Read your own religious Book carefully, almost all of it encourages positive social cohesion— if you take away the added bits inserted by humans—for whatever other agendas they had in mind at their historical times.

*Remove religion and it will be replaced with other ideas, for instance state-worship, or neo-religion of sorts, like neo-fascism. or communism, with the top echelons doing all the taking, while promoting "equality for all."*

Someone may still insist on doing away with organized religion, saying religion is responsible for many a war. They may stubbornly insist on evidence. They may ask, "What do we get if we take away religion?"

*What do we get?*

We get chaos, mayhem and leaders wanting to control others with power and brute force. We get Pol Pot with 1.5 to 2 million dead under his leadership, Stalin with about 20 million dead, and Mao Tse Tung with about 45 million dead.[31] That is what we get. Still not keen on organized religion? Then we are going to get an "organized something" — possibly, and very likely, *organized mass murder.*

Usurpers of power with their wiles keep popping up here and there. There will never be any shortage of people wanting to sway the emotionally-swayable to achieve nefarious ends.

Then there are some very clever people who know how to rile up masses by using religion. They prey on the unwary; the credulous ones made to believe that they are "serving god" by following this "leader." These "leaders" twist select passages from the Bible, or Quran, or other religious books,

---------------

31  https://www.theguardian.com/world/2015/apr/16/forty-years-after-genocide-cambodia-finds-complicated-truth-hard-to-bear; https://www.independent.co.uk/news/people/who-said-it-joseph-stalin-or-oliver-cromwell-9017590.html; https://www.theguardian.com/commentisfree/2013/jul/02/religion-wars-conflict; https://www.independent.co.uk/arts-entertainment/books/news/maos-great-leap-forward-killed-45-million-in-four-years-2081630.html

and, in most cases, reading them out of context to incite people. *There are those who also claim to be secularists. Then they go about life crucifying those who do not agree with them. They belong to a special religious creed called the secular creed. Same thing, just another name for another formal doctrine.* We must acknowledge that these kinds of people do exist. We just need to fortify our defenses by knowledge, appreciate differences in religion, culture, color, and language. Humanity should be like the woven blanket with different colored fibers, each strand strengthening the other, making a whole, to keep us warm and comfortable.

I shall relate to you a ***story about the four bulls and the lion***, to show you what I mean. I promise to make it a little quirky in case you wanted to read it to the teenage grandkids at the campfire while eating marshmallows.

## Melanin: Simple science for dorks

There were four bulls. They were friends.

One was called "black" because nature had endowed him with more melanin, an amazing adaption as his fore-parents came from sunnier climes. The melanin protected him from the harmful rays of the sun and he could chew cud while standing peacefully in the sun without needing to buy sunscreen.

"Don't you wish you had more melanin so you could eat out here with the sun shining in your face?" he asked.

"Yep," one of the bulls answered. "It is a good adaptation provided by nature to bestow a positive adaptation in sunnier climes where your fore-parents come from" The other bulls nodded their massive heads in assent.

"We are all beautiful and unique. Take, for example, the Panda. It is black and white, and it is beautiful," the darker hued added politely. He did not want to be misinterpreted or sound racist, as his intentions were good and sincere, and he did not harbor feelings of superiority.

The bulls got along well with each other and recognized that each one was unique and special. They loved listening to each other's distinct accents. They liked how each one was slightly different from the others. Some were taller, some had distinct colorations, and some had abilities to find succulent roots by removing soil in certain spots with their hooves. They would regularly share their abilities and tidbits. They lived in harmony because they appreciated differences that existed among them. Differences were not a matter of contention.

The second bull was called "native" as he was of a generous nature and the native of the land. He had welcomed all to share the bounties of the Mighty Spirit, and he would even share the last blade of grass if times were tough. He believed that all species of plants, animals, and insects complemented each other in a myriad of intricate interwoven ways in this amazing circle of life. He was always wary that he not be made to sign any paper that would confer his ancestral rights to the land merely by placing a mark on a piece of paper. He had heard what happened to many natives in Australia, New Zealand, and the Americas.

The third was called "Muslim" because he had a nice hairy chin which looked like a beard. He had moved to this new land because the province he came from in Canada, Quebec, had *bulldozed* in bull 21—or was it bill 21?—a piece of legislation in which any "ostentatious" of religious symbols was a no-no. They said they were secular, and were probably reading the bill with bowed heads, replacing a formal religion with another one, the secular one. It seemed there was no getting away with religion, after all. Despite the façade that goes with such legislations, most knew it was mainly meant to wrench the headscarves off women who were minding their own business. Muslim women, to be precise. The bull was taking no chances and concluded that soon enough any display of long beards, long horns, or hair covers would be tantamount to being ejected from livestock wagons. He wasn't too sure about the beards, but given the general mood of the politicians looking at the external appearance than the internal quality of residents, he was just being cautious. He wasn't going to allow someone to remark on his luxurious beard. Instead of focusing on the economy, the legislators were now eyeing the picture of mother Mary with a head-cover, and the picture of Jesus Christ with a beard, wondering how to deal with such things.

Some legislative buffaloes in that large province of Canada also had big ostentatious religious symbols in some legislative chambers, *sheepishly* scurrying past them pretending to be under the influence of "secular-weeds," mucking around with the Bill of Rights happily like hippy hippos, saying hypocrisy was okay. So, the "Muslim" walked everywhere with a *ruminative* look on his face. He had this contemplative look on his face as if reflecting on the purpose of his higher existence than the mere chewing of cud and travelling in livestock wagons without top covers.

The wagons in the province had no ostentatious top covers as they symbolized some sort of religious affiliation. Doctors and nurses in hospitals were being ejected if they happened to wear face masks and hair covers while performing surgeries on the frost-bitten ears of construction workers (who could not wear balaclavas to keep their ears warm in -30ºC). The surgeons stood outside, dazed and without hoodies, unable to protect their poor ears from the Canadian cold. Covid-19 appeared, and the legislators—despite their aversion to masks and face covers —were doing a quick rethink. Food preparers were being told not to wear a head covers while preparing food and shiny strands of hair started to appear, mixed in with pasta, giving rise to mixed feelings. Cartoon books were being revised and poor little red riding hood was told "no-no" to covering her hair, appearing a little upset without her hood. The parliamentarians had become too enthusiastic and did not know where to stop.

"Ostentatious, my foot!" he exclaimed, looking at his cloven hoof.

The fourth was called "white" as he was lighter in color, smiled easily, was polite, and fought for justice wherever he saw wrong being done. He came and looked at the "Muslim" staring at his cloven hoof. Then he looked at his own. They were not much different. "Nothing makes sense to me nowadays. Politicians want to make a big deal out of nothing to get votes." He was disgusted as to how his friend was being treated. "I wear a big ring in me nostril. I wear it *religiously*. Why don't they say anything about that, eh?" He was sympathetic to the ruminating bull.

The bulls were beautiful in their own unique ways. They were overjoyed when July 2018 rolled around and when announcements were made in Canada that "weed" would be plentiful. They hoped they would then chew cud while, as one of them said, "Swimming in the clods—sorry, clouds."

Though the bulls were generally happy in this land, they had but one problem: Lurking in the shadows was a lion called "*Supremacist Purpleneck*" as his mane had a twinge of purple for lying too long in a field of lavender. He smelt good too, because of the lavender, but his nature left much to be desired.

The lion carried a religious book of sorts and he would consult it from time to time, making sure to choose verses, out of context of course, to give himself some legitimacy in doing wrong to others. For example, he would read something like, "*Kindly admonish the heathens and usurp not their properties*," and he would read aloud only part of the passage, "*admonish the heathens and usurp*." (He was really good at taking things out of context, as some modern-day zealots do) Then he would kill little critters and usurp their burrows. Little critters were easy, the problem was the bulls.

The lion was no match for the four large bulls. Whenever he made an attack, the four backed up into a tight formation, brandishing their horns on all four sides. The one time he persisted in an attack resulted in such a good *hiding* that he had to go lie in the bed of lavender to nurse his wounds. He went back to his book and consulted it out of context again.

After feeling energized once again, the lion renewed his attacks. He made his attacks so many times that the four bulls did not have time to forage. The lion was a persistent nuisance.

One day, three bulls consulted with each other and decided that if they left one bull to wander further afield and not warn him when the lion came, he would be killed, and the lion would not pester the rest of the bulls again. The lion would be satisfied, so they hoped. So that is exactly what they did. The lion attacked the lone bull and killed it.

One bull gone, three left.

After a month, the lion had finished gorging on the poor dead bull and was hungry again for bull meat. The lion was now stronger, confident, emboldened with his first bull success, and so he renewed his attacks with greater gusto.

So, one day, two bulls decided that this was too much, and they conspired to let another one of them be killed so the two could live in peace. When the lion attacked, the two pretended not to hear the bellows of help.

Second bull gone; two left.

Peace, finally? No, for after another month when the second dead bull was now only bones, the lavender-smelling lion was back at it again; stronger still, further emboldened, and the bully really relished bull meat. It did not take long for the lion to kill the remaining two bulls as they could not protect themselves by making an effective formation.

*Moral of the story:* I know it has something to do with lavender. No, wait. The moral has nothing to do with lavender.

The moral is that one should never think that racism and injustice only affect others because he or she is not directly affected by what is happening to others. Eventually, injustice is going to catch up with him or her; if not now, very possibly in the near or far future, with his or her children, grandchildren or future progeny.

Our children and grandchildren will intermarry among different ethnicities. We probably will not even be here. Racism, a sanctimonious "I-am-better-than-thou" attitude, oppression, indifference, the causing of dissension among people, and insensitivity towards others (who do not resemble the self) allow greed and evil to go unchallenged. Our attitude will affect those who come after us.

Silence or apathy is never an option; we are part and parcel of the entire "Circle of Life." Our actions or inactions have a profound effect upon the whole.

If you read the autobiography of the famous boxer Muhammad Ali, you will note that his true mettle was not merely physical strength, but more so his intellectual fortitude against any oppression. He stated, *"Hating people because of their color is wrong. And it does not matter which color does the hating. It's just plain wrong."* He had true grit. This should sum it up: true grit is not muscles, guns, or cowering behind a façade of legislative writ. *It is mental fortitude against any persecution, or any injustice—against anyone.* Legislative buffaloes would do well to learn this.

## The science of activism, compromise, and tact

Too often we hear "ignorance breeds contempt," and that Muslims need to increase social engagement. Well said and all that. Let us say it again, "Ignorance breeds contempt."

*For heaven's sake, let us dispense with clichés, and get to work.* I am talking to Muslims, so bear with me a bit. Muslims need to be seen doing good works while wearing the hijab (that many Muslim women wear) or sporting a beard (for some Muslim men who do let their beards grow). This way, Muslims are *seen* to be participating in civic society, thus dispelling ignorance that undoubtedly breeds contempt in the mind that has already been subject to the negative stereotype.

When there are marches, or events being held to advocate for animal or human rights, my wife and her mother often attend these kinds of peaceful demonstrations, even if it is freezing cold outside, dressed in their Islamic attire complete with a hijab, as they normally would do for an Islamic event. Invariably, the media notice the two of them, since they would not be accustomed to seeing Muslims marching for social causes that do not have a direct religious connotation. They would often approach them for a brief interview and their pictures would be posted in the papers or on TV. The idea of seeing Muslims marching alongside non-Muslims in support of moral and social causes as being something *newsworthy* by reporters indicates to what is perceived to be general apathy among Muslims when it comes to fighting for social justice. Muslim engagement must be very common at such events. Muslims should be front and center when it comes to advocating for everything good. That is Islam in action.

There are many causes that are fundamentally Islamic (attending mosques and performing ritual prayers are not the only Islamic obligations taught by Prophet Mohammed, as many Muslims very well know), such as environmental protection, nature advocacy, advocating for human rights and animal rights, participating in inter-faith dialogue, assisting the homeless, feeding the poor, and so much more. It is time, that we, as Muslims, gave more thought to our social responsibility—and since we know that we have been slow on the take for many years—we need now to drastically increase our social engagement to undo the damage done by standing for too long on the sidelines till we are seen to be developing varicose veins, and attracting an exasperated, "tut-tuts" from the public health department.

When we see injustices being inflicted on the native population of a country by economically more powerful and dominant population of that state, their cause becomes our cause. *Oppression against one is oppression against all.* If we see women being paid less for the same amount and type of work as their male counterparts, their struggle to achieve equality in pay becomes our struggle.

When the Muslim stands up for prayer and recites the verse, *"Let there arise from you a group of people inviting to all that is good, enjoining what is right and forbidding all that is wrong, and those will be the successful ones"* (Quran 3:104), it is a call for action. The verse is meant to transform the ritual into "walking the talk."

I advise my fellow faith members to keep mosques accessible to the public and create spaces where non-Muslims can come and watch you pray and listen to the sermons; let the sermons reflect the fact that the congregation includes people who may be non-Muslims coming to learn about Islam.

Have a representative available when there is a major event to provide any further information or clarification sought by the media. Make sure, though, that the representative is properly educated in Islam; is abreast of current developments; has tact; knows how to speak good English or French, or the dominant language of the country in question; and is smart enough to know when the questioner is trying to lead the representative to make statements intended to tarnish the image of Islam. Being cognizant of norms and nuances could be of great help.

A good grasp of the locality's dominant language and of local etiquette is also important. Courtesy and composure must be maintained at all times, however tough the questions being posed in an acrid environment due to recent negative events in which Muslims may have been thought to have been culpable—regardless of the validity of accusations. Muslim representatives need to have exquisite manners, emulating the words of their Prophet.

> Aishah, the wife of Prophet Mohammed, said, *"I heard the Prophet—peace be upon him— say, 'Indeed the believer by his good manners reaches the ranks of those who spend the whole night in prayer and fasting'"* [32]

Prophet Mohammed also said:

> *Nothing weighs heavier in the balance on the Day of Judgment than good character. God hates that which is wanton and base.*[33]

To take the moral high ground is also essential when dealing with negative rhetoric. I was listening to Paul Kennedy's *Ideas* program on CBC one night. The topic was philosophy and children.[34] I smiled with wonder at one child answering a question on how to deal with a bully. I am not quoting exactly, but the gist I got from the child's answer to the question amounted to this: If a bully comes to you and says, *"I don't like your shoes,"* do not fight back in a similar negative fashion. Instead, if you were to reply with, *"I like your shoes,"* it leaves the bully confused, caught off-guard, and he would often not know how to engage in further negative comment.

I reflected on these words of wisdom coming from a child: the person would not have criticized his or her own shoes, did not stoop lower to counter the negative, nor invite further tit-for-tat. In fact, such a response might often engender goodwill from the bully, or at least leave the bully searching for words while you make a confident exit. Muslims must learn to engage with similar tact, wisdom, confidence, a superior moral stance, and with consistency.

We all need to learn wisdom from a pure mind, no matter the age.

Muslim leaders must appoint a media person for each mosque or organization. This should be done in advance, not scrambling to find one when the media representative is knocking at the door. If you have to, then provide training for the person who will represent your mosque or the Muslim community at large.

In this age of social media, words can be disseminated widely. Imams need to be acutely aware that words need to be nuanced enough since they will spread to different people from many backgrounds, cultures, and perspectives.

The Imam may know how to conduct exceptional prayers, but not know how to navigate skillfully with the media.

Many Imams in traditional madressas (teaching houses), especially from the Indian-subcontinent and Asian-run madressas in the West, have been busy churning out *parrots*. These human-parrots spend years learning how to recite the Quran beautifully without knowing a single meaning from a single verse. Some of these students emerge and commit crimes that tarnish the image of Islam. The companions of the Prophet would not proceed to the next verse *until* they put into *practice* the instruction from the previous verse. ***They walked the talk.***

My advise: If an Imam is going to teach your innocent child to recite the whole Quran merely like a melodious parrot, you are better off teaching the child **one verse with its meaning**, at home, yourself. The Prophet said, "*One Faqih (knowledgeable man) is more formidable against the Satan than one thousand devoted worshipers.*"

When a reporter from a paper known as *The Untainted Press* read a book about Muslims who were trying to be understood, he got quite interested. But he did not want to get caught in long sermons at a mosque. *Being a fair man, he wanted to give Muslims a fair shot in the media.* So, he picks up the phone and calls the author of an Islamic book…

# CHAPTER 3

# SENSE AND SIMILARITY

*It's an universal law—*
*intolerance is the first sign of an inadequate education.*
*An ill-educated person behaves with arrogant impatience,*
*whereas truly profound education breeds humility.*

—ALEKSANDR I. SOLZHENITSYN

A reporter working for a popular weekly publication, known as *The Untainted Press*, having read a chapter of *A Seedling of Hope* and deciding that he liked it, phones an Imam, an author of *another* book on Islam. This author is a friendly and polite man who is living in the same city. The reporter asks him if he would kindly come to the press office for an interview for the next issue of the weekly.

The author is happy to do so and arrives promptly on time. His wife wanted to go shopping and came along since they have only one car. He had asked her to wait in the car while he went in for the interview, saying he would be back in a jiffy. An hour soon flies by for the author. He suddenly looks at his watch. He has spent more time with the reporter than he anticipated. He jumps up, apologizes to the reporter, "Sorry, need to make a quick call. I will be back soon," the author says and disappears down the hall to look through the glass window at the cars parked below. The reporter goes to replenish his coffee cup.

"Now what was the author talking about," the reporter asks himself after filling his cup with some coffee. "Oh, yes. He was going to give me some papers to explain some basics of Islam. He was trying to explain the emphasis the Quran places on humans to *reflect deeply* on the world around them." The reporter wants some definitions cleared up before he lets the author go. He looks at the author hurrying back.

AUTHOR: Sorry. I had to make a quick call to my wife who was wondering where I was since she has been waiting in the car for an hour. I had told her I would be back shortly, but time just flew by while I was trying to explain things to you. I just phoned her and she told me she was going home in the car as her toes were freezing and she does not like to keep the car idling. I will have to take a bus. I am going to be in big trouble when I get home.

REPORTER: I hope you came up with a good excuse.

AUTHOR: I could not lie. I told her that I was asking the reporter to *reflect* on the marvelous world we inhabit, and that it took a little too long. She told me I will have a lot of *reflecting* to do when I get back home because she will not open the door so I can get a chance to *reflect* on the state of toes in freezing temperatures. She told me that this marvelous world I inhabit may not be much for me to *reflect* upon if I come home late. I ruined her frying pan last weekend and now this.

REPORTER: Ha! Ha! What is this about the frying pan? I am curious to know, if you do not mind. I find human nature very interesting. And you do not look like a fella who could get into trouble.

AUTHOR: Yes, I can. I get into trouble often. Last weekend I thought I would give my wife a surprise and prepare breakfast before she got up. It was a Saturday and she was still sleeping soundly. I got up early and used her favorite pan to make some pancakes. I put the batter on the pan and went to grab the newspaper. The headlines caught my eye and I started reading and promptly forgot about the batter. The fire alarm went off waking the whole household up with a jolt. As my wife came rushing down, I saw to my horror that I had ruined her favorite pan. She saw it too through the thick smoke. As she ran into the kitchen to get hold of a utensil to use it for a purpose not within the manufacturer's guidelines, I ran out the front door in my pajamas, with disheveled hair and without my slippers, to escape any potential wrath upon myself. My quiet elderly neighbor, who has bad knees, was puttering in the garden as I rushed out. The commotion made him jump and he bolted into his own house. I have never seen a man with bad knees run as fast as he did. I felt very embarrassed and pretended I had seen something on the front lawn. I saw him peering out of the window at me looking at some blades of grass. I saw him later in the day looking at the spot where I had been looking. He must be wondering what was so special about the particular patch of grass that caused me such excitement. He must have thought the Muslim next door had finally flipped. I don't think I have made a good impression on the neighbor.

**Reporter:** Ha! Ha! I think you should go and explain to him what happened. You must let him know that your senses are intact.

**Author:** Thanks. I think I will do that. But since that day, he goes inside his house as soon as he hears me coming out. I will have to come out quietly, creep up on him and pat him on the shoulder before he goes into the house.

**Reporter:** No, no! Don't do that. You will give the elderly chap a heart attack. He already has a negative opinion formed of you. Do it some other way. Give him a ring and invite him over for tea or something. At least that will start the ice to thaw. Explain what happened over the phone.

**Author:** Good idea. Thanks.

**Reporter:** You are welcome. You said you would write up on some basics on Islam and bring it with you. Did you get the chance to write up some stuff?

**Author:** Yes, yes. I did. Aah! Here they are. I kept some explanations short in case you wanted to use them for your weekly.

The author hands some papers to the reporter. He looks at the reporter's face with anticipation as the reporter reads.

## Allah

In the Arabic language, God is known simply by the name "Allah". We know that not all Arabs speak English, so if you approach a bunch of Arabs drinking coffee and conversing in Arabic, and pat one on the shoulder and ask him, "Who is God?", he may give you a blank unhappy look; and you should not be quick to assume it has something to do with drinking bitter black coffee in tiny cups and he feels hard done by without having a bigger cup and some milk and sugar in his coffee. (Some *prefer* bitter coffee in tiny cups. It is just the way it is, and we should just accept it.) It is more probable that he is unhappy as he knows not a word of English. The Arab-speaking group, when talking about the Lord and Creator, will not use the English word "God"; they will use the word "Allah." Simple so far, I hope.

Now comes the difficult part: there are some "enlightened" zealots who think that "Allah" is a form of a deity that Muslims falsely worship, when they should instead be worshipping "God" (the capital "g" one, silly), and they are on the internet denouncing "Allah" not knowing that it is an Arabic word for "God." Sometimes, in their zeal, the zealots catch an Arab unawares, prod him in the back while he is holding hot coffee which causes him to spill it on himself, and after ignoring his expletives, sincerely try to explain that the Arab got it all wrong and he should worship God, not Allah. The Arab, thoroughly confused since he does not speak English, keeps muttering in vain, *"Ana la atahadath al Inglizia. Ana murtabik"* ("I do not understand a word of English. If you do not stop now, I will leave you talking to yourself, or I will wring your English neck till you stop talking in this foreign tongue." Well, not in so many words). He says he does not speak English and he does not understand what they said. Half of the clever zealots go away with a huff denouncing the ignorant Arab who can't even hold the coffee without spilling it on himself.

So far, so good; half the zealots get it, half still do not. These remaining English-speaking monolingual diehards are still denouncing the Arabs for using the word "Allah" instead of "God." So, let us take one of these ultraconservative fossils to France.

Point the religious zealot in the direction of a proud French guy eating lunch and enjoying his French fries with escargot. Watch him as he persists in using the word "God" and gives the French guy (who does not speak English) a long lecture on "God." At the end, observe him as he gives the French guy a gentle pat on the shoulder for being such a good listener. Watch the zealot closely as he asks the French guy if he has any questions. Do not laugh when the zealot falls off his chair when the French guy says, *"Pardon? Je n'ai pas bien compris ce que vous avez dit. Ma nourriture est devenue froide a cause de toi"* ("Excuse me? I did not understand what you said. My food has gone cold because of you.")

God is "Dieu" in the French language.

Only about a dozen zealots still remain. They are still adamant people should worship "God," and no other deity. They still do not understand that God is Allah in Arabic. So, let us take one of them to a Christian village in the Middle East.

If the zealot asks an Arab *Christian* reading the Bible written in Arabic what they call God in his native Arabic tongue and he says, "Allah," make sure the zealot has a firm grip on the chair. Too many bumps on the head falling off chairs for hardheads causes damage to heads. Or concrete floors if the noggin is very solid and unyielding.

*Assyrian Christians use the word* **Elaha** *or* **Alaha** *for God. Jesus and his disciples would have spoken* **Aramaic,** *a Semitic language and the lingua franca of his time. The word for God in Aramaic is* **Al-Ilah.**

Allah, when addressing *Himself* in the Quran, will often use the Arabic word *Nahnu*, translated loosely as "We," as is used in many other languages in a royal context. In the French language, such use is employed even when addressing a single person, as a sign of respect.

A king may address himself in colloquial English as the imperial "We," such as in, "We decree that henceforth…". Many ancient languages use the term "we" instead of "I" as a term of ennoblement intrinsic in the self. This is not to be confused with multiplicity.

Arabs do not have any confusion about the term "we," as they use this liberally and without contradiction, knowing exactly the context in which it is used.

Why am I focusing on the word "we" and what am I trying to get at? It is all because of a group of young enthusiasts who came knocking at my door one weekend, wanting to educate me about Islam since I looked droopy without my morning cup of coffee. I went slowly to open the door, and blinked in the bright sunlight. New faces greeted me. "Oh. Hello. Do you guys want to come in?" I said. They did not, but they had something to show the "ignorant Muslim" because I had probably got it all wrong.

## A groggy Muslim on a weekend

So here I was looking at some enthusiastic young Jehovah's Witnesses. I was going to be taught about Islam and the "We" phenomenon. The leader (I assumed he must be the leader as he was doing most of the talking) looked at me with a smug but polite grin, as if I had not noticed this glaring fact in the Quran. Here were Muslims saying, "God is One," and here was proof that we got it all wrong since God sometimes addressed himself as "We" in the Quran. "We" according to him denoted multiplicity.

I asked them, "Do you have a copy of the Quran?"

The leader answered, "No."

"Have you read the Quran?" I asked him.

"No," he answered, "but I know someone who does. He is one of our leaders and he says he reads the Quran."

"Oh. Does he know Arabic?"

"No. I don't think so. He has a copy of the translation."

"Then how would he know, if he is reading from a translation of the Quran, in which context the term 'We' is used?" I asked politely, wanting to clarify this simple point of contention.

I explained to the group that the term "We" was used in the Quran as an innate form of dominion, glory, and respect. I asked if someone from their group spoke French, and was pleased when they pointed to a tall member of the team. I addressed the French-speaking member of the team and asked him if a similar term was not also used in the French language as a term of respect: "Don't you use *nous* as a term of respect, instead of *je*? And don't you use *vous* instead of *tu* to a person to whom you want to address with respect?" The others looked at the French-speaking person nodding in affirmation.

Since the eager group had been showing me passages from the Bible that they had with them, and as I had spent some considerable time listening to them, I felt I was justified in bringing out my copy of the Quran to dispel the confusion that the youths obviously had.

Unfortunately, the now uncomfortable team, who just minutes ago were so eager to spend time quoting the Quran out of context, were suddenly constrained for time and did not want to look at my copy of the Quran, as if the book was going to cast a spell on them. They made a hasty retreat when I invited them inside for tea so I could bring the Quran out from my home library and clarify some other points of contention that they had been erroneously (I use that lightly) taught about the Holy Book of Muslims at their places of learning.

*We are taught to look at both sides of the story in civil engagement and discourse, especially when rendering judgment. The attitude of not hearing out the other party, especially in this century of much touted progress, is naïve and regressive.*

As they walked away, I admired their suits and ties, for indeed they presented themselves well. They seemed to be good people; no doubt eager to "save" people from their wayward ways. They were polite. How good it would be if we could all sit at a table and have a wholesome and dynamic discussion and come to a common platform! The eager group had come in peace, and was leaving in peace. I hoped it would always stay that way. In the end, if all else fails, we can agree to disagree and still be civil about it.

Unfortunately, that is not always the case. You will often notice "holier-than-thou" and "gun-toting and religious-book-carrying" people from all walks of life using vile means to try to achieve an objective that is contradictory to the words they preach, "Believe in the Book and look at these nice passages (selected to serve my passions and avarice, you nasty ignorant heathen, but of course I am not saying it. It's all in me heart, y'know. By the way, give me your land you ignorant native and let my imported slaves work the field. I am happy you are doing this peacefully 'cos I have this firearm here, see?)" These phenomena have vestiges in various forms still present on a distant planet in a land called the Southern State.

Many politicians and religious leaders, eager to keep their grip on power, appear to suffer particularly from this malady; I bet they must have failed their anthropology and social sciences exams. The zero tolerance on differences among humans and the big "0" on their exam paper may well indicate proportionate material inside the cranium.

## Prophet Mohammed

Muslims are commanded in the Quran to accord proper salutation to Prophet Mohammed when referring of him; and this often comes in the form of reciting the following salutation: *Peace Be Upon Him (PBUH)*. Though I may not state the salutation every time I mention Prophet Mohammed in this book, *A Seedling of Hope*, I nevertheless mean it to be there as a recurring postscript. The name Mohammed in this book refers to Mohammed bin Abdullah, the Prophet of Islam, born in Mecca 1,400 years ago and believed by Muslims to be the final messenger of God, and not that other Mr. Mohammed, your next-door neighbor, now seen with his pajamas peering curiously at something on his driveway, something the cat brought.

Prophet Mohammed was born about 570 years after Jesus (peace be upon them both), the son of Mary. Muslims are commanded to pronounce peace upon their prophets and to honor them. Most Muslims generally pronounce the salutation of "peace" not only when Prophet Mohammed is mentioned, but also other prophets of God. Prophet Mohammed said that they are his brothers (in faith). You will not find Muslims denigrating any prophet, and this basic fact is only one of the many platforms on which relationships between faiths can be built. *In fact, there is a chapter in the Quran titled Mary, and she is mentioned with much endearment as is Jesus*.

When Aisha (the wife of Prophet Mohammed) was asked to describe the character of her husband, she said he was an embodiment of the Quran. Prophet Mohammed (peace be upon him) lived a life of austerity, was quick to forgive, firm in carrying out God's command, extremely generous, and resolute in times of hardship. Almost without contention, these qualities of Prophet Mohammed have been widely accepted, including among non-Muslim scholars.

Michael H. Hart's book, titled *The 100: A Ranking of the Most Influential Persons in History* is a fascinating read.[35] Guess who has been given the **number one spot**? Mohammed. Why this man? Study Mohammed in *authentic* sources and you will know why. Mr. Hart, a non-Muslim, objectively compares such figures as Isaac Newton, Aristotle, George Washington, Jesus, Moses, Charles Darwin, Karl Marx, John F. Kennedy, Confucius, Albert Einstein, and others who are considered the most influential figures in history. He is quoted as saying, "My choice of Muhammad to lead the list of the world's most influential persons may surprise some readers and may be questioned by others, but he was the only man in history who was supremely successful on both the religious and secular level."

The book has garnered rave reviews in publications such as the *Los Angeles Times*, the *Wall Street Journal*, the *Daily Mail* (U.K.), and many others, having sold half a million copies in 15 languages.

## Quran

> The legislation of Quran will spread all over the world, because it agrees with the mind, logic and wisdom.
>
> —LEO TOLSTOY

The Quran is the Holy Book for Muslims; Muslims believe it is the Final Revelation from Allah to Prophet Mohammed, who then

---

35 Michael H. Hart, The 100: A Ranking of the Most Influential Persons in History (New York: Citadel Press, 1978/1992)

transmitted the message of the Quran to his followers. Simply put, the Quran is an instruction manual from God Almighty. The Quran has remained unchanged for 1,400 years, and this fact is undisputed, even by Christians and contemporary historians. *Muslims believe that Almighty God revealed the same basic message of monotheism via different messengers (such as Abraham, Noah, Moses, Jesus, and Mohammed; peace be on them all).* Though there were certain different do's and don'ts for each community based upon the historical times each lived, one thing remained *a constant*; the creed of monotheism.

*Muslims honor all messengers—and even hold Jesus in very high esteem as one of the messengers of God—**but believe that the other religious books have undergone some change through human interference, with insertions, deletions, and/or alteration**. Muslims also believe that **<u>allegations</u> of marked indecent behavior** (such as incest) against the prophets of God (except for minor failings) in the Bible **are human insertions**. The Quran addresses all the prophets with honor, **rejecting** all such accusations of immoral behavior.*

Muslims believe that the Quran remains unchanged, as Allah has taken it upon Himself to safeguard it, as is quoted in the Quran: *"We have, without doubt, sent down the Message (the Quran); and We will assuredly guard it (from corruption)"* (Quran 15:9).

The Quranic verses were revealed t o Prophet Mohammed over a period of 23 years by Archangel Jibreel (Gabriel). Prophet Mohammed himself was "unlettered," meaning he did not know how to read or write. Thus, the assertion occasionally made that he copied texts from ancient scriptures is inaccurate. Prophet Mohammed recited the Quranic verses to his companions, who would memorize them, inscribe them on parchment, leather, or other materials, and repeat them to him to ensure accuracy. Every year the Prophet recited the whole Quran to Angel Jibreel, and vice versa, as he would love to hear the Quran from the angel.

Though the Quran is a large "manual," it is indeed amazing in that even a ten-year-old child is able to memorize it easily from cover to cover, so that there are hundreds of thousands of children and adults (men and women) in almost every corner of the world able to recite the Quran word for word without a single mistake. A *haffidh* is a person who has mastered the art of recitation and committed the entire Quran to memory. Memorizers of the Quran are known in Arabic as *huffadh* (plural of *haffidh*), meaning "Protectors" of the Quran.

My son, a *haffidh*, even at the tender age of 14 would often lead the prayers at different mosques with much older men standing behind him, an honorable privilege given to those who can recite the Quran accurately and from memory.

Prior to the advent of mass printing, the *huffadh* traveled widely across the Islamic Empire and were received with great respect wherever they went. There are many competitions on the art of Quran recitation across the world, which are easily accessible on the internet, for those wishing to sample the rhythm, tone, and techniques of different reciters and experience how the Quran sounds in mosques.

One of the oldest copies of the Quran (owned previously by Uthman, one of the closest companions of the Prophet) is displayed in the Topkapi Museum in Turkey (there are other ancient copies and parchments in such varied locations as England, Germany, and even the Vatican).[36] Amazingly, the latest copy of the Quran in circulation remains unchanged from the copy in the Topkapi Museum.

The legacy of the Quran is stored within the bosoms of countless Muslims in every part of the globe, who recite verses in their daily ritual of five prayer sessions. If the sound of these recitations were to be gathered in one place, the reverberations from the entire Muslim

---

36  https://commons.wikimedia.org/wiki/File:The_%E2%80%98Uthman_
Qur'an_-_Kufic.jpg; https://www.livescience.com/51638-quran-manuscript-oldest-
known-copy.html (University of Birmingham); https://www.moroccoworldnews.
com/2014/11/144270/researchers-discover-oldest-copy-of-the-quran-in-germany/;
http://www.oldest.org/religion/qurans/

population around the globe would indeed rise to an intense and profound crescendo; God praised with great intensity every minute of every day. Of the Quran, Allah (God) states, *"No falsehood will come to it, in the present or in the future; a revelation from the One who is Wise and Praiseworthy"* (Quran 41:42).

## Hadith

> *Qais ibn Sa'd, one of the companions of Prophet Mohammed reported: A funeral passed by the Messenger of Allah, peace and blessings be upon him, and he stood up. Someone said to him, "the person was a Jew." The Prophet replied, "Was he not a soul?"* [37]

The above quote is an example of a *Hadith*. A *Hadith* is a saying or counsel given by the Prophet as instruction. This Hadith appears in two of the most authentic books—*Bukhari*, and *Muslim*—and by consensus among Muslim scholars they meet extremely stringent standards of authenticity—about the life of the Prophet. Now that we know what the Quran is, the term "Hadith" is easier to understand. The instruction manual (Quran) from Allah was sent to Prophet Mohammed so that he could teach his followers how to apply the message, as well as appreciate its nuances, subtleties, and complexities. Prophet Mohammed's life and sayings form what is called the Hadith (singular), or Ahadith (plural). Hadith is how the Prophet conducted his affairs, leading his life through example and instructing his followers on the do's and don'ts of Islam.

The question would arise in an inquiring mind: why send a messenger when God only needed to send the Book? There is a

---

37 https://sunnah.com/muslim/11/103

Chinese proverb which states, *"Tell me and I will forget. Show me and I will remember. But involve me and I will understand."* What beautiful words of wisdom! God in His Infinite Wisdom sent not only these manuals (such as the Torah, the Bible, and the Quran) but also teachers (such as Moses, Jesus, and Mohammed—Peace be upon them all), who then demonstrated the *application* of the Book to their respective nations.

These compilations of Hadith are recorded in several collections of books such as *Bukhari, Muslim, Tirmidhi, Muwatta,* among others. For example, the quote above, by Qais, has been authenticated by the books of *Bukhari* and *Muslim.*

*I have used only the most authentically stringent sources of Ahadith in this book.*

## Islam

> *I challenge anyone to understand Islam, its spirit, and not to love it. It is a beautiful religion of brotherhood and devotion.*
> —Yann Martel, *Life of Pi*

Though some Muslims believe that the word "Islam" means *peace,* the true meaning is in fact *submission* to the Will of God. In Islam, the belief is that when someone submits to the Will of God, that person attains peace (*Salama*).

Unfortunately, what you see is not always what you get. Many Muslims have drifted far from their religious inheritance of practicing altruism, forgiveness, kindness, compassion, and firmness in carrying out God's commands. This book attempts to clarify for non-Muslims what true Islam is, and what it stands for. It is also a call for Muslims to return to the true message of Islam and practice goodness, compassion, and mercy to all of God's creatures, as well as live a life of honesty and good citizenship.

## Muslims

> *The religiosity of Muslims deserves respect. It is impossible not to admire, for example, their fidelity to prayer. The image of believers in Allah who, without caring about time or place, fall to their knees and immerse themselves in prayer remains a model for all those who invoke the true God, in particular for those Christians who, having deserted their magnificent cathedrals, pray only a little or not at all.*
>
> —POPE JOHN PAUL II

Muslims are people who follow the religion of Islam. Simply bearing a Muslim-sounding name and professing to be a Muslim does not make a person a true Muslim. If one says he is king of a country, does it make him the king? In his delusion he may feel he is a king, strutting about in his fantasy; while we wink at each other knowing very well he is not.

It is sad that sometimes Muslims offer lip-service in a manner that is un-Islamic, and thus tarnish the image of Islam. Being born into a Muslim household or converting to Islam is not a guarantee of righteous living. One needs to embody the faith and practice the Islamic behavior of fairness, goodness, and justice. One must live by the Quranic injunction that states, *"(And) lo! Those who believe and do good works are the best of created beings"* (Quran 98:7).

We often blame the media for biased reporting. But how can the media make a distinction as to who is a good Muslim and who is not? The media, often unintentionally, report crimes committed by (non-practicing) Muslims emphasizing the religious dimension, raising the question of why these members of a religion preaching peace would commit such crimes.

How might an objective media—and an objective readership and viewership—avoid the pitfall of painting all Muslims with the same brush? Here is one way: If they were to examine those who commit crimes against others, and dig a little more deeply, they would often find that these "Muslims" do not pray regularly and consistently, year after year, as commanded by God; that they do not give regularly to charity as commanded; that they are not truthful consistently; that they may have a criminal record; that they break promises thoughtlessly and unrepentantly; or that they have just recently put a pause on an un-Islamic lifestyle and want to redeem themselves quickly, often violently. Dig a bit more deeply, and the "Muslim" tag is just that: a tag. This tag is synonymous with a price label that is attached to a shirt in a store, easily replaced by another tag if circumstances change.

Price fluctuates, tag changes. There is no permanency to such tags.

A true Muslim, on the other hand—where is he? His tag is tattooed onto his heart and soul with indelible but invisible ink. He is busy doing simple chores, earning an honest living, and putting food on the table. He is a permanent fixture with a label whose value does not change. He is well-versed in his religious obligations. He is compassionate, forgiving, and hates to hurt others. He is aggrieved when he sees injustice. He may even sit down and write a book trying to dispel confusion and stereotypic behavior, and advocate for unity. You are not going to hear about this guy in the tabloids.

Consistency in small acts of kindness, as any leader of any religious denomination will tell you, builds a good solid character, and it is no different when it comes to true practicing Muslims. As the American entrepreneur, author, and motivational speaker Emanuel James Rohn put it, "Success is neither magical nor mysterious.

Success is the natural consequence of consistently applying basic fundamentals."

The reporter lays down the papers. He had a better idea, n o w he hoped, of the Muslim mindset. It would be good if other people knew it too so that they would know how deal with Muslims. They would also know how to present their own religion to the Muslims. Mutual discourse would whisk away the ignorance of the other. They would learn to empathize, and learn to tolerate each other. They would stop fearing the other.

Was that part of the formula so that members of different faiths could learn to live with each other in harmony? Interfaith dialogue looked promising. Perhaps more of it was needed in a torn planet, the reporter reflected. But he wasn't done yet. *He wanted to know if God really existed. He had read the book by Darwin, and the idea of "Evolution" and the "Origin of Species" had appealed to him. How did this Muslim think of God?*

*"You seem to have firm faith in the existence of God. <u>Is there a God?</u>* "He knew he had been a little too abrupt, and he hadn't phrased it politely enough to the man sitting in front of him. What was the author going to say?

"Of course, *there is a God.* I was writing about the existence of an ingenious Creator just last week for our youth program. Wait, I think I have some papers here." He rummages through his briefcase. "I created two simple scenarios, or stories, with lessons for a contemplative mind. Ah. Here they are." The author hands some papers to the reporter.

The reporter reads. He pauses often, reflects deeply for brief moments at some passages, and then resumes reading. It is a bit long, but *fascinating.* This is what he reads:

## The Creator

You can address the Creator, or God, or Allah, by His many attributes. There is no separate deity for every religious group out there. It is the same Creator. I will sometimes use Allah and sometimes God in this book, to indicate The One True God, Creator of all things. There are 99 names for God in the Quran and Hadith, each one of the attributes of God worth reflecting upon. As the Quran states, *"He is Allah, the Creator, the Inventor of all things, the Bestower of forms. to Him belong the Best Names. All that is in the heavens and the earth glorify Him. And He is the All-Mighty, the All-Wise"* (Quran 59:24).

In the Quran, God constantly exhorts us to reflect on His signs; within His creation is *proof* of His existence, His power, and His infinite knowledge. Instead of asking us to "just believe, have faith, and do not ask questions," the approach the Quran takes is that of *reflection and of contemplation*; it appears to promise that for people who strive sincerely in their attempt to look for truth, the answers will come fairly quickly and with clarity, while the answers will elude those whose motives are insincere.

Trying to be true to this exhortation, I will attempt to simplify a few of God's attributes using two conversations to underscore some concepts.

## Bill meets Peter Pompus, a rocket-propulsion scientist, at the space station

Bill was sitting with his friend Peter at the Space Headquarters having had special clearance by security for a special invitation courtesy of his friend. The security team was thorough, and he had felt embarrassed when they extracted something from his pocket. They had gathered around to look at the crumpled aluminum foil and gingerly opened it, one holding his gun holster at the ready. It was a used chewing gum and Bill had forgotten to throw it away before he came in. Oops.

But now he was relaxed, enjoying the company of his friend, who was trying to explain what the giant flashing screens overhead were meant to convey. He had, however, noticed that his friend had walked over to him with his head held a little too high as he walked past other scientists who cowered when he went by. This was unlike Peter who was normally so genial that one would never know he was one of the greatest scientists the world has ever known, a master when it came to spaceships and propulsion.

Bill had known Peter since childhood and they normally conversed frankly and with ease. Peter takes a bite from an apple and offers Bill the basket of fruit that is sitting on his desk. There are bananas, apples, oranges, grapes, pears and a myriad of other fruit. These guys must eat well to keep their grey cells working full tilt, reflects Bill.

"No, thanks Peter. I just had a sandwich as I was driving in. Now, now, Peter, no need to get so haughty with your fellow scientists. I saw you. You walked past the other scientists with your head held a little too high. That is unlike you. You need to be brought down a peg, my friend, and I am gonna help do it for your own sake. We certainly do value the invention of this complex spaceship that can travel beyond the Earth, even as far as Mars, with most of the propulsion dynamics perfected by you. I am not trying to belittle your contribution to this spaceship, for it is indeed amazing."

Bill surveys the people running around, engaged in their specialized tasks at the base-of-operations space hub, giant screens flashing information that only people with advanced technical knowledge would know how to decipher. Bill felt himself break into a sweat, for it was indeed overwhelming. He lifts a paper from Peter's desk and reads its contents. It is from NASA: "The US National Aeronautics and Space Administration (NASA) seeks proposed solutions for fecal, urine, and menstrual management systems to be used in the crew's launch and entry suits over a continuous duration of up to 144 hours. An in-suit waste management system would be beneficial for contingency scenarios or for any long duration tasks."[38] NASA was offering $30,000 to anyone who could help them overcome the problem. Bill puts the paper down and continues, "Have you solved the problem with defecation by the astronauts that you guys were working on?"

"The poop problem, you mean," Peter smiles. "Not yet. We have now sent an invitation to the whole planet's scientists to help us solve this problem that happens when the astronauts 'have to go' and can't hold anymore. No success so far. We are still working on how to get rid of body waste efficiently. We think we are so clever, but now we feel so humbled."

"Peter, I am going to tell you something about the ultimate designer and creator, and knowing you, I am sure you will not take offence. Here it is. Despite all your technological knowledge, you must accept the fact that you have had to invite the whole world and its community of scientists to solve the simple—or maybe not so simple after all—problem of defecation by the astronauts. The world's intellectuals are scratching their heads and holding conferences to solve the poop problem. Yet look at this amazing world—how everything is coordinated in such fine balance that we not only get rid of our body waste but it gets recycled to fertilize and produce new growth in complex recycling pathways, and all with such ease. Then we eat sweet fruit from fodder we defecate, while we dispute the existence of God with an apple in hand."

"Interesting," says Peter. He glances at the apple in hand but knows Bill was only using a scientific metaphor. "Go on."

"My dear Peter, it is God who created you and your brain and the materials you used to construct the spaceship, isn't it? Your spaceship will have to pull away from the gravitational force that God created, to planets he set into motion with such precision that they do not collide with each other. The precision of gravitational forces

38  https://www.natureworldnews.com/articles/33135/20161130/win-nasa-30-000-space-poop-challenge.htm

they exert do not exceed even minutely to cause heavenly catastrophe. He also gave you means, materials, and combustible fuels to put things into motion. He gave you eyes to see, and fingers to compute the mechanics of propulsion on paper. He gave you nerves and the CNS to control every motion within your body; and ears to hear your colleagues as you put things together. Can we not marvel at the Being who gave all this to man?"

"I guess we can," concedes Peter.

"Peter, I will tell you something very profound," says Bill, placing a hand on Peter's shoulder to make certain the words will get due attention. *"even before the ear is created to perceive sound, one has to have the concept of sound. even before the eye as an organ is made to see, one has to have the concept of sight.* Isaac Newton—the scientist who discovered the phenomenon of gravity—that same Newton you scientists have to deal with in order to design your spaceship's propulsion to overcome the force of gravity. Commenting on this Powerful Being, Newton said, *"Gravity explains the motions of the planets, but it cannot explain who sets the planets in motion."* Peter, think with the brain that God made for you: did you not use this same brain to enable you to travel through the deep space, the deep space that *He* created."

"Interesting," says Peter. "I guess I did use the brain, a brain that was not of my making. Go on," says Peter. He is not offended and he knows his friend means well.

"We value your contribution to science, and it is indeed praiseworthy," continues Bill. "Nevertheless Peter, if you are truthful and humble, to *Whom* should we direct the ultimate praise?"

"I guess the one who created the brain," says Peter. "Go on."

"I was reading about hearing and sight and I came across a very interesting verse in the Quran that Muslims say came from God," says Bill. He pulls out a piece of paper from his shirt pocket. "Here is one. I can't find the other piece of paper. This one is from verse 16:78 of the Quran. It says, 'And it is God who brought you forth from your mothers' wombs, and He appointed for you hearing, and sight, and hearts, that haply you will be thankful.'"

Peter is about to take another bite from the apple, but Bill's words have a striking naked truth to them. His hand stops, the apple hovering near his open mouth. It seems many seconds before he takes a bite. The fruit tastes different, more juicy and sweeter, and he suddenly becomes aware of the possible existence of an ingenious designer. He reflects particularly on why we always have to use the word "nature" to sound more scientific. "Nature did this" or "We owe it to nature."

He wondered why the scientific community seemed to make a deliberate effort *not* to assign praise to an intelligent creator. A Creator who had furthermore surely endowed him with incisors to take the bite from the apple, a hand with which to hold the apple, eyes to see its vivid colors, nostrils to smell its sweet aroma, taste buds able to partake of the sweet taste, and a digestive system to extract energy from the food—everything fitting into the circle of life in intricate and intertwined pathways. This miracle in itself was greater than the spaceship that people with intelligence and body parts—these also given to them by a higher power—were attempting to perfect.

Bill has been going through his pocket while Peter was thinking, chewing the apple slowly. Bill finds the other piece of paper he is looking for and offers it to his friend. When Peter picks it up and reads the second paper, he nearly drops the apple that he is holding in the other hand: "*Soon, We will show them Our signs in the universe, and even in their own bodies, until it becomes amply clear to them that, indeed, this (Qur'an) is the truth. Is it not enough for you that your Lord (watches and) witnesses every single thing?*" (Quran 41:53).

Had Peter heard what Betty on the other side of the planet was saying to her friend Mary, he would probably have choked on the fruit.

## Betty and Mary, scientist friends, somewhere in the Sahara

Sweat dripping down her brow, Mary stumbles into the tent, flushed not only with the searing midday heat of the Sahara Desert, but also with excitement. She puts her rucksack on the lone table inside, grabs a bottle of water from those on the table, and pours the entire contents over her head. "Aah! Heavenly!" she exclaims, looking at Betty, who had jumped up quickly from where she was sitting reading a book, fanning herself, and is now staring aghast with wonder at her friend.

As water makes its way right down to Mary's ankles and into her boots, she grabs another bottle and drains it down her throat in two deep gulps. "Water! The liquid of life! Marvelous $H_2O$! A thumbs-up to whoever thought of creating this wonderful substance. From it springs all life and we need it to keep alive, and yet we do not give water a second thought when we have it aplenty! One more bottle over the head and my shower is done for the day!" They both laugh. Mary then motions to the rucksack. "I have something interesting to show you."

"I can't wait, but you need to relax first." Betty resumes fanning herself. "I told Abdullah not to take you too far. Best to go when the sun is about to go down. He is used to heat but we are not. How did you fare with the camel?"

"I think I am getting better at controlling the camel. Though the ride is a bit jaunty; sitting higher up is more comfortable as the sand was really hot when I came down. I can't understand how camels' hooves can withstand such scalding sand. The 'ship of the desert,' they call it. It is so well adapted to the heat and dryness, and its huge eyelashes and a special third clear eyelid keeps dust at bay during desert storms. I learnt that it can go without actually drinking water for many months in the Sahara winter months when it is a little cooler, whereas humans can only last a few days without drinking."

"How does the camel accomplish that?"

"It has oval-shaped red blood cells that keep the blood flowing when the volume of blood goes down in times of water scarcity," Betty replies. "Human red blood cells are spherical, and would have difficulty flowing if the volume were to go down. Did you know the camel's hump stores abundant reserves of energy and water which the animal can use when food and water resources are minimal? I am developing a real affection for such a beautiful animal, though many people do not think of it is as being pretty. I love its huge eyes. I do not care what people say. It *is* beautiful, as all creatures are in their own special ways!"[39]

As seasoned adventurers, Mary and Betty had gone up into the mountains of Nepal, traversed the farther reaches of Alaska with sleds pulled by huskies, had dove deep into the turquoise blue ocean off Australia to touch dolphins, and had even been chased by an irate female elephant when they had gotten too close to one of the herd's babies. It was a moment of truth, a moment each one knew for certain who would be speedier when it came to a heated race. The elephant, its huge ears flapping, gave a final warning trumpet and ambled off when the two suddenly vanished from sight behind some trees, with tired wheezing the only sign of their presence when they peeped cautiously to check if they were still being followed. That was in Kenya, on their most recent trip.

Betty was an anthropologist and Mary a wildlife biologist. Every year, the two scientists would save up funds and go for two to three months on distant trips to marvel at the wonders the Earth had to offer, taking pictures, writing articles and advocating for the Earth's protection. Their husbands understood their passion, and though they would accompany them at times, they preferred to remain behind, claiming busy work schedules for their successful private companies. Only the golf course personnel knew what "busy schedules" really meant. But Mary and her friend knew the urgency of their tasks:

---

39 https://www.livescience.com/27503-camels.html

time was running out, species were disappearing, fragile habitats were under greater threat with each passing day; human greed unabated—indeed accelerating. Betty was known among her peers as one who loved to write; many of her articles published in scientific journals drew rave reviews, and some of her books delved into issues that fomented considerable ire from the scientific community, but also acclaim from a segment that was not content in towing the conventional academic line; critical reviews abounded from both the media and the analytically studious. When she wrote, people took notice.

Mary opens the rucksack and pulls out a skeleton arm. Betty jumps back. "Whoa!" she exclaims. "What in heaven is that?"

Mary motions to a watch loosely strapped to the skeletal arm. "I found this in the desert. There were several skeletons dispersed a little distance from each other. Some poor folks probably got lost and died of thirst. This was lying close to one of the skeletons. The bones were all whitewashed by the sun, the flesh possibly picked clean by vultures and bugs. This arm struck me. The watch on it is a computer smart-watch. The battery is dead, of course."

Betty approaches, looks closely at the watch, and then picks up the skeleton arm. The battery has leaked, leaving a dried stain on the underside, while component parts inside were loose and falling apart. *"Entropy,"* Betty says. *"All things in nature fall apart and deteriorate and disintegrate over time."*

"How about diamonds?" asks Mary.

"Even the hardest materials like diamonds have a half-life. There is no exception," replies Betty.

Betty motions to the chairs and indicates they should both sit down. Mary sits. Betty moves her chair closer to Mary and sits.

"The arm bones confirm the evidence that they came from a living human who was born, ate, grew into adulthood, breathed air to sustain life, and used his body parts in a multitude of ways," says Betty. "The bone structure indicates it may have been a male. The person did not on his own accord decide to construct himself and put life within his own body. Most of the body is gone now; the bones too will eventually disintegrate. The watch remains, though it is falling apart. Some people, somewhere, possibly with many of them working together in a complex factory, and with precision and technological knowledge to guide them, must have put this complex watch together. No sane person would believe it came together by mere chance. Even if you tell me a thousand scientists have concluded that it came together by mere happenstance, common sense tells me someone made it."

Mary looks at the pile of books in the place where Betty had been sitting. "I see you have been reading thought-provoking books again. Are those religious books you have been reading? No wonder you have gone on a spill about the deeper meanings of life!"

Betty smiles at the comment. Her brows then furrow and she falls into deep thought. After a moment, she resumes the conversation. "Things do not come together miraculously, fall into place in a fine balance, and start functioning on their own, especially if they have many component parts, with distinct functions, each one working in amazing harmonious concert with each other: a human being, for example, with cells and organs to make a whole; or a mere insect with unique eyes or multitudes of fish in the oceans, each adapted uniquely to their environment. Entropy: given time, all things will fall into disarray and break down. *If you take atoms and molecules colliding with each other for millions of years, they do not come together and give themselves 'life' and start functioning.* Even if I were to give the Earth billions of years, the number of unique species cannot occur by mere chance. There is something out there the scientific community must come to terms with. Shunning truth with the excuse that this is mere "chance" is too naïve to be credible. What do you think, Mary?"

"I agree with you, Betty," responds Mary, as she gazes into her friend's deep blue eyes. She had not realized that Betty reflected so deeply into things they saw on their travels. She inwardly sighs with relief. She had been struggling inwardly about an Ingenious Creator and here was someone who felt as *she* did. There were things in life that could not be explained simply by allowing others to do our thinking for us, and then following their directions.

"I ask you, Mary, who created this amazing, intricate, precisely functioning world and all that is within?" Betty moves her chair closer. She motions to her friend to do the same. Mary knows her friend wanted her undivided attention. Betty continues: "We are still trying to understand how things work in amazing balance, harmony, and interdependence. Could it be by 'chance'? Science tells us that things fall apart over time and that there is gradual decline into disorder for all things, known as entropy. Obviously, this cell phone did not come together by chance even if we give millions of years of colliding atoms and molecules. The cell phone went through entropy and the human went through entropy. They both deteriorated over time. I do not believe that things accidentally come together in harmony to form functioning entities with millions of units working together in coordinated precision. Take the human body, for example ..."

"Betty, I have just come in from the heat. My mind is slow on the uptake. Simplify things, for heaven's sake." Mary takes a fan and also starts to fan herself.

"You certainly are hot! You are all flushed." Betty pauses for a few moments to give her friend some time to grab a bottle of water. She resumes after making sure her friend is feeling better, "Let me give you the example of the eye, simply one organ from the many within our own bodies. The eye has many component parts—like the lens and the muscles that control it to bring things into focus, the rods and cones for vision and color differentiation, the optic nerve to carry signals—all the individual parts uniquely designed for specific functions, composed of millions of cells, individual parts coming together in precise harmony and working together to form an image somewhere in the dark interiors of brain. It isn't really the eye that sees—it is the brain that forms the image in that convoluted dark mass in that protective cranium. I am simplifying this, of course."[40]

"Have the physicians fully understood how the eye and the brain work in tandem?" Mary asks.

"Our best physicians are still trying to understand the complexities of the eye and the brain," Betty answers. "Merely to understand it, Mary—never mind how it was formed, how individual components came together in an amazing complexity to make the eye function, its ability to see in light and dark, discerning the myriad colors and distances; to say nothing of those animals with eyes specially suited to their own unique environments! The signs of God are all around us, *the truth* is plain to, to ..." She falters as she tries to find the right words.

"Truth is plain to see for those who seek, especially since we are talking about the eyes?" suggests Mary.

"I like that. See for those who seek. See for those who seek the truth, that is. Now, Mary, imagine every creature and its special characteristics, the universe, and a myriad of other intricately connected things. *one has to have the concept of sound in order to create the ear.* One has to have the concept of taste to create taste buds. Do you not think there is a 'Being' out there who had the knowledge of the concepts of touch or smell or light or taste to create the body parts or organs to sense the same? *We know sound and touch and smell and taste only after **experiencing** these things. Can you imagine the ingenuity of the 'originator' of these stimuli, and then go on to create body organs to **perceive** these stimuli? Is it merely evolution? Is evolution so astonishingly clever that it creates the concepts of sound, hearing, sight, touch, and taste and then go about creating organs to perceive the same? or is there an Ingenious Creator who created such breathtaking phenomena?"*

---

40 https://www.brainfacts.org/Thinking-Sensing-and-Behaving/Vision/2012/Vision-Processing-Information

"Wow! I never reflected deeply on these phenomena which are so easy to see now that you point them out. These things elude so many of us as we wander like sheep moving towards a precipitous cliff of delusion on a dark night!" Mary exclaims, hoping to sound as clever as her friend.

"Some people reduce this huge, mind-boggling phenomenon to simple terms such as 'evolution' or 'adaptation.' I do not have a problem with that, but we must not stop there. *To a certain degree the phenomenon of evolution and adaptation is indeed certainly true. No argument there.* But we must go beyond the simple, and give ourselves greater credit with the intelligence we have been endowed with. With God's amazing power and ultimate creativity, is it not possible that He has formulated within creatures an amazing ability to *adapt and evolve*? We humans too are now trying to design 'smart' computers and robots with AI (artificial intelligence). A smart robot with AI can be programmed to learn from its interaction with its environment or from challenges it faces, and based on this experience, incorporate further strategies and expand its knowledge base and with this more enhanced potential re-interact again with its environment; in other words, *it can become smarter with each interaction, potentially indefinitely.* I'm sure you've heard of the IBM designed supercomputer Deep Blue and the chess match with world chess champion Kasparov about which the documentary film *The Man Vs The Machine* was made?"[41]

"Yes, I did. But it was a long time ago," replies Mary. "Refresh my memory."

"In this documentary film," continues Betty, "Kasparov won the first tournament in 1996, but was defeated by Deep Blue in 1997—the supercomputer kept incorporating more and more strategies with each interaction. Now we have much smaller but more intelligent off-the-shelf computers than Deep Blue. How can it be that God—

41 "Signals: The Man vs. The Machine," espn.go.com. ESPN.

with His awesome power of intricate creation and who designed the human brain to do amazing things—failed to include as part of His creation such systems that would withstand challenges that must occur in such a dynamic multifaceted world as ours?"

Mary interjects when Betty pauses: "But Betty, people are going to say that evolution and adaptation cannot coexist with creationism. It is either evolution or creation, not both. This choice is the main reason that many have rejected God or the idea of a Creator. How do you reconcile what appear to be polar opposites?"

Betty answers with a retrospective question, "Why have we, as intelligent humans created a dichotomy which says that if the one paradigm were to exist—for example, say, evolution—the other—for example, say, creation—should not?"

"*Are you saying God created animals and then put complex evolutionary mechanics within them that allows them to take optimal advantage of the challenges—or forces, or dynamics—they face or shall face on Earth?*" asks Mary.

Betty admires how quick Mary grasps the gist. "You get the general idea. Let us take the example of air or water. Air is invisible, occupies space, and is in a gaseous form. Three paradigms coexist in air in those three properties. Water is liquid, and it is tasteless, odorless, and it occupies space, flows freely if it is liquid, and can be turned into solid if you freeze it; six paradigms. Yes, different paradigms can exist at the same time. Now the interesting part: do you not think that God can, in His Infinite Power, Wisdom and Knowledge—such amazing Knowledge and Artistry that we cannot even begin to fathom or comprehend—create all these myriads of complex creatures and at the same incorporate within these creature's certain adaptive and replicative mechanisms—we may call it adaptive genetic mutations or adaptive evolutionary gene transformations or a myriad of other names—for survival in a dynamic and changing environment? *Why have humans decided to put a dichotomy that says that if evolution were to exist, God cannot exist?* Why are humans trying to limit the power of God, the Incomparable and Absolutely Ingenious Creator, who has the ability to create species and place within these species the ability to evolve and adapt? *Deep Blue incorporated adaptive skills into its hard drive; living things do the same into their DNA, by God's Ingenious Design.* Betty, the power, might, and wisdom of God in His creation must be truly amazing, and I really cannot find words that can accurately describe it; I did marvel, however, at a phrase in the Quran that those Muslims read. It is in verse 67:4 and goes like this:

> *"Then look again and yet again [and however often you do so, with whatever instruments to aid your looking] your sight will fall back to you dazzled [by the splendor of God's creation], and awed and weakened [being unable to discern any flaw to support any excuse for claiming that there could be any sharing in the dominion of the universe]".*

Mary is stunned and can only whisper, "Wow!"

Betty pauses briefly to look amusingly at her wide-eyed friend, and then continues slowly, "One very amazing thing about the Quran is this, Mary: I have read many religious books from most religions, and there is much good in all of them, but the Quran is unique in that it is God speaking through the medium of the Angel Gabriel, whom the Muslims call Jibreel, and then via Mohammed to us folks. It is a direct conversation with each one of us. It is not merely a historical account of events that occurred in the past, given in the third person, as we find in the Bible and some other religious books. I am not in any way saying anything negative about the Bible since it too came from God, but humans interfered by using human perspectives when translating or transmitting it. In the Quran, the essential quality is that God is the author, and He speaks directly to us. He addresses each individual directly via the Angel Gabriel and then through Mohammed. Open the Quran and see what I mean. It is as if God is speaking to *you*."

"I did not know you to be overly religious, Betty. Have you been hiding something from me?" Mary asks.

"No, not really. Regardless of religion, we must be willing to accept reason and open up conversations when the scientists roll up their sleeves and tell us it is taboo. Mary, I think that when God decided to place man on Earth, there was *already* a myriad of animals such as dinosaurs as well as plants and other living things that He had earlier created. Much later on, man was placed on earth after the dinosaurs had died out from whatever causes He decreed for them. When I was reading the Quran, I discovered that the angels asked God why He wanted to place man on Earth when the angels were already doing things He willed. The angels were not only aware of the existence of the Earth, but also that the creatures God now intended to place there might shed blood. The Quran phrases it thus:

> *And [remember] when your Lord said to the angels: "Verily, I am going to place [mankind] generations after generations on earth." The angels said, "Will You place therein those who will make mischief therein and shed blood, —while we glorify You with praises and thanks (Exalted be You above all that they associate with You as partners) and sanctify You." He [Allah] said, "I know that which you do not know."* (Quran 2:30)

"I understand this to mean that the Earth was already there, inhabited by creatures other than man, and then God placed man on Earth much later on in his overall creation. The angels addressing God had a concept of blood and the shedding of blood. From where did they get that idea? I assume that they knew of life that existed on Earth—

the creatures on Earth must have been shedding blood as we had predators and prey on the planet—before the human was placed on Earth. That is why we find simple and complex fossils spread through the Earth. He originates creation, puts formulas of adaptation and evolution into His creation, and then repeats this amazing original creation in a multitude of ways. The human appears to have been placed in the form of Adam and Eve and they too divided into nations and tribes. In verse 49:13 of the Quran, it reads:"

> *O humankind! Surely We have created you from a single [pair of] male and female, and made you into tribes and families so that you may know one another [and so build mutuality and co-operative relationships, not so that you may take pride in your differences of race or social rank, and breed enmities]. Surely the noblest, most honorable of you in God's sight is the one best in piety, righteousness, and reverence for God. Surely God is All-Knowing, All-Aware.*

"Wow!" Mary exclaims. "You have surely made a profound statement, Betty. *But can you point out the passage to me that deals with this concept of original creation and its repetition in later creations?*"

Betty picks up the Quran that she had been reading when she was interrupted by Mary stumbling into the tent. She flicks through the pages to a yellow highlighted portion.

Mary laughs: "You have been marking the Quran at certain selected passages that interest you, haven't you? I bet even the imams would have to consult you for your observations!"

Betty smiles; charmed at her friend's comment. She puts her finger on a passage and reads:

*Say to them (O, Mohammed): "Travel through the earth and see how Allah originates the creation, then creates the later creation. Surely Allah has power over everything."* (Quran 29:20)

Betty continues, "Let me give you my reflections, Mary. This in no way means that humans evolved and crossed species into what we are today. Yes, we evolve and adapt, but not from a slug to man. One of the ways evolutionists explain themselves is that we evolve to a *better* form, yet we find apes still present among us. The way some of us behave, I sometimes wonder who came first."

"Hah!" Mary grins, amused. "I guess so, seeing some of our antics!"

"It is not easy to dismiss the stunning complexity of life and the immense precision mosaic of the heavens simply by stating 'natural phenomenon', 'nature did this', and 'evolution did this'– and evolutionary scientists are getting stumped at every corner and whichever way they look. Evolution does exist, and we are in concurrence on that one, but the scientists haven't figured 'how', yet. True scientists need to accept divergent views instead of looking at everything with yellow colored glasses that tend to make every living thing appear jaundiced. Plants are so much more efficient than animals. They extract materials from the Earth and use sunlight to manufacture food. Living things could have remained in plant form if evolution's mode was only "survival". Plants can manufacture their own food and are better at using things readily available. But God willed more than just plants or microbes."

"I guess you are right. But you know how scientists are. They will soon be rolling up their sleeves to counter your views," Mary cautions.

Betty is undeterred. She has intellectual grit, and is not one to cower. "Let me give the scientist with yellow glasses another amazing scenario to ponder upon: on this Earth we have man and woman, separate sexes, a male and a female, so that they can reproduce using special organs to produce children who will grow up and continue the cycle, generation upon generation. Then we have a male giraffe and a female giraffe, a lovely pair. We have *pairs* of thousands and thousands of species such as a male walrus and a female walrus far away in the Arctic, a male ostrich and a female ostrich in Africa, a male platypus and a female platypus down under in Australia, and so on. Look up and you find a male elephant chasing a gorgeous female elephant and you better run for your life because you do not want to look like a pancake. Look down and there is a male squirrel giving you a telling off for having stepped on his wife's tail while you were running away from the elephant. In fact, if the haughty scientist were to go deep into a forest that has never been explored by humans and lose his way because he was wearing dark yellow glasses, he could very well stumble upon new species of animals and be surprised that they came in pairs—male and female—keeping their progeny going strong."

"It's true. Never thought of it in that way before," says Mary. "There are pairs of thousands of creatures on Earth."

"Yep," says Betty. "In hundreds of thousands of years, millions even, there could have been thousands of different *types* of sexes in the animals that we could easily think of, if evolution was in full swing—a small change here, a big one there. Now let us see what we have: will the result be amazingly perfect or will it be absolute chaos? Remarkably, we have fascinating pairs of creatures with organs or methods that allow the establishment of successions of progenies; a female and a male counterpart that ensure the continuation of the species. *Did all the thousands upon thousands of animals, fish, insects, and birds sit at a table one day and decide that they should make themselves into exact complementary pairs—a male and a reciprocal female?* How ridiculous would that be? Indeed, there must be an ingenious Designer out there. It makes so much more scientific sense to accept the presence of a divine Creator than go about in circles picking at tiny yellow straws while wearing yellow 'evolutionary' glasses to justify His absence."

"So how would you advise the chap with dark yellow 'evolutionary' glasses, Betty?" Mary asks.

"My advice to the poor chap?" Betty's eyes twinkle with humor. "I would first ask him to get rid of the yellow glasses because they make him look *ridiculous!*"

Both of them burst into laughter.

Betty continues, "I would ask this evolution-scientist, who likes to follow others like an obedient lamb, that he tries hard and think for himself, and accept that this beautiful system of 'male and female' did not come about by 'chance'. Next, I would also give him a Tylenol to get rid of the whopping headache that's been brought on by squinting through the yellow fogginess to see *light*. It is so much more scientific to accept the presence of a magnificent Creator than otherwise. The only reason I think people do not want to accept the presence of a Creator is that if they were to do so, then they would feel obliged to abide by His laws, and therefore restrain themselves from doing that which would displease God, like lying and cheating and adultery. Some humans do not want restraints and so they invent theories to appease themselves and feel comfortable about the whole thing. Regardless, God exists and is ever-existing."

"What if someone firmly believes that God does not exist?" asks Mary.

"If one were to resolutely convince himself that God did not exist, would that suddenly make God disappear? No, of course not— it is simply self-deception. It is like the scientist who wants to find something to argue about, presenting numbers and figures so he is always looked upon with awe. If you tell him the sky is blue, he says, 'Not entirely. See that little cloud swimming in the sky. So, I say it is not all blue. And it is not blue at night. So there!' And if you bring out the Quran, that Muslims consider to be from God, which says, '*And we created pairs of everything that you may contemplate*' (Quran

51:49), he presents the idea of a hermaphrodite. The *general truth* is staring him in the face, but he is busy digging the poor worm from its soil, looking for *exceptions* from the general rule, and chasing little yellow clouds in a blue sky while wearing those ridiculous yellow glasses so that he can dispute its not a blue sky."

Betty pauses, lifts a bottle of water, takes a drink, and pours the rest over her head. "Time for a little shower, like you had!" They both laugh.

Mary is a good listener, keen to know more. "Go on, Betty," she prompts her friend. "I am all ears. But there is something that bothers me. Most major religions believe that God is *'infinite'* and *'eternal'*. How can you explain such things?"

Betty nods kindly. "God has placed *limits* on every creature, Mary. Let's imagine a clever frog in a well. The *well* is his *universe*."

"Is his name *Kermit*?" Mary asks with a mischievous grin.

"Ha! Ha! No, you smart aleck! Y've been watching too many *Sesame Street*s. His name is not Kermit, but he is clever nevertheless. From a tadpole, he has grown, and is now starting to ask questions. As we all do. He wants to know how big the universe is, and space, and time, and the concept of infinity. His world is limited by the walls of the well, outside of which he has no knowledge. The sun he sees is there for a very short time as it passes over the opening of the top of the well. These, therefore, are the *limits* beyond which he has no knowledge."

"Poor froggie," remarks Mary.

"Yes, poor froggie. Only if he were to go out of the well would he know that in fact there is a bigger universe beyond the well, and that time is different for humans living outside the well. The humans see the sun for a longer time. But even humans outside the well are constrained by the limits imposed upon them. They live on top of the Earth; they see the sun rising and the sun setting over a bigger horizon. That is their day. It is a longer day. Someone living outside the solar system has a different limit. Our day, dictated by the rising of the sun and the setting of the sun, is not the same for God who created the sun and the Earth. He exists *outside* those limits. God is the One who *created* space and time, and the sun and the Earth, and evolutionary mechanisms, and amazing creatures with specialized functions that fit precisely into ecosystems. He is not constrained by the limiting factors of time, space, Earth, and the sun, and constraints humans foolishly place on God with their own limited understanding of creation."

"Since you have been reading the Quran, is there anything about the 'essence of time'? That would be really interesting." Mary is eager to know more.

"In fact, there is," affirms Betty. "There is an interesting verse on 'time' in the Quran. The angel's day is equivalent to 50,000 years of our days, as per the Quran. In verse 70:4 of the Quran it says, 'The angels and the Spirit ascend to Him in a day, the measure of which is fifty thousand years.' Our minds can only contemplate God by how much He allows us to understand Him. *"Infinity," "Eternal," and "A God who does not beget and is not begotten" is beyond our grasp, because to us humans, all living things are "born." and must therefore "die". As Humans, our brains are constrained by the limits imposed upon them. If you take a mathematical calculator and ask it a question on the human brain, it will say, 'E'; for error. It has limits; it is programmed to do only so much and no more. The human mind also has limits.*"

"I wish all humanity would not quarrel and learn to love one another," Mary says. "It is the same God who created us all, and He would obviously want us to love one another as we are all *His* creation."

"I agree," Betty responds. "No religion has monopoly on God. You bring coherent proof and ignorant people will bring ten ridiculous arguments to discredit you; as if their god is better than the others person's god. They do not realize that they are talking about the same Universal God who created all of them. They are shallow, ill-educated, and arrogant. However, there are good sincere people among humankind; they acknowledge that most religions know God is eternal and that He is merciful. We know God by His attributes that He wants us to know Him by, such as mercy, love, and justice. I have tried to simplify the concepts of 'eternal' and 'infinite,' of course, but you get the gist."

"Wow! Quite a bit to take in," says Mary.

Betty opens the tent flap to let in a breeze that has arisen with the sun going down. The air is no longer hot, but has a touch of coolness about it. The twilight is casting long shadows.

Betty motions to a nearby open tent. All its sides have been furled up. Abdullah is busy laying different types of fruit on the table under the open tent. "Our vocabulary itself is limited, Mary," Betty says as she points to the fruit on the table outside. "Since we only perceive the outside world from the human perspective or paradigm, how can we truly understand God unless He gives us the wisdom to know Him? For instance, besides the watermelons and grapes and oranges Abdullah is laying down for us on the table, there are thousands of different varieties of fruit all over the world, each with its unique sweetness, the sweetness of mango quite different from that of the banana and so on for thousands of other fruits. Yet we and our smart scientists could only conjure up the word 'sweet' to describe the multitude of types of sweetness that exist—unless, of course, you count the use of the name of the fruit itself to describe its type of sweetness, such as apple-sweet, mango-sweet, pineapple-sweet, and so on."

"Interesting the way you describe this. It is very sweet the way you describe sweet!"

"Thanks, Mary. I know your mouth is watering for that watermelon. Let's go eat."

They both greet Abdullah and he responds with a broad smile. Mary and Betty treat him well, and he tries to reciprocate in his own way. Today he has gathered some cactus fruit on his forays into the desert. He has carefully peeled away the skin so they would not have to do it, as the sharp spines can be quite a pain to remove if they went into the fingers. He says he is going to pray his sundown prayer and exits, carrying his prayer mat with him.

While Mary is eating the watermelon, Betty continues, "Betty, if you reflect, God has placed within our tongue the ability to differentiate between the different *types* of sweetness, and yet we have been eating these fruits all our lives without having given this 'sweet' phenomenon a second thought in our headlong rush through a life of consumerism, materialism, and oblivion to God's awesome creative power," Betty continues. "These fruits come from plants that extract materials from soil, and yet the soil is not sweet. Grainy, bland, even yucky-tasting earth if we were put a handful in the mouth! Yet, from this earth comes different fruits, with different textures, different shapes, and different sizes. Sweet and yummy! A grace from God"

"I agree" accepts Mary. "And from the earth we get cucumbers, potatoes, and onions. They have different nutrients and different tastes. I am coming to love this earth!"

"We must acknowledge with humility the awesome power of God. If we are humble, He shall grant us the wisdom to know Him better," continues Betty. "*We are running all over the world, arrogant with the little knowledge we have, causing destruction and mayhem.* One day our great scientific community says the egg causes health risks and the next day it is retracting its statement to advise us to eat eggs as they are good for us. One day we are taking dozens of cholesterol-fighting medications and the next day we are busy trying to debunk the whole cholesterol hype.[42] When we contemplate God with humility and take a little time to reflect, rather than blunder through life like sheep running towards the precipice of a cliff, we are able to reflect on His awesome power—and He will show us more of His signs."

---

42 https://www.nhs.uk/news/heart-and-lungs/study-says-theres-no-link-between-cholesterol-and-heart-disease/

"Little knowledge combined with arrogance is indeed a dangerous thing," responds Mary, admiring Betty's ability to sum up what was on her mind. "Go on, Betty," she urges.

"Mary, don't you think we should consider the views of other people, such as those who claim that there exists an ingenious Creator?" Betty looks at her friend; a glint of determination is clearly visible in the deep blue eyes. When Betty is stirred, there is no knowing what she may come up with. "Do you think that if we are to call ourselves 'true' scientists and get the pat of approval from the scientific community, we necessarily have to—as has become fashionable nowadays—refute the existence of God? God says in the Quran:

> *Your God is but one God. There is no god other than Him, Compassionate and Merciful. In the creation of the heavens and the earth, in the alternation of night and day, in the ships that ply the seas to the benefit of man, in the water sent down from the heavens to revive the earth after its death, in the different species of animals scattered across the earth, in the rotation of the winds, in the clouds that are subordinate to God's command between heaven and earth, in all of this, there are signs for men who use their intellects.* (Quran 2:163–4)

> *Tell men to reflect with care and see what things the heavens and the earth contain.* (Quran 10:10)"

༄

The reporter finishes reading and looks at his watch. It is getting late, and he is worried about the author, "Whoa, man! Do you know it is minus 35 degrees centigrade outside? Did your wife not warn you to return home by five?"

"Oops. I know you wanted more information, but I have to consider my health like you said. Would you mind asking me a few questions that are on your mind so we can wrap this thing up?"

"Okay," The reporter is happy to get an opening to ask some difficult questions that have been nagging him. "Tell me, why are Muslims allowed to marry multiple wives whereas we Christians do not?"

"Fair question," the author replies. "As to the question of multiple wives, Islam did not invent this concept. This concept *predates* Islam. The Bible mentions Abraham, Solomon, David, and other people of God having multiple wives. David had six wives. Solomon 700. In fact, Islam put a **_restriction_** on how many wives one can have if they are treated with equanimity and justice. Four is the maximum but the rules are so rigid in their demands for equity that most Muslims marry only one. They must each be given a separate abode, or dwelling. Each must be provided *equitably* of one's time, attention, and resources to the best of one's abilities. I, for example, am married to one."

"Do you want to marry another woman?" the reporter asks.

"No, I am happy with the woman I married. Even if I wanted to, I would not feel confident I would be able to do justice in treating them equitably as demanded by the Quran. So, no. Let me complete the answer that you asked. Did you know that the Bible has verses on men having multiple wives, such as Exodus 21:10, 1 Kings 11:3, and Genesis 4:19. I hope that clarifies some things for you?"

"Yes, it does. I really did not pay that close an attention to the Bible, but you are right. Christians were marrying multiple wives before the advent of Islam. Now tell me, why do your women cover their hair whereas we Christians do not?"

"I have seen many Mennonite women using a hair cover, and they *are* Christians, are they not?" the author replies gently. "As to why Muslim women cover their hair—it is in obedience to God and nothing to do with subjugation to the husband as is often cited by some Christian adherents who read from the Bible. Muslim women have been commanded by God to do it for the purpose of modesty so that they may not be molested by some uncouth elements in society. Men have been commanded by God to lower their gazes too in modesty and respect when in the presence of women. *Both commands are to preserve modesty in society.* Both these commands are in the same verse and they have nothing to do with subjugation."

"Are unmarried Muslim women also required to wear a headscarf?" asks the reporter.

"Yes. Even unmarried Muslim women cover their hair. By the way, have you ever seen Mary the mother of Jesus with her head uncovered in all the pictures and statues you have ever seen of her? Have you seen a nun or the Queen of England without a headscarf or a hat in any recent photo? Did you see many people demonstrating against these noble women wanting to cover their hair? *Muslim women are living up to what should be Christian standards and instead of supporting their stance; they face animosity by folks who should rather marvel at their courage.*"

"I personally think veils look good, but I don't think the womenfolk in my house would ever wear a veil or a headscarf," reflects the reporter.

"I will tell you something remarkable. You may be surprised that even those folks who are so against the veil may know someone in their families—or maybe themselves even—who have worn a head cover or veil. Are you married? Do you have a daughter who got married, or a picture of your mother or aunt when she got married? Yes? Maybe they wore a nice white wedding dress and lifted that *veil*, or called *hijab* in Arabic, for the kiss?"

"Ha! Ha! Never thought of that. It's funny the way you put it." The reporter is clearly amused.

"I believe that if women want to wear a head cover, let them. We should learn to stay out of women's wardrobes."

"Can I ask some more questions?" More questions have been popping into the reporter's head.

"Certainly."

"Why do Muslim men sport a beard? Why do they wear a cap? You will not find many Christians doing that. Why are Muslims trying to be different?" Though they are quite direct questions, the reporter frames them in a gentle tone so as not to sound impolite.

"I will answer that with some rhetorical questions. Isn't Jesus, in the all pictures you have seen of him, sporting a beard? Have you seen the Pope in a recent photo? Does he not wear a small cap?"

The reporter laughs. "Do all Muslims think the way you do? You seem to know quite a bit. Can I ask a few more questions? I will not ask too many more, I promise."

"Go ahead, please. Ask any number you want. I will try my best to answer," the author smiles encouragingly.

"Muslims greet each other with '*Asalamualaikum*.' I know it means 'peace be on you.' But why not just say 'hello' in your language? Keep it simple, y'know, like most people. Also why do Muslims assume a ritual prostrate position on the ground while praying to God? That is a lot of work. Sorry, I do not mean to sound rude, but why complicate things? Why do you do have special greetings and pray in a way than most of us do not?"

"Fair questions. You know Muslims love and respect Jesus. They respect all prophets. Muslims say, 'peace be on you' translated as 'Asalamualaikum.' That is absolutely correct. Did you know Jesus is reputed to have done the same in the Bible?"

"Well ... no."

"In Luke 24:36, Jesus says *'Peace be upon you'* to his disciples. This phrase, if translated in Arabic, is *'Asalamualaikum.'* It means the same thing."

"How about prostration? Is this unique to you guys?" The reporter repeats.

"No. Others do it too. In fact, *there are many instances in the Bible where other prophets have fallen prostrate to God in prayer.* For example, Moses, in verses 16:22 and 20:6 in the New International Version of the Bible, is recorded to have fallen prostrate on his face in worship. In the Old Testament, Genesis 17:3, Prophet Abraham is recorded to have fallen on his face in prayer. In fact, Jesus himself is recorded to have prayed by prostrating. You can read this in the New Testament, in Matthew 26:39. It says, *'And he (Jesus) went a little farther, and fell on his face, and prayed...'* I am not making this up. Do you want me to show this to you in the Bible?"

"No, no. It is okay. I can check it, because if it is there, I would find it very interesting."

The reporter pauses briefly, thinks on how he will phrase the next question, takes a sip from his cup, and asks, "I have a lot of experience interviewing people. I find that the true character of a man or a woman is not truly revealed in short meetings. I find people tend to present themselves in a different light when they go out or meet acquaintances for short periods. People are very different when they are at home. If you look at it, it is the spouse who lives with his or her companion for several years who truly knows the character of the man or woman since all is revealed at home: the temper tantrums, the patience, the love, the respect, the art of compromising with the other, the racist undertones, the habits, the cleanliness, and so much more."

"You are absolutely correct. I am of the same opinion. My wife truly knows all my failings, and there are many."

"Exactly. The spouse is the one who understands the other's true colors. Tell me, what did the spouses of Mohammed say about him, since some lived long after he had passed away from Earth?"

The author takes a book out of his bag. "I was going to write something about this very question. Aah! Here it is!" He flips some pages. "Let me read this to you. Prophet Mohammed said, '*The believers who show the most perfect faith are those who have the best behavior, and the best of you are those who are the best to their wives.*'[43] A consensus exists among Muslim scholars and historians that Prophet Mohammed was extremely kind to his wives and attentive to their needs, doing house chores to help, and never known to have spoken an unkind word to any of them. His wives missed him dearly when he finally passed away. Years later, they continued to miss him, and continued to transmit his sayings and of how he conducted himself within the households, until they too left this world for the abode of the hereafter."

"How about you? What would your wife say of you today if she were candid?" the reporter asks, with a mischievous twinkle in his eyes.

"Not many good things," the author replies unhappily. "Not many good things at all, especially after what happened today."

---

43 https://sunnah.com/riyadussaliheen/1/278

# CHAPTER 4

# WORD PLAY

*"Not all of us can do great things.*
*But we can do small things with great love."*

—Mother Teresa

The above quote, in large print, has taken its prominent position for several years on the front wall by the receptionist's desk in my clinic, "*we can do small things with great love …*" I like that. It is from a noble lady, a Christian, and it has great wisdom. The words have sincerity. There is no word play here. We make an effort to apply that at the clinic. It is still there today.

On the waiting room TV screen (to keep my patients occupied in case I am late to take them in, as sometimes a difficult clinical case inside may have detained me) I have some funny bits about foot specialists, medicine, some amazing things about animals, and some quotes. These bits scroll in a continuous loop. One of the quotes is by Abraham Joshua Heschel: "*Racism is man's gravest threat to man —the maximum of hatred for a minimum of reason.*"

The clinic is a smoking-free zone with a "do not smoke" sticker stuck on a wall. The clinic is also a racist-free zone too.

The message? Do not do either. It is bad for my health. In fact, do not do either; both are bad for *your* health.

Intolerance is bad. *But tolerating the intolerant is worse*; do not expect me to keep quiet if racist overtones shall be thrown about. All are welcome and all shall be treated with utmost dignity. I love you, yes. Just do not push it because I have patients from all castes, colors and creeds. And I love them too.

Back to my book.

If I were invited to give a lecture and asked two questions—"Does the end justify the means?" and, "Would I have the guts to tell my fellow Muslims the hard truths without someone drawing out the scimitar?"—I would come wearing an armored suit onto the platform, peer through a crack in the armored head-piece to see that that no one had come into the room carrying sharp objects, and then state some hard truths. Just kidding.

I think the scimitar will stay in its scabbard even if someone still carries ancient weaponry. The Muslim may feel a bit offended and wince as he pulls a few strands from his beard, but I think he will agree with me in most of what I have to say. We are at the crossroads, and we need to accept that there is much we need to improve upon.

Given the degree of social upheaval in many countries, increased mobility at both the global and local levels of the socio-economic platform, increased social media interaction, faster and more varied international travel, and increased physical interaction amongst people of all races; Muslims and non-Muslims are ready for common-ground dialogue. *They want to talk.*

## You never know what's under the ashes

Great battles have been fought over religion: for example, the Spanish Inquisition, the Crusades, or the war in Bosnia. Bigots have this worked out to a fine art and they know the exact formula to rile people up. After giving a subversive agenda a religious flavor or a flavor of superiority—provocateurs essentially playing with words where they say *your* religion or race is better,—adeptly mixing in a little bit of crude science and a bit of oil as they do this— they sit back and watch how they can hot things up for low-burning bigots lying under the ashes.

What do I mean by "crude science"? Well, take, for instance, the case of Samuel Morton, who collected skulls—a famous one being that of an Irish convict—placed lead shot into the craniums, and decanted them to see the volume within skulls. His theory proposed that the greater the volume within the skull, the greater the intellect. Then h e d i v i d e d people into categories, with Native Americans and blacks placed at the bottom of the intellectual scale.[44]

*See the problem with this crude science and science-based word play?* There is little consideration of relevant factors such as the size of the individual, their age, the genetic determinant of body size—such as that of a pigmy whose size is genetically determined—and so on; yet, the theory was zealously taken up by those wishing to perpetuate racism.

A "superiority flavor"—be it of race, or religion, or gender, or ethnic background, or any of a multitude of differences between us—can wreak havoc in society, as detailed below.

Many religions have at some time promulgated color superiority, which at times, essentially allowed people to justify slavery. An amazing number, 10 to 12.5 million Africans, were shipped to the New World during the slave trade.[45]

The feeling of one *race* being superior to another has allowed some to justify ethnic cleansing (think Rwanda, with about a million dead, comprising about 70–84 percent of the Tutsi population), or the Rohingya in Myanmar (with 700,000 refugees and a conservative estimate of 10,000 dead).[46]

The idea of *race* and *color* superiority has also allowed members of one race of people to subjugate another of a different color and race. Think of the Uyghurs in China. Think of apartheid or the plunder of nations by European imperialists.[47]

The idea of one person being superior to a counterpart of another *gender* has justified for some the disbursement of unfair treatment to women— thus we needed bitter social upheaval in the form of the women's suffrage movement to allow women the right to vote or the more recent 'me-too' movement against sexual harassment that has brought down more than 200 previously untouchable and powerful men.[48] Harvey Weinstein becoming the recent casualty, despite power and wealth.

45 https://www.britannica.com/topic/transatlantic-slave-trade; https://www.encyclopediavirginia.org/Transatlantic_Slave_Trade_The; M. Rediker, *The Slave Ship: A Human History* (New York: Viking, 2007)

46 R. Dallaire and B. Beardsley, *Shake Hands with the Devil: The Failure of Humanity in Rwanda* (Toronto: Random House Canada, 2003); https://www.bbc.com/news/world-africa-13431486; https://www.cairn-int.info/article-E_POPU_504_0401—the-death-toll-of-the-rwandan-genocide-a.htm; https://www.bbc.com/news/world-asia-41566561; https://www.un.org/press/en/2018/sc13552.doc.htm

47 https://www.theguardian.com/politics/2005/aug/20/past.hearafrica05; F. Fanon, The Wretched of the Earth (New York: Grove Press, 1963)

48 http://www.nwhp.org/resources/womens-rights-movement/detailed-timeline/; https://www.nytimes.com/interactive/2018/10/23/us/metoo-replacements.html; https://www.theguardian.com/world/2018/oct/08/metoo-one-year-on-hollywood-reaction

We think we can wash our hands of all this bias, inequality, and racism if we can simply and verbally affirm, "We would never do such a thing." This is simplistic and naïve. We are often participants, willing or not, when we elect officials who represent us to carry out wrong, or when our taxes are diverted to war machinery and the manufacture and sale of weapons to subjugate the masses by autocratic despots and the unleashing of death and mayhem around the world. Where are the sit-ins, the hunger strikes, and the civil disobedience? Where are the loud demonstrations, and the work strikes to make our elected officials reevaluate that their positions in office are not blank cheques?

In 2016, the worldwide arms sales of the U.S. government totaled some U.S.$40 billion.[49] As if this is not enough, we also have Russia and China contributing to the arming of the world, for they too have realized that selling weapons is a lucrative business—*money in coffers in exchange for people in coffins.* China has been on the march while we were busy buying their plastics and focusing all our energies on the Arabs; governments all over the world (especially African countries) and their lands, ports and roadways, rare earth minerals, and even cultures under sway when state-sanctioned Chinese arrive offering cheap loans ("Kudos", once only, to Trump for standing up to China for some of the things they do, like putting *Uyghurs in internment camps.* Isn't there a children's book that says feeding the Chinese Dragon a little bit too much chowder and then poking it will make it flex its muscles? If not, here is an idea for an aspiring author). *Isn't it funny that countries that become militarily powerful somehow also transform themselves into "peacemakers" while fingering a nuke?* It is finely rehearsed "word play" given to the state-media to trumpet and the duped to spread it around. There are too many bad weapons out there now, and corporate gluttons going around steadily arming the world.

---

49 https://www.reuters.com/article/us-airshow-britain-usa-arms-idUSKCN0ZT0ZH

Keep your fingers crossed that there is no Third World War. *Because there may never be a Fourth World War.*

## "Better than thou" phenomenon

We sometimes do things that we would otherwise find distasteful or even abhorrent. If we keep quiet when bad things are done to others, *we are silent partners.*

If some people (I mean us, folks) are not ready to carry out the bidding of demagogues with subversive agendas, all these provocateurs have to do is play some more with words—bring forth a few religious doctrines, pick and choose a few verses, quote them out of context, and then sit back and watch as the community rallies with zeal (including pitchforks, machetes, AK-47s; and—for the social-media connected, the spreading of false news and innuendo).

Look around you: there is a deeply ingrained color, ethnicity, or religious sense of superiority in the bosoms of the multitudes, who think they are better than others.

Muslims have been taught that many prophets and messengers were sent to mankind by the one Creator, delivering essentially the same message of worshiping only One God and to remain faithful in obeying His commands, including those relating to justice, kindness, forbearance, forgiveness, and tolerance. I would draw your attention to one particular verse in the Quran which might come as a surprise to non-Muslims and which Muslims would do well to heed at all times. God commands Prophet Mohammed to state, *"We believe in God and in that which has been revealed to us and in that which was revealed to Abraham, Ishmael, Isaac, Jacob, and their descendants. We believe in that which was given to Moses, Jesus, and the other Prophets by their Lord. We make no distinction between them and we have submitted ourselves to the will of God"* (Quran 3:84). With a few exceptions, most of us would rather submit to the lower desires of the "self" and find ways to divide ourselves along religious, ethnic, color, social, national, and monetary lines.

We have Shia vs. Sunni, with neighbors staring at each other across the borders of Saudi Arabia, Iraq, Iran, and Yemen, ready to take a potshot at anyone who doesn't wear the same color turban.

We have among us the older-generation sanctimonious believers vs. the newer-generation hypocritical smug atheists.

Then we have the Chosen vs. the Goyim, Protestants vs. the Catholics, and so on. Some people have found that the best way to get other people riled up is to use religion, in the knowledge that most folks would not have really bothered to learn what their religion requires of them, and so would be easily susceptible to manipulation.

Had the masses bothered to pick up their religious books, they would have learnt that at the core of all religions is goodness, empathy and "not do unto others what you would not want to have done unto you," presented in a variety of forms:

> Those will be given their reward twice for what they patiently endured and they repel evil with good, and they spend from what We have provided them. (Quran 28:54)

> Treat others as you want to be treated, for this sums up the Law and the prophets. (Matthew 7:12)

> What is hateful to you, do not do to your neighbor. This is the whole Torah; all the rest is commentary. Now go and study. (Babylonian Talmud, Shabbat 31a)

> Don't do to others what you don't want them to do to you. (Confucius, Analects 15:23)

None of you have faith until you love for your neighbor what you love for yourself. (Prophet Mohammed)

Like the rest of humanity, some Muslims do not always live by their religious dictates, and they often fall prey to religious extremism, the pursuit of "materialism," the appeasement of baser desires, and similar shortcomings. Muslims are not unique in this respect, there are members of other religious factions that do it too; self-righteously pointing at the dirty feet of others while one is standing deep in mud is—if I may phrase it crudely—the type of bogged-down hypocrisy from which we need to free ourselves.

The concept of the Day of Judgment is very important for Muslims. Muslims have a firm belief that on that Awesome Day, they shall each be questioned and good and bad deeds weighed on the scales of True Justice, which will then determine Success (Gardens of Bliss) or Loss (the Fire of Hell).

Whereas in the past most Muslims studied the Quran and applied its verses in everyday life—such as kindness to animals, study of the sciences, the obligation to uphold women's rights, keeping promises, honesty in business, upholding the Truth even when it is against themselves—many Muslims now imagine that simply practicing rituals and reciting the Quran with a beautiful voice will be enough for their salvation on the Day of Reckoning/Judgment.

The idea of *ritualizing religion* is also true of many faiths throughout the world; most adherents to a religious order ritualize worship and have elaborate ceremonial protocol and, after (lip) service, go about life in the same manner they always did, with scarcely any change. The moments (often emotional, and sometimes with tears) of life in prayer-chambers, such as the church, synagogue, temple, or mosque, *remain entombed* within these chambers, with most people emerging unaffected to carry on life as usual despite having just heard passionate sermons about changing their behavior!

As a former president of ICONO (Islamic Centre of Northern Ontario), based in Sudbury, Ontario, I have encouraged the use of posters on foyer walls advocating for human rights, animal rights, and our obligation to the environment. These posters are there today, printed on vinyl to be more permanent, with verses from the Quran and Hadith to make them more relevant to the challenges we face today.

When given the opportunity to deliver sermons in the absence of our regular imam, I tend to focus on present-day challenges and ways to overcome them. In general, the effect these sermons on young people, though initially positive and infectious, is unfortunately temporary, what with the overpowering attraction of social media. The effect on the elderly and many members also appears to be minimal: they are generally content to reminisce about bygone days and content to follow habits and *rituals for rituals' sake.*

There is the earnest hope that Muslims (and members of other faiths) will once again foster understanding among peoples of different faiths by continuing to reach out to each other. I have seen change slowly happening both at the micro-level in individuals interacting with members of other faiths; and at the macro-level in mosques, churches, universities, and other venues that promote interfaith dialogue.

Many good politicians, intelligent leaders, objective media outlets and fair-minded populations of many countries appear to be sincerely seeking some kind of formula in their relationship with Muslims that would bring about fruitful dialogue and the elusive common goal of restoring peace in a torn world.

Is there a workable yet simple formula that we can be applied without alienating large segments of society? Yes, there is, and the answer lies in this phrase: "ignorance of the other breeds contempt; knowledge of the other often engenders love and understanding." It is a simple formula. Someone may say, "Should we not be looking for sophisticated, unconventional and state-of-the-art strategic plans to bring about harmony in a torn world?"

Leonardo da Vinci made a rather succinct observation: *simplicity is the ultimate sophistication.*

We do not need a sophisticated hodgepodge. We need simplicity to bind us. We all need to make more use of this simple formula by attempting to learn about the other so that we can remove the hatred that originates from an ignorance of the other's perspective and lifestyle.

So, should we try to understand why white supremacists feel the way they do? *Why not?* Many such individuals may believe (rightly or wrongly) that their way of life is being threatened by rapid cultural change and new social dynamics. How are we going to engage meaningfully with them if we stay in our bubble and they stay in theirs? Unless we try to have a substantial engagement with them, presenting our statistical evidence—scientific, religious, humanitarian, anthropological, social, economic, geographical—in a measured fashion, we will allow the feelings of 'us vs. them' to grow and fester.

Some may obstinately want to remain in the bubble they create, but persistence and the deployment of sound knowledge will make many entrapped within these cocoons reconsider their position. At the end of the exercise, most will surely realize that we are not that different after all.

## Even real hawks would probably give them a wide berth

There are a  hawkish few who believe that they must crush Islam to achieve their nefarious ends and are prepared to employ various techniques such as manipulation, subversion, misinterpretation, and sometimes downright lies about the belief system of true Muslims. They also play with words to rile people up.

They often concoct lies and attribute them to Prophet Mohammed. They are adept at choosing and quoting passages out of context from the Quran and Hadith to tarnish the image of Islam. They may even employ weaponry upon practicing Muslims and their institutions.

These belligerent hotheads believe that by employing such methods, their subversive endeavors will be met with success. "Let the end justify the means," they would say—think Kashmir, the Uyghurs in China, the Rohingya in Burma, and think of Bosnia and what happened there. However, this approach has been met with failure, repeatedly; history appears to affirm that the *only thing we learn from history is that we do not learn from history.* As Winston Churchill remarked, "Those that fail to learn from history are bound to repeat it." Instead of peace, we have created more discord.

Repeatedly pelting stones (be it stones coated with sugar) on a beehive full of bees minding their own business is apt to anger one or two bees who may not take kindly to the affront (we see that happening all over the world by more powerful nations, but instead of stones they use lethal weapons upon a populace minding its own business). If perchance one of the bees comes out of the hive and gives the smirking lark a sting on the behind, do not blame the bee, or worse still, the entire beehive. Not every bee will be happy with an outsider stealing its honey (should I have said oil and minerals instead?) or placing a wasp as a puppet to subjugate the bee populace. *The autocratic wasps placed as puppets in Egypt and Saudi Arabia must to be deadlier than the executioner wasp, one of the deadliest wasps on the planet.*

Is there such a thing as an *"executioner wasp"*? Yes, there is. It is called *Polistes carnifex*. It is found in South and Central America. *The human form is found in Egypt and Saudi Arabia in the echelons of power among kings, princes, and military tyrants.*

Do we see places that have earned the reputation of being pariahs simply because they resist being easy walkovers? Maybe Cuba, Nepal? Feel free to fill a few more blanks here.

People who resist being subjugated must be, your politicians will make you believe, "really bad." The powerful bourgeois want you to be submit and obey without resistance, and if you do that, you get the label of being "good," of being freedom-fighters, liberators, and heroes. Definitions can be juggled around and the powerful can label whom they will, at will. If you resist, you may end up becoming another label: rebel, terrorist, or anarchist. It is word play at its best, and they hold the dictionary close to their chests.

What is the formula for establishing harmony, a harmony that will encompass Muslims endeavoring to show patience and tolerance, and continuing to practice goodness despite being maligned or subjected to a barrage of negative rhetoric by a few boorish bureaucrats?

*First, do not pelt them with stones.*

Second, let Muslim scholars and imams continue to teach authentic lessons of goodness to the Muslim masses. The powers that be in the West should encourage them to continue with this work, rather than try to undermine them. These scholars are engaged in the difficult and important task of presenting true Islam that advocates peace. Do not make it tougher for them than it already is. To give you an idea, go to the local mosque to listen to a sermon on a Friday. A typical sermon might include recitation of Quran 5:32, which states that "*if any one killed a person, it would be as if he killed the whole of mankind; and if any one saved a life, it would be as if he saved the life of the whole of mankind.*" Islam strictly forbids harming *any* innocent person—indeed, any living creature—and there are numerous references to this subject in the Quran and in the life of Prophet Mohammed and his companions. I shall consider some of these in more detail below to make it absolutely clear to both non-Muslim and Muslim that this has always been a central tenet of the Prophet of Islam.

"Ahem" someone may mutter, wanting some clarification. "Why then do some Muslims commit heinous crimes that would boggle any sane mind?"

After scratching the noggin (to un-boggle the confused neurons inside), I would start by recalling a Hadith (saying) of Prophet Mohammed in which he warned that many Muslims will not pay heed to their religious obligations in the distant future (which appears to be the present times):

> *In the end of time there shall come men who will swindle the world with religion, deceiving the people in soft skins of sheep, their tongues are sweeter than sugar and their hearts are the hearts of wolves.*[50]

I would also recall Prophet Mohammed's Hadith,

> *At the end of time, among this nation, there will appear people who will recite the Qur'an but it will not go any deeper than their collarbones or their throats.*[51]

Then, after recalling this, I would answer, "*If you look at the lives of those so-called 'Muslims' who have committed crimes, you will invariably find that in almost all such cases the perpetrators have a half-baked knowledge of Islam and, contrary to what the Quran and Ahadith advocate, they end up doing the very opposite of what is expected of them by Islam.*"

Such "Muslims" do not pray regularly and are not very charitable (giving 2.5 percent of your wealth to the poor is mandatory in Islam, known as *Zakat*, and giving above that is considered meritorious, deserving of great reward from the Lord), and are often not very good to neighbors and to members of society or respectful of other faiths.

---

50  https://sunnah.com/tirmidhi/36/102

51  https://sunnah.com/urn/1251740

Islam teaches that one commits wrong if he eats his fill while his neighbor goes hungry. Islam advocates that to give something which one loves, to the extent of giving something while in *need* of that very thing oneself, earns the giver a great heavenly reward. *Tell me now if this not a beautiful religion?*

The properly educated Muslim, who knows what his religion demands, will strive to be compassionate, forgiving, and helpful, and a good and honorable member of society.

There are several verses that précis this effectively: The Quran says, *"You will not attain righteousness till you spend in charity of the things you love" (Quran 3:92).*

Another verse states, *"And they are those who give food—in spite of their own need, to the needy, and the orphan, and the captive (saying in their hearts), 'We only feed you for the sake of God, and we desire nothing in return from you, not even a word of thanks"* (Quran 76:8–9).

## Thinking outside the box

I remember a Podiatric Medicine continuing-education course I once did at a conference for podiatrists in Saskatchewan, Canada, a few years ago. It was on the efficacy and incorporation of laser therapy and extra-corporeal shock-wave therapy in the podiatric clinic setting, and why we needed to use these newer modalities to treat heel spurs and other ligament, tendon, and joint injuries in the affected foot.

The present method of treating such conditions is generally achieved by using devices known as custom-made orthotic insoles that fit into shoes to alleviate pressure and address the biomechanical cause of the complaint. Though orthotic insoles work in many such cases, recalcitrant pain needs a rethink. If orthotics did not work for a particular patient after a number of attempts, alter the method. Simply using the same method of treatment again and again is likely to produce the same result.

So, to introduce my audience to the idea of applying other newer forms of treatment for such conditions—such as laser and extra-corporeal shock-wave therapies—I prepared a PowerPoint presentation late into the night and came well prepared the next day. Podiatrists had come from different parts of the province, and some did not know me well yet.

The first slide introduced the speaker: Dr. R. Bagha, Podiatrist, Regina. Some podiatrists were still talking to each other. A head dipped down to look at his cell phone; it was just going to be another long lecture. The second slide projected onto the screen was purposefully done in large print. It was a quote from Abraham Maslow: *"If your only tool is a hammer, then every problem looks like a nail."* A few podiatrists chuckled; the foot specialist peering down at his phone raised his head. I had their full attention and hence an opening to elaborate on the importance of thinking outside the box (as of this writing, some clinics in the province have now acquired laser units to treat heel pain. I get calls from these friendly podiatrists in Saskatchewan as to what laser units would give the deepest penetration for best clinical outcome).

*The point I am trying to make?*

The point (hopefully not at the end of the needle and not on my chair) is this: we sometimes need to think outside the box—there may be an idea out there that we may not have considered. Policymakers in the echelons of power need to move away from the established narrative of bombing and keep bombing to achieve an objective, though they may have sophisticated weaponry and are itching to use them. To hotheads every "Muslim problem" (especially if they refuse to give away their oil for cheap), is a nail. And what do hotheads do? Grab a hammer, of course. If throwing a bomb has not won you friends, throwing more bombs is still not going to win you friends. Policymakers in France, the U.K., America, Russia, Saudi Arabia, need to think outside the box. For example, sophisticated Western weaponry being used over and over again against poor Yemenis is not going to win over the minds of the people. What they need is food for starving children, medicine for easily treatable diseases such as cholera, and aid in various forms. *Not bombs!*

I was in Yemen for a family holiday many years ago, prior to the war, and I found a proud, polite, and generous people. As we toured the country, we would often find ourselves being invited by total strangers to share in their humble and meager meals, preferring us over their own selves as they proffered us more of their food than they would take themselves, smiling happily—feeling honored— that we had accepted their invitation. They would ask for nothing in return, and if we gave them a small gift, they would add something extra and respond with a gift that exceeded our small offering. We felt truly humbled by their generosity and started to decline such invitations because of their circumstances.

*Bombs do not win friends—they alienate people. If the Americans started throwing essential everyday items like soap and reusable baby diapers and medicine from their planes, most of Yemen would love them, wanting them to come so they could honor them with hugs, kisses, and kebobs.*

Sending unmanned drones to drop bombs do not engender goodwill either. Whether Muslim or not, if civilians die, the whole population invariably turns against the perpetrators, no matter how sweetly iced the rhetoric on the proverbial powdered keg, sorry, cake.

## State-sanctioned terrorism and word play

When states are involved in the destabilization of other states in order to impose their own belief systems, seize land, or pilfer economic assets—think Iraq, Afghanistan, Yemen, Libya (and a multitude of other countries that you are certainly aware of)—then for the politicians concerned to argue that such actions are "justified" simply because it has the support of a majority of politicians in that militarily powerful country is pure bull, for want of a better description.

We need to understand that there are real people—real children who love to play, mothers who care for their families like we do— on the receiving end of those falling bombs. John Perkins demonstrates in his bestseller, *Confessions of an Economic Hit Man*, how some of our state institutions manipulate leaders and policymakers in other countries to get what they want by use of subversion, deceit—and worse.[52]

Many people in uniform are ready to give their lives to establish justice, and over the years I have had the privilege of having many as my patients. Many veterans have offered me insights into their lives that few others will have had. I try to give them ample time to relate their personal stories: treating them with humility and dignity, for many were sincere in wanting to achieve true justice when they went overseas; think of those who served in Bosnia, in the Second World War, and in Rwanda, for example. One common theme that tends to emerge from these recollections is that war is terrible, and must be avoided at whatever cost.

Who better to learn from than those who have served on the frontlines? We will certainly learn more from these people than the guy in his smart suit sitting in his Oval Office, who would probably run for cover if he heard a loud pop from someone opening a soda can in order to celebrate getting congressional authorization to send more troops overseas.

*A war that is state-sanctioned is not necessarily right*, for we have often found that there were hidden agendas behind emotional rhetoric for which our brave servicemen and women have often had to pay a heavy price. State-sanctioned use of weaponry and/

---

52 John Perkins, Confessions of an *Economic Hit Man: The Shocking Story of How America Really Took Over the World* (London: Ebury Press, 2005)

or sanctions against civilian populations cause mass deaths and suffering for future generations. The damaged economic, social, and political infrastructure of the targeted countries will need decades to be repaired and restored. Such things breed terrorism and anarchy.

*We call ourselves peacemakers—state-sanctioned peacemakers.* We conjure up *smart lingo to mask what is in reality state-sanctioned terrorism.* Think of the countries that engage in this behavior—for there are many besides dark and sinister North Korea—countries that use their power and wealth quite openly to appropriate not only stale cookies from another country's cookie jar, but also its land, its waters, and its deposits—lock, stock and oil barrel.

We are in denial and participate in this chicanery: governments send our young men and women to fight wars while the political elite sit in comfortable offices drinking expensive café lattes and using emotional rhetoric to keep the public in line—and line them up with new laws when they are needed.

We are willing participants in this word-play game for the gullible. Media, often controlled by the corporate greedy ("you will not get to carry our million dollar ads if you state truths we do not like") show select red-color pixel images to rouse the senses, the war-drum beating in the background, while we stare entranced, mouths open wide, as they call for more blood. We are complicit in being spoon-fed state-sanctioned terrorism.

The Quran sums this up nicely with the observation:

> *When it is said to them: "Make not mischief on the earth," they say: "Why, we only want to make peace!"* (Quran 2:11)

Word play. That reminds me of something else. The hungry chap stealing a banana and a blanket from a supermarket is a thief. What about the lawyers defending the CEOs of corporations who declared bankruptcy and jointly stole millions and built villas in Bermuda and other exotic places (from penny-saving folks like us who put our money in trusts or in stocks)? Oh dear! These poor guys (with Cadillacs and villas) are bankrupt.

I thought bankrupt meant that even the shirts on their backs were up for grabs, and some of us naïve souls were even keeping extra blankets in our closets in case they felt cold. They are not thieves. And they certainly do not need our blankets because they reside in sunny locations on million-dollar yachts eating ice-lollies. They are just "smart" people who play with words and *play* the system. The Panama Papers and Paradise Papers have exposed the inequalities and the injustice in our society.

Penalize the banana thief stealing a banana for his grandma but reward the lawyers and CEOs because they know how the game is played. Governments—despite knowing that they were being complicit in many a chicanery by corporates—keep allowing these guys to open corporations bearing distinct entities as in real humans with flesh and bones—who then go about declaring bankruptcies leaving the CEO's and owners of the corporation unscathed. Better go give the blanket you saved to the banana thief's grandma as her grandchild is sitting in jail. Hopefully she will sell it to buy some bananas. She is probably starving because corporates reduced her stocks to zilch.

We must be honest with ourselves. Stealing is wrong. Enriching ourselves to the cost of others is wrong—even though some governments seem to sanction it with finely rehearsed word play. If stealing a banana at the grocery store is wrong, then devaluing the currencies of poor nations—and thereby "stealing" their coffee at prices that keep them poor—is wrong too. We need to acknowledge that we have been unjust, and that Might may not always be Right, despite the seeming endorsement of such actions by the World Bank, the IMF and powerful military-industrial nations. That delicious chocolate we are about to eat originates with families who cultivate cocoa but who are exploited by the system that primarily benefits Western consumers.

*For those cheap chocolates we enjoy and those fancy shirts we adorn ourselves with, someone, somewhere, is having to pay a heavy price. Let me draw an analogy of why poor people want to immigrate to the affluent West: If there are chickens in the field and we go and steal the seeds and amass them by the plenty in a nice comfortable shelter,* **should they not come to roost where there is fodder? So, what are we complaining about?**

## The old and the new colonialists

Stealing of lands is wrong—we all know that. But if it is done cleverly employing clever word play, we may find ourselves sitting outside our own homes. Let us see how. The old colonialist's history might go like this:

The stranger came knocking at ( North American) door and the indigenous person tolerantly allowed the chap to come in. Soon the chap had taken over the kitchen and the living room, made a polluted mess of the water the resident owner had kept in a container (for the grandchildren before they were forcibly sent to a "residential school" so they could unlearn their indigenous culture). Not content, the invader next ate all the bison in the fridge (and his buddies started killing all the millions of other ones roaming in the prairies), sprayed pesticide all over the carpet (grassland), and then rudely forced the owner to step into the garage (reserve) to live there.

The stranger is not done yet.

He then brings his friends over, establishes a court system of sorts—the native has no idea how this ancient law system works—with its ye olde law terms such as estover, ejectment, deodand, and assumpsit jargon, which even today would give most of us ye olde headaches—and knowing the native sometimes does not understand the English language, or sometimes cannot read at all, tells him to put a mark on a piece of paper. Finely refined word play facilitates the obtaining of the mark on the appropriate line. There is a kindly smile. The mark is obtained. The resident owner soon finds himself outside his own home, because he made the mark (strong liquor cleverly supplied by the wily invader have played important roles in many unwilling cases).

Then the new owner says he will buy beaver pelts from the native.

"All the beaver pelts?" the native asks.

"Yes," he says. "I reward those who loyally supply me with fine pelts since I have to ship these things to my kith and kin back home across the ocean. You can bring mink pelts too, and some other exotic pelts. You do not have to worry about supplying me with other animals such as the bison. My friends have been hard at work in the prairies with their guns (so that the 'circle of life' that you believe in ceases and you become perpetually dependent on us). You can come buy some beef from our cattle ranches with the money you get from selling beaver pelts. We will not starve you. We have beef and you have beaver pelts. Fair exchange, eh?" Thinking himself gracious and since he has been reading about being good to his neighbors, he gives the native a dirty blanket (infested with an exotic disease which will nearly wipe out most of the native's kinfolks).

Time passes.

The new colonialists blame the atrocities that occur on the old colonialists, "Our forefathers did some bad things, but we are not like that. In the twenty-first century, with a good standard of living dependent on oil, we would not perpetrate such injustices." The native's progeny is living in the garage (reserve) and they have accepted their lot in life, unjust though it is.

But the new colonialist is not done yet. It has been "word play" all the while, and since some duped, or innocent, or even well-meaning folks haven't figured it out yet, he is going to do it again. He is soon eyeing the native's garage. He wants to dig underneath it to frack some oil and pollute the little water in a little pond the native had kept pristine for his great grandchildren who have finally come home. He now wants to destroy the rest of what the native holds dear. The new colonialist now wants finite oil while destroying the one thing that matters most: the infinitely good earth and good water, the essentials of good living.

As the native sees the new colonialist approaching with gigantic machinery, he thinks to himself, "He has already taken our best lands and waters. He has devastated and polluted those. As if that was not enough, he is now eyeing my garage. He has taken all that was on the top, now he even wants things under the earth!" He sadly looks around to see where he should go and live, who would understand his plight, and who would truly feel as he does.

*And there are people who think this is just another story.*

## As a Canadian I have some heroes. Please introduce yours.

The confused "Muslim" carrying that suspicious potato sack with wires jutting out of it and winding around him (as in an old induction-coil transformer) who now enters a crowded civilian area, with a strange tick-tock sound coming from the old sack, needs to understand what his religion *really* requires of him: suicide bombings of civilians causes only mayhem and death and does not and *will not* give any ultimate moral objective any legitimacy, regardless of the initial grievance. He has probably been won over by word play from some nasty people. He should have read the Quran instead. Then he would have approached innocent people with compassion and understanding, as this is what the Quran advocates.

*The end shall not justify the means*; Almighty Allah shall never grant success to those who use means that *He* has forbidden. You only need to look at the lives of Gandhi, Nelson Mandela, or Martin

Luther King Jr. When confronted with a more powerful adversary, they adopted the strategy of peaceful engagement and achieved far more than if they had resorted to violence. They won because they were morally superior to their adversaries. They used bodies and soul, and they used words. They used words, finely articulated, to achieve their objective.

Extremist actions by hard-heads such as Boko Haram, Al Shabab, Daesh, KKK, and twenty-first century neo-intolerant-chaps contradict the teachings of their religion and are, therefore, and rightfully so, almost universally rejected by the world's majority. These chaps must have a hard time sleeping on soft pillows unless they have intolerable solid gun barrels under the pillows making dents in unyielding heads. Their heads get dents and we get the headache.

As a Canadian, I am proud of the good Canada has been able to contribute to the world. We not only use words to bring about change, but we also use our bodies and souls to bring about change in the world. Though we gave the world insulin, peanut butter, and poutine and we pretend to be humble about them, humility must be cast aside because we also gave the world Madame Louise Arbour, who served as the UN High Commissioner for Human Rights and Chief Prosecutor of the International Criminal Tribunals for Yugoslavia and Rwanda.

We gave the world Roméo Dallaire, who founded the Roméo Dallaire Child Soldiers Initiative to help reintegrate child soldiers into society and who pleaded for and eventually got some help from the UN to stop the genocide in Rwanda (albeit the help came a little too late).

Canadians are not finished yet. We have among us David Suzuki, a science broadcaster and environmentalist and the host of the popular series *The Nature of Things*; Bob Hunter and the other founders of Greenpeace; Jody Williams and the various Canadians involved in the Mine Ban Treaty; "Captain" Paul Watson, the founder of the Sea Shepherd Conservation Society—and many more of the same ilk.

We keep producing determined Canadians. Maybe it is the good water and the good soil. Maybe it is the Canadian winter that freezes the toes and legs and all the blood goes to the brain to make it boil and work harder, churning new ideas.

*Human, environmental and animal advocacy needs to be given prominence in our common vision of good for all. Good is good, and to remind Muslims—it does not necessarily need to have a Muslim-sounding name.* We need to acknowledge good and support all those who endeavor to establish justice. They make up the best of humanity, and if we join their cause, then we, as Muslims, engage in our common aspiration of *good*, as taught by the Prophet, and live up to the higher ideals that our religion demands of us. As the Quran states, *"Is the reward of goodness aught save goodness?"* (Quran 55:60).

Citizens in the U.K., U.S., Australia, New Zealand, Germany, Sweden, and Switzerland are some of the countries with the best record in terms of their citizens' engagement in good works, especially when advocating for animal and environmental rights.

I said citizens. Not politicians. Aren't politicians also citizens? Most behave as if they have been cast from outer space when the Martians got fed up with their antics. I think you will agree that for now most stand pretty much alone—in defiance, in arrogance and demanding a special spot on a conceited platform above the general citizenry. *Most think being "public servants" means the public are their servants.* But then there are *rare gems* who are not afraid of public perception or votes when they opted to do good, like *New Zealand's Jacinda Ardern* who wore a hijab proudly in solidarity with Muslims in their time of distress when many were killed in a mosque; and *Germany's Angela Merkel* who continued to assist Syrian refugees despite political backlash, both leaders exhibiting strength in times of adversity, exuding warmth and compassion to untold millions. I can assure you Germany will benefit with the Syrian refugees. They are enterprising people, with thousands of years of business and trade experience gained at the crossroads of major civilizations. Time will indeed tell a more favorable story after the initial hiccups. These leaders' words bring light to millions living in a dark world.

Talking of heroes, there is a *universal hero* common to all Muslims. His name is Mohammed. They love him dearly, yet strictly adhere to the Quran and Prophet Mohammed's injunction that he should not be deified. If one knows the man, it is almost guaranteed the person would love him too. *What is it about Prophet Mohammed, peace be upon him, that evokes such passion? We shall examine why in chapter six. It will be a revelation to many. First, did you know he was an orphan?* More later.

## The love for Mohammed among his companions

Prophet Mohammed was a truthful man. He did not play with words. There was no dispute on the sagacity and honesty of this noble man such that even enemies of Prophet Mohammed acknowledged that he never lied. Long before he received the revelations from God—and continuing even after declaring his prophethood—he was known as *Al-ameen*, meaning *the truthful-one*. In battle, Mohammed would often forgive his staunch enemies and sometimes, to the dismay of his companions who had just won a hard-earned victory in battle, sustaining injuries and casualties, he would pardon and set free prisoners of war who were resolute opponents of Prophet Mohammed's call to the worship of One God. His words, unlike the word-play of many politicians of today, were sincere. His actions, too, were sincere. His companions, confused to see their Prophet release prisoners of war, would soon realize the wisdom of their leader: his tenacious foes, recognizing the nobility and grace of Mohammed, soon adopted his cause as their own. They became his loyal and steadfast followers, and just as ardently as they had fought *against* him, they now fought *for* him, in pursuit of his goal to set people free from the servitude of humans and idols to serve God. They saw their Prophet live a life of truth, of compassion, of frugality, and never wavering in sincerity. *The love of their Prophet by Muslims is so profound that it has amazed non-Muslims and even some contemporary historians.* A good insight into this subject can be found in several publications.[53]

One person, among multitudes, who was prepared to fight for Islam was a woman by the name of Umm Amara, who took part in the Battle of Mount Uhud, in 625 CE, in which Muslim forces fought against the polytheists. Umm Amara set off to the battlefield with her husband and her two sons—her role was to look after the wounded and to distribute water to the soldiers. Initially Prophet Mohammed's army had the upper hand, as he had posted some archers on higher ground, exposing the enemy army to flights of arrows as they tried to breach the Muslim defenses.

It was at this stage of the battle that Umm Amara decided to go meet her Prophet. As she was approaching Prophet Mohammed at a juncture when the enemy was in disarray and retreating, a number of Muslim archers left their high vantage posts, lured away by the prospect of booty from the fallen enemy, and reassured by the perception that the rest of the enemy army was already in retreat.

*It was a fatal mistake.*

Seeing a break in the Muslim defenses, a section of cavalry led by an astute military leader and tactician (by the name of Khalid ibn al-Walid, who would later embrace Islam) saw his chance. He circled back with a section of the cavalry and made a ferocious attack,

53 M. Lings, *Muhammad: His Life Based on the Earliest Sources* (Rochester, VT: Inner Traditions, 2006); Safi ur Rahman Al Mubarakpuri, Ar-Raheeq Al-Makhtum (The Sealed Nectar) (Darussalam: n.p., 2002); Muhammad Husayn Haykal, *The Life of Muhammad* (Selangor: Islamic Book Trust, 2008); John Esposito, *Islam: The Straight Path* (Oxford: Oxford University Press, 1998); Y. Emerick, *The Life and Work of Muhammad* (Indianapolis, IN: Alpha, 2002).

breaching the defenses near Prophet Mohammed. Many Muslims were killed in the process, while others fell into disarray with the force of attack, exposing Prophet Mohammed to the enemy. About a dozen undaunted companions quickly surrounded the Prophet to protect him but were greatly outnumbered by the enemy horsemen. Umm Amara and her family ran to the Prophet to shield him. A shield was thrown to her on the order of the Prophet, so she could protect herself.

Umm Amara repelled many of the attackers with a discarded sword she had picked up ensuring that the enemy would not get closer to Prophet Mohammed, suffering many wounds in the process. One of her sons sustained a grievous injury, which Umm Amara quickly dressed and then had him return to the battle. At one point she was struck in the neck by an enemy sword, leaving a large gaping wound, which Prophet Mohammed ordered one of her sons to attend to, in order to staunch the flow of blood. Bleeding and weak, Umm Amara returned to the fight.

The battle resulted in losses on both sides, and there was no clear-cut winner. Prophet Mohammed was saved but sustained a number of injuries. Before both armies returned to their respective camps, the leader of the polytheists, Abu Sufyaan (who later also embraced Islam), shouted towards the place he believed to be occupied by Prophet Mohammed and his companions, *"This compensates for our loss at Badr."* (In the Battle of Badr, a year earlier, a greatly outnumbered group of Muslims—including the Prophet— poorly armed and mostly on foot, had faced a well-armed polytheist army with a formidable cavalry, routing the enemy with a decisive victory.)

In response to Abu Sufyaan, Umar ibn Al Khattab, a close companion of the Prophet, yelled back a repartee, *"We are not equal: our slain are in paradise, yours are in the fire."*[54]

---

54 Lings, *Muhammad*, 190

Umm Amara participated in many battles, in one of which, the Battle of Yamama, she sustained many wounds and lost an arm. She continued to support the cause of her Prophet throughout her life until she passed away. For her, the Prophet was more beloved than her own self or family.

*Umm Amara, like many of her contemporaries, recognized that Prophet Mohammed stood for a great cause that encompassed ending the subjugation of the poor and the weak by the rich and the powerful, the establishment of gender equality, and the practice of monotheism, whereby God alone reigns supreme. Like many of the Prophet's companions, Umm Amara was willing to give up everything she possessed so that justice might be established on earth, recognizing that such a goal sometimes called for enormous sacrifice.*

On another occasion, when polytheists captured Zayd ibn ad-Dathima, a companion of the Prophet, and were about to execute him, the polytheist leader, Abu Sufyan ibn Harb, said to the captive, *"I ask you by Allah, Zayd, don't you wish that Muhammed were with us now to take your place so that we could cut off his head instead, and you were with your family?"* Zayd replied, his words sincere, *"By Allah, I would not wish Mohammed to be now in a place where even a thorn could hurt him, if that was the condition for me being with my family!"* At this, Abu Sufyan remarked, *"I have not seen any people love anyone the way the companions of Mohammed love Mohammed."*

## War and prisoners of war

History has witnessed many such acts of heroism demonstrated by the followers of Prophet Mohammed. What is it about this man that inspired, and still inspires, such passion that one would not hesitate to sacrifice one's own life for his cause? What is this "cause"? What made enemies change heart and start to love this man? Even now, there are many people who in their ignorance blame Prophet Mohammed, but when they study what this man truly represented, they start to defend his honor (as a way of example, search van Klaveren online, a far-right Dutch MP who started to write a book against Islam and what happened as he reached partway into his book). The life Prophet Mohammed and the teaching of the Quran can provide the answers to these questions and illustrate the cause or causes that the Prophet advanced.

History is replete with examples of magnanimity shown by Muslim armies and their commanders, who had learnt by example from their commander-in-chief and spiritual leader Prophet Mohammed.

They applied prophet Mohammed's lessons of remaining steadfast in battle, and even if the battle was hard fought with heavy casualties sustained by the Muslim army, even though the opposing armies might have committed atrocities against them, the victorious Muslims refrained from retaliating in kind. Rather, to the utter bewilderment of their vanquished foes, the victorious Muslims treated them with dignity, ensured that they were fed well (sometimes better than the victors themselves), and then either set free after paying compensation or freed without penalty if they had no money.[55]

***Centuries before the Geneva Convention on the rights of prisoners of war, Islam had already set a precedent for the humane treatment of captured soldiers.*** Prophet Mohammed's words are etched in classic authentic books of Hadith. He set down certain rules for his followers in the conduct of war. They were not to desecrate or destroy places of worship or to abuse those in holy orders or who were engaged in ritual worship; they were not to cut down fruit-bearing trees or palm trees, or destroy cultivated fields, crops, or vegetation; they were not to kill cattle, sheep, and camels except for food, not kill

---

55 Books of Hadith: Musnad of Ahmed ibn Hanbal, Al Muwatta of Imam Malik, Sahih Bukhari, and Sunnan of Abu Dawud; Mubarakpuri, *The Sealed Nectar: Biography of the Noble Prophet* (Darussalam: Riyadh, 2015)

the vulnerable, such as children, women, the sick, and the elderly.[56] The Prophet's companions heeded his injunctions and the sincerity of his words. They observed the Quranic praise that says, *"And they give food despite their own need for it to the needy, the orphan, and the captive (Saying), 'We feed you only for the countenance of Allah. We wish not from you reward or gratitude'"* (Quran 76:8–9).

Historical narratives, by both Muslims and non-Muslims, demonstrate these acts of generosity, benevolence, and magnanimity when Muslims were victorious in battle. Though not all Muslim armies strictly applied these rules in dealing with their vanquished foes, the better disciplined Muslim armies did observe the injunction in the Quran that says, *"Good and evil are not equal. Repel evil with good, and the person who was your enemy becomes like an intimate friend"* (Quran 41:34).

Thus, we find that when Saladin recaptured the city of Jerusalem, he provided safe passage and protection for the prisoners of war. The book, *Saladin: Noble Prince of Islam* by Diane Stanley, is well-researched and a fine read detailing a prince-warrior of courage, piety, tolerance, and wisdom.[57] *This was in stark contrast to the actions of the Crusaders, who had indiscriminately slaughtered the city's residents—the elderly, men, women, and children; Muslims, Jews, and even those Christians who did not conform to their version of Christianity—such that the streets flowed with blood.* How could one not admire the discipline and generosity of the victorious Muslim forces?

The idea that Islam was spread by the sword is *false*, essentially word-play duping the lay. Muslims were indeed prepared to fight, but only in order to stop the subjugation of one group of people by another; to establish the reign of One God (monotheism); and in self-defense.

---

56  Bahā' al-Dīn Yūsuf ibn Rāfi' Ibn Shaddād; D. S. Richards, *The Rare and Excellent History of Saladin* (London: Routledge, 2002)

57  Diane Stanley, *Saladin: Noble Prince of Islam* (New York: HarperCollins, 2002)

Through conquest, education and commerce, Muslims left indelible marks in parts of Africa and Asia, including the Caucasus region of Russia, parts of China, and into the Balkans. Mosques and minarets were built in Spain, where Cordoba, under Muslim rule, had 50 hospitals centuries before Europe had any major hospital. Hisham ibn Abdur-Rahman, the governor of Cordoba, transformed that part of Spain into a center of learning, where people from various parts of the world came to study.[58] Muslims, Jews and Christians lived and thrived in a general atmosphere of acceptance of the other. *At that time, Spain surpassed the rest of Europe in the fields of medicine, botany, mathematics, and astronomy. once the land had been militarily won over, the sword was laid aside for the pen.*

When Andalusia, Spain, was eventually wrested from the Muslims and the population subjected to the Spanish Inquisition, many *Jews, Muslims, and even minority sects of Christians were forced to flee*, a significant number finding refuge in Ottoman Turkey.[59]

In 1847, when Ireland experienced the Great Famine, Turkey sent five ships laden with food to relieve the distress of *their Christian brethren.*[60]

Today, more than ever, we need love and compassion flowing from and into every (human heart) port, just as those ships did, for are we not but one humanity? We need sincere words, words of

----

58 https://www.nationalgeographic.com/archaeology-and-history/ magazine/2016/11-12/muslim-medicine-scientific-discovery-islam/; https://www. ncbi.nlm.nih.gov/pubmed/28468023; M. R. Menocal, *The Ornament of the World: How Muslims, Jews, and Christians Created a Culture of Tolerance in Medieval Spain* (Boston: Little, Brown and Company, 2002)

59 https://www.aa.com.tr/en/culture-and-art/ottoman-empire-welcomed-jews-exiled-from-spain/1220028; https://rlp.hds.harvard.edu/faq/judaism-turkey

60 https://www.irishcentral.com/roots/history/little-known-tale-of-generous-turkish-aid-to-the-irish-during-the-great-hunger; https://www.irishexaminer. com/lifestyle/features/turkish-aid-to-irish-famine-was-highest-form-of-compassion-275281.html

compassion, not word-play. One needs to study Prophet Mohammed, as many great contemporaries and intellectuals from all faiths have done, and if one did so in an impartial manner, one would not fail to admire and be inspired by this great man. The Quran confirms Prophet Mohammed's character:

> *only through the Divine Mercy have you [Mohammed] been able to deal with your followers so gently. If you had been stern and hard-hearted, they would all have deserted you a long time ago. Forgive them and ask God to forgive [their sins] and consult with them in certain matters. But, when you reach a decision, trust God. God loves those who trust Him.*
> (Quran 3:159)

## Taking lessons from children

If Muslims hold fast to the Quran and the Sunnah (the way of life of Prophet Mohammed) then compassion, forgiveness, and mercy will again be the hallmarks of their lifestyle throughout the world. Non-Muslims, on the other hand, need to give credit where credit is due. This is called *bridge building*, something that few people attempt or even think about. Non-Muslims should *not* hide the positive work done by Muslims and focus only on the negative. Muslims must do the same in return.

Of course, there will always be the "ignorant ones," who, no matter what you do, are so entrenched in their animosity that no reasoned discourse and no bridge-building effort will sway them. Yet, even when faced with the negative, we should not retaliate in kind. I would personally let such a person cook and broil in his or her own anger-juices, for that is what they want to do. In response to those who are set in a negative stance, and nothing, no matter how profound is going to sway them, I personally adopt the strategy advised by the Quran: *"Make due allowance for man's nature, and enjoin the doing of what is right; and leave alone all those who choose to remain ignorant"* (Quran 7:199).

We should follow the example of little children. Go to a playground and see how kids play with each other: they laugh, tussle, and tumble, and they don't give a hoot about their differences in color or religion—good is good and bad is bad, and it is that simple. One may sulk if someone gets too rough, but soon they are back at it again, the past forgotten. Color is not a divisive issue because children are not infected by adult prejudices.

There is no sinister "word play" with a hidden agenda at the children's playground. It is what it is, and it is sincere. There is often more wisdom on display in a children's playground than in the corridors of power.

*For academicians, the playground is an institution for great scholarship!* As Shashi Tharoor—author, politician, United Nations peacekeeper, refugee worker, and human rights activist—has noted:

> *Malaysians talk with Mauritians, Arabs with Australians, South Africans with Sri Lankans, and Iranians with Indonesians. The Indian Ocean serves as both a sea separating them and a bridge linking them together.*

## The art of using words

Words can hurt and condemn, and words can also motivate. Media would be wise to print some positive achievements by Muslims. There is too much focus on the negative. When Muslims are given recognition for their achievements and allowed to practice Islam freely without prejudice, and share their knowledge without animosity, all will benefit. *Muslims engaged in protecting wildlife and their habitats, preserving the waters, advocating for domestic animal welfare, and practicing environmental sustainability benefit the non-Muslims as well.*

After all, with 1.8 billion Muslims inhabiting this planet, does it really make sense to keep demonizing them? Imagine the benefits for everyone, if a quarter of the human population—yes, that is how many Muslims there are in this world—were to follow the injunctions of their religion. There would be a revival of charitable giving and kindness shown to all living things. Muslims have the potential to have a positive impact on all aspects of civilized society.

Unfortunately, Muslims face attack on an almost daily basis whether from demagogic politicians, a biased media, or tyrannical rulers manipulated by powerful regimes (who in turn siphon off the resources of the countries they control). If this situation could be reversed, then we might all coexist peacefully, despite our differences, and foster the health, wealth, peace, and prosperity of the entire planet.

Muslims must be mindful of the commands given to them in the Quran. Verse 49:13 states, *"O mankind! Lo! We have created you male and female and have made you nations and tribes that ye may know one another. Lo! The noblest of you, in the sight of Allah, is the best in conduct. Lo! Allah is Knower, Aware."*

Another serious issue (to be discussed further in later chapters) is the rate of destruction of our natural resources and the potential elimination of many species due to the disappearance of their natural habitats.

*The impact of humankind on the land, the water, and the air through urbanization and pollution is coming to a head. The naysayer's argument that "It has not happened yet, so what is the proof that it will happen?" is apathy of the worst kind, because when it does happen, it will be too late to blame or point fingers at one another.*

*And it will not matter if they are forefingers or middle fingers.*

We have a duty to educate everyone about the dangerous path we are treading, starting with ourselves and our immediate families, then friends, neighbors, and the community at large. When the point of no return is reached, an "everyone for himself" attitude will save no one.

We should have the courage to change that which is changeable immediately: treat animals justly, whether they belong to us or not; recognize our environmental obligations, and take that first s t ep, however small; help save the planet and inspire others to do the same.

The Chinese have a wise saying: *the journey of a thousand miles begins with a single step.* Pop over to the mirror and look at the image. Guess who should take the *first* step?

Wait a bit. Before you put on your running shoes, let us fire up the barbeque. I have marinated some definitions. Let us roast them in the next chapter.

# CHAPTER 5

# SKEWERING THE DEFINITIONS

*"Philosopher, orator, apostle, legislator, warrior,*
*conqueror of ideas, restorer of rational dogmas,*
*of a cult without images; the founder of twenty terrestrial*
*empires and of one spiritual empire, that is Muhammad.*
*As regards all standards by which human greatness may be*
*measured, we may well ask, is there any man greater than he?"*

—ALPHONSE DE LAMARTINE (1790-1869)
FRENCH POET AND STATESMAN

Let us fire up the barbeque, skewer some definitions and terms, and roast them. Definitions are constraining and they limit free thought. They limit the ability to go beyond their confining borders. Give me your plate. Savor the new refined flavor.

## Atheism

China has recently witnessed the mass incarceration of Chinese Muslim Uyghurs (possibly millions) in mass concentration camps to be indoctrinated in the "new religion" of "State Worship," because that is what it is at its core.

Humans are essentially "worshiping creatures"; if humans do not worship an invisible deity, they are invariably worshiping something else: money; the state (think China under Mao Tse Tung, Russia under Stalin); a hero in human form; a figurine carved out of wood, stone, ivory, or some other material (idols), to be placed in homes or places of worship; the new Ferrari; power; the old piece of wood in the pocket that one must "knock" to keep bad omens at bay. *So, is an atheist really an atheist? Let us see.*

Say an atheist was stuck on an island with an active volcano that is starting to rumble and spew black clouds, and a frazzled looking and incantation-singing shaman happens to come along with a box that is emitting strange odors. The shaman h as seen a man with a coconut standing at the shore and senses an opportunity right before his eyes and approaches slowly, pretending to know the unknown realm. If the shaman were then to say to the atheist, "Would you be willing to worship the box and give me your last remaining coconut and the dingy that brought you to this island if I can make the volcano stop rumbling?" the chap would probably agree to the deal, knowing that the volcano was just about to erupt. They both wait while the Shaman is shaking in his torn pants.

If, perchance (as a result of natural phenomena or simply coincidence) the volcano then stopped rumbling, the "atheist" would willingly hand over the coconut, regard the shaman as his guide and augur, and become a worshiper of the box. The shaman breathes a sigh of relief. *He can't believe his luck.*

In fact, the "shaman" was actually someone who had been stuck on the island for a long time. He had a frazzled exotic appearance because he had accidentally stepped on a crusty old lion's tail. The animal had let the shaman know in no uncertain terms that causing indignities to a lion having an afternoon nap is not a good idea. Once the kerfuffle was over, the "shaman" emerged alive *but disappointed that lions had no patience listening to explanations.*

The shaman's "incantations" were in truth muffled curses in his native tongue directed at the lion and laments about his desperation to escape this abominable island whose creatures could not keep their tails tucked in. For his part, the atheist is convinced that the box must contain great power, for hadn't it stopped the volcano rumbling? Next day, when the atheist goes to find his "master," the shaman is nowhere to be found—until he looks out to sea and spies him bobbing up and down in the dingy. The shaman has escaped from the island, taking the coconut with him, leaving behind the awesome box. The chap slowly opens the box—and finds inside a *smelly old sock.*

The "atheist" had been worshiping something that *stinks.* Worship is essentially someone—or something—we are obsessed with, *religiously* sacrifice our time and efforts for, and are very attentive to: gods (with a small "g," silly), mini-gods, idols, or false deities.

We all worship something: a good home with a manicured lawn that we spend our time and effort on; our family, and doing whatever it takes to ensure their wellbeing; the business, which again consumes much time and effort; our desires of sex, power, arrogance; the body and the face and the billions we spend on them; or even an old sock.

There is no such thing as an atheist: we all venerate something; we all have something we hold dear to our hearts—even the avowed "atheist."

A paradox for the atheists: some atheists may adamantly claim to be "sincere" atheists. They hold on to that concept *religiously*, like a formal religion, and then whimsically market their *belief* as "atheism," not aware that it is an "*ism.*" Apologies to all atheists: this is only my opinion. Can we still be friends?

Then there are confused "secularists". Recently Quebec passed a bill restricting women from wearing head coverings, which almost everyone *from Michel to Michael know that the bill is targeted against Muslim women who don the hijab.* They came up with a smart (but not so smart) excuse that the head covers were "ostentatious" displays of religion. These tenacious politicians are pretty religious if you come to think of it. *They are merely preaching "secular religiosity" with passion, probably reading with bowed heads a religious book called Bill 21 in the hope of replacing one religion–the formal one–with the secular one.*

Many of us, however, would rather worship a force beyond our immediate perception: The Creator of everything, Eternal, Forgiving, Compassionate, Just, Ever Aware, and with the ability to assign hell or heaven to those He has created based upon the "life of tests" on this Earth. Others choose to worship material wealth: the "mighty dollar" for instance, or the big fancy house, the beautiful or handsome spouse, or even the golf course.

The Quran in verse 45:23 makes a remarkable observation of these mini-gods that one gives greater import, and which take various forms such as ego, base desires, caprice, fancies, whims, and vagaries, *"Then do you see the one who takes as his god his own vain desire? God has, knowing him as such, left him astray, and sealed his hearing and his heart, and put a veil on his sight. Who then will guide him after God? Will you not then receive advice?"*

In short, we all engage in worship, and we will all continue to do so. As the Quran says, "And they have chosen idols in various forms besides God, hoping that they would be a source of strength for them" (Quran 19:81).


## Jihad and Shariah

Many Muslims, especially during colonial and post-colonial exploitation of their lands by militarily powerful Western conquerors, have—and vanquished Muslims can certainly not be blamed for this—forsaken or forgotten to study the foundational principles of human rights, animal rights and environmental rights established by Prophet Mohammed. As recently as June 11, 2017, rallies were held in cities in the U.S. against "Shariah Law." Shariah is an Arabic word which means law. One can say that one prefers to follow secular Shariah (secular law) instead of Islamic Shariah.

So, lawful rallies were being held against law-law.

These types of disingenuous rallies happen when we do not take time to study what Shariah actually means; our prejudice obscures any objective discourse. To those who only feel comfortable with things "as they were," any change must be bad and must be resisted, a feeling that can be manipulated by more insidious forces.

Islamic Shariah prohibits stealing, lying and murder.

Were lawful rallies being held opposing stealing, lying, and murder? *I sat with a headache trying to figure this one out.*

It is enough to say the words "Shariah" or "Jihad" to have someone scramble up a tree to escape the coming calamity. It is not the intent of this book to give the pros and cons of "Shariah," but we must be brave enough to give thought to the matter instead of rejecting it outright (without having read the finer details of the law), weigh its pros and cons, and accept or modify or reject what we do not like. *Stealing is wrong, lying is wrong, giving false testimony is cowardly, and murder abhorrent. These are well known in Islamic Shariah.*

We need to allow a mature discussion on Islamic Shariah. Are we not still in the twenty-first century and find ourselves averse to burning people on the stake for expression of ideas or are we quickly regressing back to those brawn-but-no-brain times?

Let us take one simple example of Islamic Shariah or Islamic Law: the prohibition of gambling and the consumption of alcohol. Let us say that a hulking man called Mr. Dezert Al-Sahara comes home intoxicated after having lost large amounts of money in gambling, and the place he called home where he would normally hang his sombrero will no longer be his (since he has lost that too laying bets while inebriated). Mr. Al-Sahara is fuming mad. He wants to blame someone for his bad luck. Not knowing his own strength, he ends up inflicting grievous harm on his wife and children while still groggy.

The next day, after taking aspirins for his hangover at the jail, he is ushered to face the judge. He tells the judge that he regrets his actions and he would like to go to the hospital to visit his family as soon as he is discharged from the court. He says that all this happened because he was angry and drunk and the sombrero obscured his vision while he was swinging punches.

The judge eyes Mr. Al-Sahara with disapproval, as he has seen him before. Previously, he had been accused of driving while intoxicated, and injuring someone walking on the footpath with his dog. Mr. Al-Sahara had been represented by an experienced lawyer who was able to get him off on a technicality.

This time, Mr. Al-Sahara knows he is in trouble. He insists that Shariah be applied in his case, trying to befuddle and confound the judge. The judge agrees, much to Mr. Al-Sahara's astonishment (unbeknownst to the latter, the judge had done some reading about Shariah)[61] Mr. Al-Sahara gulps. He knows he cannot call the best lawyers and claim temporary insanity while inebriated.

His expensive lawyer is looking on from the gallery, wishing he had been hired for he could have used legal loopholes freely available in secular law (as big as school buses)—such as intoxication, addiction, unfortunate possession of a muscled body, and poorly designed sombreros that obscured his vision when he threw the punches—to get his client off and allow Mr. Al-Sahara to repeat his bad conduct in the future.

However, in Islamic Shariah, he has already broken three laws: alcohol consumption, gambling, and physical and emotional injury

---

61 https://wpisca.wpengine.com/?p=115; https://www.washingtonpost.com/opinions/five-myths-about-sharia/2016/06/24/7e3efb7a-31ef-11e6-8758-d58e76e11b12_story.html?utm_term=.747a821cd319

to his wife and children. The judge pronounces some clear-cut and unambiguous judgments: Mr. Al-Sahara has already broken the first law (intoxication) and the second law (gambling), so he needs to take full responsibility for the consequences of his actions (i.e. the emotional and physical injury to others). Mr. Al-Sahara faces several charges and lengthy sentences for each of them.

After duly paying for his crime, Mr. Al-Sahara now wants to mend the error of his ways. He wants to exercise discipline and restraint, and he also intends to strive to become a better person since he dearly loves his family. He is determined to stop hitting the bottle, so he decides to shun the bar.

He is found sitting quietly in a busy restaurant drinking fizzy pop. He fondly recalls his childhood days and remembers how his mother kept the little one on her lap and warned him against using alcohol and to not forget his mother tongue.

He decides to start using more of his mother tongue. He says quietly to himself a word that has a range of meanings—such as "strive," "discipline," "restrain," and "struggle"—the word "Jihad." He proclaims in Arabic that he will exercise Jihad upon himself and will not touch liquor again. Unfortunately, though the music in the restaurant is blaring, some people within earshot hears him muttering things in Arabic and one of the words is "Jihad."

There is a scramble for the door and the nearest tree.

When the tree is swamped by people clinging onto thorny branches, some have to swim across a nearby river to get far away from him. All this commotion, all the scratches and wet clothes because people did not ask what "Jihad" meant and instead responded to the definitions provided by non-Arabic speakers who were bent on taking it out of context.

The poor chap's personal Jihad was simply to free himself from alcohol intake since he knew that if he touched another drop, he may once again fall into the trap of abusing alcohol. Unfortunately, he had used an Arabic word for "struggle" and "strive."

Mr. Al-Sahara was last seen being shuffled back to meet the tired judge (Okay, then, if it will make you happy—the judge's name is Mike. No, I am certainly not going to tell you who made the sombrero. It was only used to give an example, for heaven's sake) because he whispered Jihad and caused a stampede. As he was being escorted in chains, he was heard asking the cop in a very loud voice, in English, in a hushed courtroom, "What did I do now?"

But nobody was listening.

Time passes.

Mr. Al-Sahara has spent quite some time behind bars (the other kind). While incarcerated, he has had time for deep reflection. He reads a lot of books on self-improvement, the art of motivating people, and leadership. He wants to give some good back to society for the kindness his adopted country has shown him and wants to become a model citizen. He resolves to become a teetotaler, to never gamble, and decides to advocate against gambling and intoxication having learnt from his mistakes.

The first thing he concludes when he walks out of the prison is never to use Arabic words unless he is on an elevated podium (that would pose some difficulty if someone decided to clamber up) when delivering a presentation to the public, a quick exit door at the back, preferably with a car parked outside, with the engine running. He decides on these simple precautions in case someone's adrenalin shot up with foreign words that cause excitement.

If the word "Jihad" is to be used, Al-Sahara decides, it must be done openly, in an educational format, with a big screen quickly flashing the English translation for any sentence he uses which has Arabic words in it. For example, when he wants to say that he wants to do "jihad" by "yuhibu" all human beings, regardless of faith, the screen would flash, "Stop. Do not get alarmed, please. I am simply saying that I want to strive (jihad) in loving (yuhibu) all human beings, regardless of faith."

Regardless, he comes wearing sprinting sports shoes in case someone could not read.

Al-Sahara becomes somewhat of a celebrity for his honest passion and his love for mankind. Soon he is getting invited to different schools, alcohol/gambling rehab centers, and public forums. At the completion of every presentation, he has someone (in armor) standing at the door to hand out pamphlets to the exiting audience. The pamphlets give some statistics on the harm gambling and alcoholism can cause to society. The printouts say the following:

> *The harmful use of alcohol is a component cause of more than 200 disease and injury conditions in individuals, most notably alcohol dependence, liver cirrhosis, cancers and injuries… In 2012, about 3.3 million deaths…, or 5.9% of all global deaths, were attributable to alcohol consumption.*[62]

> *Crashes involving alcohol and/or drugs are a leading criminal cause of death in Canada. every day, on average, up to 4 Canadians are killed and many more are injured in alcohol and/or drug-related motor vehicle crashes.*[63]

> *The likelihood of developing a gambling addiction increases 23-fold for people affected by alcohol use disorders.*[64]

---

62  https://www.who.int/substance_abuse/facts/alcohol/en/

63  https://madd.ca/pages/impaired-driving/overview/statistics/

64  https://www.addictions.com/gambling/5-alarming-gambling-addiction-statistics/

*Seventeen to 24 percent of pathological gamblers will attempt suicide during their lives.*[65]

*oregon Problem Gambling Resource states that about 10 to 17 percent of children and about 25 to 50 percent of spouses of problem gamblers have been abused.*[66]

*Roughly 50 percent of those addicted to gambling will commit crimes to support continued gambling activity.*[67]

**Islamic Law forbids alcohol consumption and gambling.**

## Shariah. Still raw. Needs a bit more roasting.

Unlike most Westerners, Muslims generally do not make a distinction between a secular, temporal lifestyle and a once-a-week religious ritual (such as the church service on Sunday, which is often considered distinctly separate from the rest of the routine of life).

Islam is a *way of life*, and Muslims understand it as such. By *way of life*, I mean that religion, and even the court of law and the government function with deference to the Quran and Sunnah (the sayings and actions of the Prophet, as instructions).

---

65  https://www.ncbi.nlm.nih.gov/pmc/articles/PMC3004711/; D. M. Ledgerwood and N. M. Petry, "Gambling and suicidality in treatment-seeking pathological gamblers," *Journal of Nervous and Mental Disease* 192, no. 10 (2004): 711–14; O. Kausch, "Suicide attempts among veterans seeking treatment for pathological gambling," *Journal of Clinical Psychiatry* 64, no. 9 (2003): 1031–8

66  https://casinorank.com/gambling-addiction/gambling-addiction-statistics/

67  https://opus.uleth.ca/bitstream/handle/10133/411/GamblinginPrisons-CJB-2005.pdf; https://www.geneushealth.com/gambling-genetic-rehab-texas;

The process of drafting and enacting laws begins with the Quran and Sunnah, the sum of these two guides forming the foundation of Shariah (Islamic Law). These give fundamental and basic guidance, from which other laws can be extrapolated.

If there is no clear guidance on a given situation in these manuals, then a consensus (*Ijmaa*) is sought from experts within the field in conjunction with scholars from Islamic jurisprudence. These scholars, known as *Faqih* (Jurists), have a deep understanding of divine Islamic Law (*Fiqh*) and can quite accurately rule on ambiguous subjects.

For example, Islam forbids using pork for food, but are there exceptions? Let us say that a Muslim is stuck on an island because he bought a used dinghy with a small leak that the previous owner assured him was too small to be of consequence. Stranded on the desolate island, he looks around for food as he is starving. There is no food on the island except for a pig looking at the Muslim with suspicion. The Muslim is thinking what the law is regarding eating pork in dire circumstances as he eyes the wary porky. He knows that the Quran forbids using pork for food. But he must live.

He wishes to live long enough to lay his hands on the man who sold him a dud dinghy. Life is at stake. Ah, yes! He remembers that Islamic scholars and physicians have ruled that in such circumstances the eating of pork is "allowed," since the saving of a life takes precedence over the prohibition on eating pork. In Shariah (viz. Islamic Law), the saving of life takes precedence over many other rules that would normally apply. The hog, observing a smirk developing on the Muslim as the memory of the ruling was slowly dawning upon the hungry man, was last seen bolting with its tail in the air.

Another example? Muslims are required to *fast* (nothing to do with speed, for many Muslims are as slow as the next guy) in the month of Ramadhan (if there is any speed, then watch the speed exhibited by youngsters at the time of breaking the fast). So, what about diabetics on insulin when it is Ramadhan? Would they not be breaking two religious dictates—that of injecting something that had a pork origin and that of eating—during the holy month? Well, the consensus ruling from physicians and Islamic scholars is that such individuals can, within reason, be allowed to eat and inject a product that has a pig source as the support for life supersedes other dictates (in the not too distant past, pig-sourced insulin was the only type available, but that is no longer the case, as insulin can now be manufactured using recombinant DNA technology). The scholars of Islam and experts within the relevant field (in this case medical doctors), consulting with each other, drew important lessons from the Quran and Hadith, and came up with an extrapolated ruling making such an allowance legitimate.

These two simple examples are merely a dip in a vast ocean of detailed and exhaustive studies and deductive analogy (*Kiyas*) that make up Islamic jurisprudence (*Fiqh*). The reason why I bring up these terms that is causing you some consternation (as all you wanted to know was what happened to the pig) is simply to demonstrate that Islam is an immersive, scientific, analytical, and methodical religion with the ability to keep current with new developments and scientific progress.

If you are thoroughly confused with all these terms, do not worry. So was the chap on the island, but things did eventually become clear (to the detriment of the pig making a dash for it). Furthermore, I can assure all animal rights activists that the pig bolted into a hole and was saved by a whisker. So was the man, by the way—in case this book is being read by human rights activists to check if I neglected to place human rights on the agenda.

## Anthropomorphize.

Say anthropomorphize five times in quick succession. Now for the general meaning: to attribute human characteristics or behavior to animals. The five times repetition was just to get you into the mood for what comes next.

Since the beginning of time and up to the present day, humans, in general, have regarded all other life forms as exploitable, since those forms do not speak any human language (and certainly not the foul words you hear when someone stubs his toe), or look (as pathetic as some of us do in the early morning), smell (try sniffing a human who has not showered for a month), walk (or crawl, like the remnants leaving the pub at closing time), or act like us (though considering how some of us act, it is best that animals don't try to mimic us).

Our idea of "intelligence" has been extremely limited—we have defined it from the human perspective. So, if an animal can use a tool, then it surely must be intelligent to some degree, but only a limited one, since we are so much more capable of using tools.

Why should the ability to use tools be regarded as an indicator of intelligence? It is one form of intelligence, yes, but let us not forget the resourcefulness of animals as they hunt (think of the intelligence of lions hunting in tandem, keeping low, stealthily approaching prey while keeping themselves upwind, positioning themselves strategically before an ambush), hide and camouflage (think of the mimic octopus, the chameleon, and the baby deer), protect their young (think of how the buffalo form a fortified circle, horns flashing outwards, to keep the lions at bay and away from their young), and communicate (think of elephants and how they communicate across hundreds of miles with others of their kind by making infrasonic rumbles beyond the range of human hearing).

Elephants: that reminds me. One of the best books I have read is a book by Lawrence Anthony titled *The Elephant Whisperer*. I have suggested to some of my friendlier patients and associates to read the book, and I have been informed by some of them that they liked the book so much that they started buying copies as gifts for their friends during Christmas and other special gift-giving events. Try this book: you will come out humbled at the intelligence, empathy, and resourcefulness of these giants and how, if humans are willing to understand and respect animals, what bountiful insights these gifts of nature can reveal.

## Macho

Shoot! Not with the gun, silly, but with the camera. Amaze us with your technique, intelligence, resourcefulness, and skill. The macho man or woman is truly macho when he or she opts to use the camera, despite having the choice to kill and deny future generations to see lives of other creatures in their dazzling array, and not the gun. Now that is *real* willpower, showing the fraudulent gun-wielding "macho" wimp that it takes more courage to choose an option that allows future generations to enjoy the beauty of *life*. True grit is this: the ability to come close to the animal, to wait patiently, and then take a stunning picture.

Then there are these fake macho's in their 4x4's, purposely revving up and honking, annoyed that they are getting late for work, as little creatures try to cross roads that we have crisscrossed in their birthing or foraging area. Many do not care to slow down when little ducklings following their mother are trying to hurry up with their tiny feet to cross the road, leaving little bodies scattered on the pavement.

One time my daughter (who is studying to become a veterinarian and has a passion for helping wild animals in distress) and I were coming home to Sudbury, three hours in on the road, having picked her up from the airport in Toronto.

It is a lovely four-hour drive home, the highway meandering around some pristine lakes, thick forests, and wetlands. We happened to see a large injured turtle on the road, its shell cracked open by a passing vehicle. It was moving very slowly across the divide, leaving a bloodied trail across the path. I braked firmly, slowed down, and parked safely on the side of the road. The turtle was partially to our side of the road. We got out, my daughter assuring me it may still be helped by gluing its shell, having taken courses at a turtle rehab center. Then we saw a big pickup truck come zooming down the opposite side, going the other way. I have no doubt it must have seen us and the turtle; we would certainly stand out like sore thumbs, since it is a lonely stretch of the highway. The vehicle pummeled down without slowing, shifting its bearing towards the turtle. The vehicle had actually maneuvered to the wrong *side* of the road and we heard the tires going over the injured animal. My daughter picked up the bloodied animal, her face wet with tears at this obvious injustice and ignorance, and the animal soon died in her arms.

One particular macho individual, knowing my love for wildlife and aware that he was making me upset, was trying to rub it in. He was a big man complaining of chronic heel pain and he had been booked in for a cortisone shot. As I loaded the syringe to inject the medication into his foot, the previously cocky guy was soon reduced to a blithering wuss at the sight of the needle. He insisted on holding his wife's hand, sweating and trembling. The lady, clearly amused, reminded the macho man that she had delivered "a few young 'uns without much ado." A few minutes earlier, this chap had been boasting about his hunting exploits, recounting gory details with such insensitivity that would make you wonder about the human species. He could not brave a small thin needle, but was brave enough to put large bullets shot with great velocity into animals, and recounting gory details with such cold detachment. If the macho chap wanted to hunt to eat, the least he could do is show respect for the animal he was going to consume, as many members of indigenous cultures, such as the Maasai of Africa, native North Americans, and the Australian aboriginals do.

And then there are people who pose with a gun, while a beautiful giraffe that one may have killed—often the intention is not to eat the animal to sustain life (you may recall some recent photographs in some major newspapers)—lies dead behind the person. No respect for life—especially when it comes to life that is not one's own. Reverse the role, and see how bravado evaporates. Animals are no match for guns and fast vehicles. Neither would humans if they were on the receiving end.

Engineers and officials responsible for building the new four-lane highway called highway 69 going south, in Sudbury, my home town, have made provisions where they have fenced major portions of the highway while creating bridges and pathways dedicated to animal crossing. It is a pleasure driving on this stretch of road with the knowledge that animals are safe (or relatively safer), and humans are safe too. When human intellect takes into account that we need to live and let live, amazing things can happen. Kudos to those highway engineers.

## Empathy

Fortunately, in the last three decades, there has been a growing appreciation of animal rights, a recognition that animals have intelligence, albeit of a different kind to humans, that they have emotions and even exhibit empathy.[68]

I have seen such empathy (not the convoluted definition concocted by certain behaviorists who are keen to point that it is not true empathy but rather complicated methods of self-survival, but the simple definition that most of us understand and appreciate)

---

68 J. P. Balcombe, *What a Fish Knows: The Inner Lives of Our Underwater Cousins* (New York: Scientific American, 2016); F. B. M. D. Waal, *Are We Smart Enough to Know How Smart Animals Are?* (New York: W.W. Norton and Company, 2016); M. Bekoff, *The Emotional Lives of Animals: A Leading Scientist Explores Animal Joy, Sorrow, and Empathy—and Why They Matter* (Novato, CA: New World Library, 2007); Eugene Linden, *The Parrot's Lament: And Other True Tales of Animal Intrigue, Intelligence, and Ingenuity* (New York: Plume, 1999/2000); Bekoff, *The Emotional Lives of Animals*

first-hand at my farm in Stouffville, Ontario. We had a number of chickens and one cockerel, kept free to range for the purposes of harvesting organic eggs. One fall, when prey birds began to migrate south prior to the winter setting in, a peregrine falcon established itself in the vicinity, and attacked our chickens for food. Unfortunately, two chickens were killed as a result. We started seeing our chickens afraid to venture into the open field, tending to tuck themselves beneath bushes in the area when foraging. One day as they ventured out, the falcon swooped down and attacked one of the chickens. The cockerel, though a distance away came rushing to fend off the attacker, and in the process was attacked and injured, but refused to abandon his mate until the falcon decided to flee.

This is not an isolated incident; I have witnessed many similar episodes. Farmers and animal behaviorists see it all the time, provided they keep their eyes open and their admiration for these beautiful creatures kindled. Regardless of whether we can prove that a certain animal has these qualities of empathy and intelligence, it behooves us to accord all animals our respect and kindness.

There are some well-meaning individuals who love animals and plants and go out on a limb trying to anthropomorphize different species to encourage humans to protect and care for them. For example, we tend to anthropomorphize monkeys or chimpanzees, assigning them certain human characteristics and attributes to justify their care and protection. Such efforts deserve our praise—but do not stop there. The care and protection we can offer should not be limited by anthropomorphic criteria.

In many ways, humans are limited in their ability to outperform many of those with whom we share this Earth, so are human characteristics really the only *relevant* criteria to assess the value of the inhabitants of our world? Let us continue to ask the smug human some questions.

How many of us can hibernate like the bear or the squirrel, for months, in deep winter? And in this challenge, we allow the human to use any amount of winter clothing and gorge as much food as they can before any competition commences.

How many of us are as nimble and sure-footed as the mountain goat (watch some YouTube videos to see what I mean). In this challenge we buy you the latest mountain shoes with steel spikes and the best mountain gear money can buy, and the human has to follow the goat-leader as it clambers along narrow rocky ledges, often suspended thousands of feet in the air, before nimbly jumping across a deep chasm onto a small cliff edge, where one slip could spell doom? ("That mark on the bottom of the valley? Oh, that was left by the last chap who took up the challenge, jumped, and missed the ledge.")

How many of us can change shapes and colors to mimic other species like the mimic octopus (again, try some YouTube videos) which can so transform itself that it blends into myriads of terrains as it moves along at speed? The mimic octopus was discovered in 1998 along the coast of Sulawesi in Indonesia. In this challenge we provide the human with as much make-up material he or she desires to try to match the octopus's ingenuity ("You don't expect me to apply make-up on the whole body now, do you?") and shape ("Can't change shape unless you give me a few months to either shed a few pounds or gain weight"). I doubt if anyone could match the mimic-ingenuity of the octopus or indeed that of lionfish, jellyfish or sea snakes.

## Bird Brain

If a bird could speak, it would probably say, "You choose to use animal names to insult other humans, call them pigs or dogs, even donkeys or turkeys. Let's talk about birds for a moment. Did you know that the swift (a bird with a bird brain—the term used with respect and not mockery), without any satellite navigation system or air traffic control guidance, can fly at the same altitude as the most sophisticated of your planes and stay on course, adjusting flight paths and speeds and maintaining accuracy both at nighttime and daytime, while, wait for it … often asleep, in flight, and staying in the air for ten months at a time? This amazing fact was just recently discovered by one of your scientists, known as Dr. Backman from Lund University in Sweden, a specialist in bird migration, using tracking radars.[69]

"Did you know that before chicks hatch, they can communicate with each other and their mother through a special sound system? Did you know that a hummingbird can fly backwards and sideways, that its weight is about the same as a penny, and that its wings beat about 100 beats per second? Try to click your tongue. It probably took a second. In that one second, the hummingbird has already beaten its wings 100 times to both boggle the mind and the poor clicking tongue. When the hummingbird dives, its wings beat 200 times per second, and those wings can rotate a full circle. The hummingbird can also hear and see better than humans. Did you know that the sooty tern sleeps only a few seconds, while in the air and still flying, and only lands to lay eggs and raise its young?

"Birds with bird brains. Yeah, right. Consider a tiny creature like the honey bee, with its highly developed community structure and the benefit it provides to humans via delicious healing honey, or in contrast the mighty elephant, with its ability to smell water buried deep in the ground, an ability that helps sustain its community and many other animals that would otherwise perish in times of drought.

"Each animal has unique characteristics, if only you took time to study us. Unfortunately, we are disappearing before you find out even more special things about us. Clumsy, greedy and wanton sanctimonious humans. You know what we call our animal kind when they underperform? We call them humans. Just kidding."

Look even at the most familiar of animals: sheep or cows. How many of us can live off grass (I do not mean that "grass," silly) for years

---

69 http://www.telegraph.co.uk/science/2016/10/27/common-swift-sets-new-record-by-staying-airborne-for-10-months-a/

on end sustaining their young and our young by producing milk? It is fodder for thought, right? Let the human compare himself to the tiny fruit fly—or "mighty" fruit fly, if you consider its ingenious design, with its miniature wings, two compound eyes and three triangular eyes, powerful sense of smell that can detect fruit from miles away, tiny muscles, miniature nerves, a GI tract that produces insulin and modulates energy, and gut microbiota that gives it immunity. Can you imagine the size of the tiny nerves that lead from the miniscule eyes to its brain? Even at that size, it can fly with tiny miniature wings controlled by tiny muscles, land vertically, and maneuver in remarkable ways.

There is no creature that could fail to fascinate us if we are humble enough. We need a dose of humility and a bigger dose of knowledge to really understand our interdependence on each other. Where do we start?

Humility. Why not start there?

> *And there is no creature on the earth or bird that flies with wings except [that they are] communities like you.* (Quran 6:38)

## Free Speech

One time I wrote a letter to the BBC—you can find this by doing a Google search—when the debate was going on about cartoons being drawn of Prophet Mohammed and the "right to free expression," as promulgated by many on the other side of the divide—but only when they are not the ones being subjected to crude attacks.

The letter goes like this:

*Please allow me to put this into context. For too many years Islam and Muslims have been demonized, ridiculed and mocked at without regard for the feelings and hurt this causes to law abiding citizens in different societies. This over-reaction, if we call it that, is a result of such actions. Most media coverage hardly mentions the positive contribution that Islam and Muslims have made or are making to the present world we live in. There appears to be a subconscious animosity regarding Muslims pervading most media likened to: "these heathens..." (with all its negative connotations). I would also like to advise Muslims that the Creator (remember I am a Muslim) created us all and there are very good people in every society and religion. We have to be very careful that we do not trample the rights of the innocent who have nothing to do with this. This reaction in almost all Muslims is a deep sense of love for the prophet of Islam and the reaction is "the straw that broke the camels back". I also view cartoons and jokes on any prophet of God, be it Moses or Jesus Christ (peace be on them all) in poor taste and make a very conscious effort not to read them, however funny they may appear to be. We all have to respect our dead who lived to teach us to do good. We all have boundaries of ethics and our rights of the freedom of expression should stop where the rights of others begin.*

—RIAZ BAGHA, SUDBURY, CANADA[70]

Freedom of speech is good and dandy so long as one is not on the receiving end. Reverse the tables and watch how quickly the freedom

---

70 http://news.bbc.co.uk/2/hi/talking_point/4684840.stm

of speech lovers swing to the other side of the pendulum if someone they love is mocked. In this letter to the BBC, I made the point that *"we all have boundaries of ethics and our rights of the freedom of expression should stop where the rights of others begin."* Muslims love their Prophet and are sensitive that he not be belittled, portrayed in a negative manner, or made fun of.

Let me put this another way for some individual clarity: If you are not okay with your street neighbors hurling abuse at your dead grandparents, or with people drawing caricatures of your children in your local paper (since it does not affect them in the way that it affects you), then would you not agree with me that your rights too are being violated? Or would you nonchalantly shrug your shoulders, or join the throng in the streets waving placards proclaiming *"Freedom of Speech"*? To those who do not see it the way you do—because to them it may be funny, abstract, or cleverly portrayed as freedom of speech—their argument will appear crude and base to you. In fact, you are still not very likely to agree with them even if they stated, "Your grandparents are dead anyway, so why do you care so much for dead people? They are not going to come back and complain, are they?" You will still not want them to be mocked.

You too would be saying the same thing— "These p eople's rights should end where my rights begin" —right?

Freedom of expression therefore has to have limits. Leave the nasty ones alone and let bygones be bygones? Raise your hands in defeat and go home? Nope. When besieged with negative rhetoric, do not cower. Give bullies a free hand and, as a psychologist will tell you, they will be encouraged to intensify their behavior. That said, should Muslims respond in kind to those who inflict abuse and deprecate them? One has to have courage not to stoop to the level of the abuser, but, rather, in the course of discourse always maintain dignity and address the other with sound knowledge and education. Education can change the strongest minds. If your first a ttempt a t imparting education fails, could it be a problem with the delivery?

Improvise and try again. If all your positive attempts fail, leave the other party in their depravity. Tit-for-tat blows will only come to an end when one party—I encourage Muslims to be the first ones—has the courage to say, "*enough! Let us have peace.*" Martin Luther King Jr. stated:

> *The old law of an eye for an eye leaves everyone blind. It destroys communities and makes humanity impossible. It creates bitterness in the survivors and brutality in the destroyers ... In winning our freedom, we will so appeal to your heart and conscience that we will win you in the process.*

## The Right and The Left (with torn pants)

A person with extreme ideologies is like the sanctimonious macho man setting himself high above all others and swinging like an ape to the extreme end and then having to bear its consequences, especially if the vine were to snap. I do not simply mean the political far right or far left, for we also have those suited guys, many of them wealthy heavyweights, who often get hold of the vine with their extreme political fringe support-base and swing to the extreme end. All you have to do is wait, for soon enough the taut vine is going to untangle and the chaps will hit the good old Earth with a mighty wallop; extreme ideas are self-limiting, and justice, like the gravitational force acting upon the load, will soon exert its influence. The Earth is becoming more cosmopolitan with each passing year and people will eventually assert their due rights.

"Aah! I get it now," someone might say, having read what happens to those who swing to one side of the human pendulum towards extreme ends (extremist ideas) and as a result damage the seat of their pants as they hit the dust. "Let us therefore keep our minds open and allow all that the people want. No more restrictions. What do you say to that?"

Besides saying, "Those who bit the dust—please first pay a visit to the local tailor to salvage the torn pants" (since we must also care for the environment and support local industry), I would add a caution: "Please don't be too hasty and swing to this other extreme which I see you beginning to contemplate." Both extremes have potential for problems if not carefully and thoroughly planned out since we cannot—in our rush to appease populism—accurately predict the different paths a quickly enacted legislation may traverse and undulate over a long term. How often have we seen governments produce legislation hurriedly because it seemed a good idea at the time, and then decades later try to enact more laws to contain the original legislation? We are being encumbered with legislations upon legislations till we have it coming out of our ears.

As an illustration, the Canadian government now allows recreational marijuana; soon enough we shall have children coming to high school with their own personal "highs." See what I mean? We have been shifting the goal posts so often that we can no longer recognize what were acceptable codes of conduct, common to all major religions and cultures. I am not saying pot is bad per se. I am saying that we must study the repercussions by means of wide consultation before taking the decision to proceed with reform.

You want another example to hand to the chaps who have happily gone into the Canadian Parliament after partaking of the legalized pot? I hope you are successful while they are feeling jovial. You can hand them this idea to debate: we are all for women's rights, yes? Yet we allow the porn industry essentially unfettered access to the Net in order to disseminate images in which many women and girls are subjected to different types of bondage—all under the guise of "art" and "freedom of expression." See where the legislative protection of "art" and "freedom of expression" has taken us? It has allowed parts of the porn industry to take advantage of this very legislation to the detriment of some of the most vulnerable: our womenfolk, the daughters and sisters of mankind, many forced to participate under duress.

A few points need to be clarified, however. Am I advocating pornography provided it is conducted properly? *No, I am not.* I am a Muslim (yes, really) and imagery is forbidden in Islam, while *great emphasis is placed on modesty.* My concern is about legalizing something without considering long-term repercussions. There have to be limits and stricter safeguards. If we are truly in favor of women's rights, we need to go all the way, and limit any potential abuse. One vulnerable woman under distress is one too many.

## Confirmation bias and Pinocchio

Adoption of extremist ideas and wanting to remain cocooned in monocultures and thought patterns—as for example, confirmation bias in which a person reads and follows only material from like-minded people who confirm one's own worldview— are essentially people nodding in unison with each other to feel good about the whole thing, whatever that thing is. I imagine a bunch of wooden-headed Pinocchios, nodding in unison, and telling tall tales till their elongated noses connect with each other all over the world in their comforting prejudice.

To travel is an idea.

Travel opens up horizons of knowledge and breaks down barriers of bigotry. Mark Twain once said, "*travel is fatal to prejudice, bigotry and narrow-mindedness.*"

Since traveling widely is good education, my wife and I have made mindful choices over the years in exposing our children to people from many different countries, consciously making an effort to interact with the locals, especially from the lower economic strata.

I will say this: we have found the welcome and the generosity of the poor unmatched wherever we have traveled. We all have so much in common, and we need to be fair. We all like to be appreciated, loved, smiled at, fed, not harmed, and treated with civility. On the subject of travel being a good idea, less chilies in some Indian restaurants would also be a great idea.

One has to be very careful not to be insidiously drawn towards denying others their due rights. Religious zealots would rather asphyxiate our minds against recognizing other perspectives. They delude themselves and others that utopia is achievable by barricading themselves behind a holier-than-thou homogeneous façade.

Extremist ideologies give rise to such things as the KKK, apartheid, the Holocaust, and the Spanish Inquisition. Such ideologies are self-destructive and you will always find them banished to historical ignominy. There are newer ones now (you will hear such things as "if you are not with us, you are with them" from new twenty-first century models), but they too shall be relegated to historical pages under the title of *transgressing thugs and goons*.

*In Islam, being moderate, and making certain that one does not stray even close to the edges, though it still be within its confining limits, is emphasized and encouraged.* In Islam this is known as *dinnul-wasat*: a religion of the middle course, adopting balance, justice between parties, and tolerance.

Prophet Mohammed said that a shepherd whose sheep stray close to his neighbors have the potential to cross over, thus causing difficulty for both sides. He warned, *"Beware of extremism in religion, for the only thing that destroyed those before you were extremisms in religion."*

Some Muslims, contrary to the direction of their Prophet, have abandoned this middle course and fallen prey to one or the other of the extremes; religious fanaticism or religious abandonment. There are fanatics in every religion. They think fanaticism is the right course in religious matters, and that religion has to be strict and unyielding. Think of the Spanish Inquisition or Daesh. They are intolerant and unkind to those who do not adhere to their brand of extremism. Prophet Mohammed advised, *"Allah is Kind and loves kindness in every matter, and kindness has been granted capacity which violence could never attain."*

Prophet Mohammed further stated, "Make things easy for the people, and do not make it difficult for them, and make them calm (with glad tidings) and do not repulse (them)."

> *And we have made you [Muslims] a Median Community [ummatan wasata—meaning a people of moderation/a balanced medium] in order that you may be a testimony or model for humanity.* (Quran 2:143)

## Apps.

Ditch ahead. Brake! The chap missed all the beauty around him while watching pixels on a screen but at least he is safe.

We need to stop, appreciate, and enjoy our surroundings; savor human-to-human and human-to-nature organic connections. We are becoming like robots with ever-present screens; inanimate objects guiding us instead of innate and instinctive principles. Even Apes would be amazed at our apps. A senior and experienced pediatrician friend recently confided to me, as we were waiting for the elevator, that practice was becoming rather challenging due to the surge in teenagers coming in with depression and anxiety. He figured it must be due to social media. Maybe he figured it right.

Whenever a trip takes me to Toronto for a conference, I take my family for an occasional treat to a restaurant to sample some ethnic cuisine. We often see couples, friends, and families peering into their cell phones the whole time they are sitting there. I imagine the text conversation would go like this:

"Hi, Nancy."

"Hi, Alfred."

"What are you doing tonight, honey?"

"Eating at a restaurant."

"Which one? With whom?" texts Alfred, a frown appearing on his forehead.

"With you, dummy. I am sitting across from you."

"Oh. Sorry. I was paying proper attention to my cell phone, honey. What are you eating?" asks Alfred, fingers typing quickly on his cell phone.

"Pasta, with some tomato-garlic sauce. Let me send you a picture."

"Wow! That looks yummy," texts Alfred, "I can almost smell the aroma."

"You should. You are sitting quite close to my plate if you haven't noticed. Once the door to the restaurant opens and a breeze comes in through the door in a north-north-easterly direction, you will be able to smell it better. I have a new app which shows wind direction."

"I think a person just walked in through the door, honey. Aah! Yes! It does smell good. I am soon to get a new cell phone with two tiny holes that will absorb and analyze smell. It will tell me if the aroma is good or not. I will not have to bother smelling things when I have the new app. And then there is another cell phone that comes with a small spoon. You press a button and a tiny spoon pops out the side of the phone. You scoop a little bit with this spoon, it automatically withdraws back into the cell phone, and an app analyzes the taste. Then out comes the tiny spoon and you clean it. It tastes the food for you. You do not have to bother tasting and savoring. You just gulp down food and then you go home."

Nancy is impressed, and sends a quick text, "This is so much fun! Can we meet again next month? At this restaurant and do this again?"

"Yes, sure!" types Alfred. "Before we meet again, honey, let me share an amazing text with you. I have reserved a helicopter flight over the Niagara Falls this summer. It's a five-minute flight. I will be sitting next to you, honey. You will be given a limited number of bytes of data courtesy of this new helicopter company. You must type your texts quickly to me. If you waste time looking at the falls, you will miss out on the free data. It is best you look at some aerial pictures of Niagara Falls before you come, honey, otherwise you will miss this amazing data deal."

"Wow! Thanks!" Nancy texts back, sending a smiling emoji to the chap sitting across from her. "Please don't forget to charge your cell phone like you did last time. You ruined our dinner by not being observant."

We are losing good old face-to-face social bonding, replacing real physical touch and interaction with screens. Maybe I am overreacting to, "Sorry, what did you say?" culture. I often have to tell my younger patients as they sit on the treatment table glued to their cell phones (and the cell phone virus has now even jumped my older patients!) that I need information so that I can properly assess the medical condition they came complaining of, "Kindly look at me, sir, 'cos I asked you an important question" Recently I have been thinking whether I should text the questions as they sit across from me.

I only hope I won't turn into a cell junkie too.

That said, I agree most of us make good use of cell phone technology. We can search, research, communicate with families and friends, and call an emergency service or family when in trouble.

I said *most* of us. Then there are some who think cell phones are toys. Give them a cell phone and chaos may well result. Especially if they do not understand that, when in a position of authority, one cannot just go ahead and tweet, worldwide, off the cuff and without foresight, on an emotional cue.

If it be tweets, I hope you agree with me that they be from cute feathery creatures sitting atop trees, from true bird brains and not fake ones, *real tits–not twits*. Out on the tree in the yard *outside* the White House, and not *inside*.

# CHAPTER 6

# PROPHET MOHAMMED

*"History makes it clear, however, that the legend of fanatical*
*Muslims sweeping through the world and forcing Islam at*
*the point of sword upon conquered races is one of the most*
*fantastically absurd myths that historians have ever repeated."*

—DE LACY O'LEARY,
*ISLAM AT THE CROSSROADS*

## An orphan was about to change history

Mohammed was born in a polytheistic idol-worshipping community, with some 360 idols in the immediate vicinity of Mecca alone. Mohammed was of noble lineage, descended from a family of chieftains. Both his parents had died by the time he was six years old, leaving him an orphan at a young age. The custody of Mohammed fell to his 80-year-old grandfather, the leader of his tribe.

The grandfather loved him dearly, and when the old man passed away two years later, he had already entrusted the care of Mohammed to his son, Abu Talib. Abu Talib, Mohammed's uncle, took good care of Mohammed for many years, unaware that the child in his care was about to unite the superstitious, warring, and idol-worshipping desert tribes into a unified force under the flag of monotheism.

The idolaters performed special rituals in respect of their idols, the main ones called Hubal, Al-lat, Al-Uzza, and Manat. The idols had very special status, with people often swearing oaths upon them to confirm agreements or contracts, or seeking their protection or blessing. The numerous tribes of the surrounding regions would often come to the Kaaba (a cube-like structure, originally dedicated to the worship of One God by Prophet Abraham and the center of pilgrimage since ancient times) to offer sacrifices and perform rituals at the location of these stone or wood idols, covering them with expensive clothing materials, and embalming them with oils and precious perfumes.

Mecca is isolated in a harsh desert environment. Most tribespeople lived a nomadic existence, grazing animals, or were involved in trade. The two main powers of the time, the Persian and Roman empires, had little control over these tribes, perceiving them to be uncivilized and not worth subjugating or colonizing. Furthermore, these communities were difficult to reach, living in harsh, hot environments, generally poor, and lacking the basic resources of water and good agricultural land.

These isolated polytheistic communities of the time developed crude rituals, practiced female infanticide, enslaved other peoples, and generally treated women like chattels: used, abused, and "disposed" of at whim. Animals were treated cruelly and made to work and carry burdens beyond their capacity. Tribal affiliations determined power, so the more populous and wealthier tribes tended to oppress those who lacked these attributes.

Prophet Mohammed was about to transform these idol-worshipping pagan Arabs into a nation that would submit to the worship of One God (monotheism). Once he began this mission, the infuriated Meccans used every means to get Mohammed to abandon his call of monotheism: promising him wealth in such abundance that they would make him the richest among them, offering him the most beautiful and noblest of women to marry, and promising to make him chief over all other chiefs in Mecca. When he refused to accept their bribes, the chiefs plotted to assassinate him.

They would have done this easily had Mohammed not been from a powerful tribe. Though a majority of the members from Mohammed's tribe—the noblest among the tribes of the time—disagreed with his call, they were duty-bound to protect him and to retaliate if he was killed.

The enemy chiefs therefore plotted to select elite warriors from each tribe in the region (with the exception of Mohammed's tribe) who would attack and kill Mohammed in the middle of the night. Because all the other tribes would share responsibility for this deed, Mohammed's tribe would not be strong enough to retaliate against such numbers (do you see a similar method being used whereby some militarily powerful nations gather together and unify so that the blame is equally shared, and then isolate a country refusing to be subjugated and impose sanctions on it?)

However, the plot was revealed to Prophet Mohammed by the Archangel Gabriel (Jibreel), and when the warriors stormed the house, Mohammed had already escaped with his best friend and companion, Abu Bakar, making a difficult journey to Medina (his mother's town). Rich rewards were offered by the conspirators to foil Mohammed's escape, but these attempts were unsuccessful.

The call to monotheism continued from Medina: Prophet Mohammed insisted he would not abandon this objective since it was not merely a choice he had made, but a *command* from God. Here was a man giving up everything he had to fulfill the mission assigned to him by God. In the end, he was ready to forsake all his possessions—including his home, and his beloved town.

Mohammed's call for monotheism faced strong opposition from the outset: wars, battles and skirmishes; an economic and social boycott of his fledgling movement by rich and powerful chiefs and businessmen; ridicule and mockery; torture and the murder of the poorer residents and slaves who had dared to forsake idolatry; assassination attempts; attempts at bribery by offering positions of power and wealth. And when such attempts failed to dissuade Mohammed's followers, they were forced into exile. The BBC documentary *Life of Muhammad* and the PBS documentary *Empire of Faith* provide an excellent glimpse of the challenges facing Prophet Mohammed at this time.

A little history at this point, perhaps, would help in understanding these idol-worshipping Arabs at the Kaaba, in Mecca. Abraham, to whom the three main monotheistic religions (Judaism, Christianity, and Islam) trace their roots, had historically built and dedicated this house to the worship of the One True God. With the passage of time, however, the true purpose of the Kaaba was "corrupted and adulterated," but remained a focus of worship for polytheists.

People over a large area still attributed to the Kaaba a religious significance and came from near and far to deposit their idols inside it. For the Meccans, the Kaaba was a source of pride and financial benefit (as is Hollywood for newer-model entertainment pilgrims). As caretakers of this place of worship, the leaders capitalized on its prestige and power, receiving dignitaries and numerous gifts. As people came from afar to deposit and worship their idols in the immediate precincts, they also conducted trade at this focal point, enriching the inhabitants. For the caretakers of the Kaaba, therefore, the more idols stored at the site, the merrier.

For the leaders, this perspective of more idols for increased trade was going to be turned on its head.

A major reason for the animosity displayed by the leaders and some residents of Mecca towards Mohammed was an economic one; more tribes coming to the area with their individual gods increased commerce, and yet this man was asking people to worship only One God. He was reciting verses openly—at God's command, he claimed—such as, *"Say (O'Prophet Mohammed, to the people): He is Allah, One; The Self-Sufficient Master, Whom all creatures need, He neither eats nor drinks; He begets not, nor was He born; and there is none co-equal or comparable unto Him"* (Quran 112:1–6). History was to prove the chiefs' fears unfounded, for as soon as the religion was established in distant lands, throngs of people flocked to Mecca to do pilgrimage. They came not only from the Arabian Peninsula, but from all over the world (in fact, for many years now, Saudi Arabia has had to impose quotas on many countries whose residents want to come and perform pilgrimage. This may simply be due to a logistical headache trying to accommodate millions more wanting to come by the plane load! Since those ancient times, the whole region has seen commerce increase many folds. Saudi Arabia does not have to have oil to support its economy or spend millions to promote tourism; all they have to do is open the human-entry floodgates and people will come to do pilgrimage and spend billions of dollars there).

The leaders of Mecca were of one mind: Mohammed's message must be resisted at all costs. They realized that if his message was accepted by the masses, their status would be challenged sooner or later. They preferred the status quo. But here was a man, a Meccan like themselves, preaching a radical message to the resident idolaters and the idolaters who came during pilgrimage: women and men earn good and evil for the sake of their own souls; women are inherently and distinctly free, even in marriage, and not "owned" (in Islam, women keep their own surnames even after marriage); women have a right to inherit and vote (known as b*ayyah*, personal freedom to exercise the oath of allegiance, 1,400 years ago, in contrast to women in the U.S. only gaining the right to vote in 1920). Mohammed was encouraging the masters to eat with their servants promising that such actions were noble and would earn them the pleasure of God. He preached that men are born free and cannot be enslaved and bondage was permissible only during times of war when opposing fighters were vanquished and captured (as was practiced universally in those times).

He also insisted that to free a slave would earn the master a place in heaven. The directives in the Quran and the Prophet's life made so many references on manumitting slaves that any occasions that presented a sin, the absolution of the sin would be to free a slave (compare that to a bitter civil war in the U.S. to establish—on paper, at least—since discrimination is less overt but still exists entrenched subtly in various forms—rights for blacks and other races of color). Prophet Mohammed encouraged the master not only to dine with his slaves and servants and to share the same type of food with them, but also to clothe them as he would clothe himself. He enforced the worshipers to stand shoulder to shoulder during prayers in order to unite their hearts (be ye rich or poor or be ye king or servant).[71]

Mothers were given an elevated status in this new religion, which taught that a person could earn his place in heaven simply by serving his mother with kindness, and a man could lose his place in heaven by being unkind to his parents though he may have done other good works. *Tell me now: Is Islam truly that bad?*

Prophet Mohammed taught aspects of basic empathy one may easily overlook, such as counseling his followers that while on horseback the horses were to be treated with empathy and were meant for riding and not meant to be used as couches while the riders engaged in idle talk. He taught people that they are duty-bound not to neglect the animals under their care: show compassion to them, feed them properly, and never overburden them. Hunting for sport was prohibited, using animals for target practice strictly forbidden, as was adorning oneself with the skin of wild animals.[72]

---

71 http://www.gowister.com/sahihmuslim-4093.html; https://sunnah.com/bukhari/70/89; https://sunnah.com/bukhari/10/119

72 http://www.beautifulislam.net/animals/islam_animal_kingdom.htm

Likewise; prisoners of war must be fed properly and treated with justice.[73] *Tell me now: Is Islam truly that bad?*

A mandatory "tax" of 2.5 percent was to be levied on the rich (to help the poor) to be paid yearly. This is known as *Zakat* in Islam.[74]

These were such revolutionary directives that they angered the idolaters and were even frowned upon by the early followers. But then, slowly, albeit reluctantly at first, they were soon embraced by the populace as they saw the wisdom and justice inherent in this new approach. *Tell me now: is Islam truly that bad?*

The pagan Arabs who had at one time fought vehemently *against* Mohammed now began to fight *for* him—with even greater zeal, ready to lay down their lives for the religion of One God. Thereafter, with a poorly armed and much smaller contingent of fighters, Prophet Mohammed would go on to challenge the power of the Roman and Persian empires with their advanced weaponry and well-trained armies, liberating many from the autocracy of man and showing them in its place the power of God.

Readers may not immediately appreciate the profound nature of these directives, as society has undergone much change in the 1,400 years since Prophet Mohammed lived. His were truly revolutionary messages of the time: in almost the whole world over, basic human rights were minimal, women were treated like chattels; slavery was an accepted norm; "might" was "right," and conquerors dictated the fate of the vanquished—often putting the males to death with little remorse, while the women of the defeated enemy, if lucky, would be taken as slaves and concubines. A question for those who hate Prophet Mohammed: *does this look like a person who deserves malevolent balderdash?*

---

73 https://islamqa.info/en/answers/13241/treatment-of-prisoners-of-war-in-islam; https://www.bbc.co.uk/religion/religions/islam/islamethics/war.shtml

74 http://www.bbc.co.uk/religion/religions/islam/practices/zakat.shtml

Thomas Carlyle, the Scottish philosopher, had the correct perspective on Prophet Mohammed:

> *The lies [Western slander] which well-meaning zeal has heaped round this man [Mohammed] are disgraceful to ourselves only ... How one man single-handedly, could weld warring tribes and wandering Bedouins into a most powerful and civilized nation in less than two decades ... A silent great soul, one of that who cannot but be earnest. He was to kindle the world; the world's Maker had ordered so.* (Heroes and Hero Worship)

## Why Mohammed? Why the desert? Why Arabic?

One can only conjecture as to why God acts in the way He does. God does not need human sanction as to whom and where He chooses to send His revelations. God dictates and is not to be dictated to. Abraham, Jesus, and Moses were also chosen by God. He did not need our approval when He chose them. God chose Jesus from one Semitic people, the Jews; and He chose Mohammed from another Semitic people, the Arabs. It is as simple—or as difficult, if one wishes—as that.

The Arabs of the region had developed governance systems based on tribal affiliations without strong central authority. The harsh life of the desert gave the Arabs fierce independence at an individual level while at the same time the threat of famine or scarcity of water meant the need to maintain tight tribal affiliation. Tribes engaged in skillful and sensitive negotiations to ensure harmony between each other, conscious that misplaced words or actions would easily give rise to offence and bloodshed that would last generations for these proud people.

Furthermore, since communication was conducted primarily by the spoken rather than the written word, perfection in the use of language was all-important. The settled Arabs and the Bedouin Arabs developed great accuracy of expression using words, phrases and language to such an extent that poets would travel far and wide to display their skills.

It was important that the right words be chosen for each subject and occasion. For example, a bare dinner table is called a *kheewan*. When it is laden with food it becomes a *maa'idah*. Wind is called *reeh*, a gust of wind is *asfah*, and a blast of wind is referred to as *habah*, while a gentle wind, or breeze, is known as *naseem*, and so forth. There are about 300 words and epithets for lion in classic Arabic to indicate the context in which the word is used. For example, *Asad* is lion; *al-Afdah* is a lion whose coat blends with the early morning; *al-awf*, a lion who stalks in the night; *al-muzafar*, a lion whose coat has a reddish tinge; *Sibl*, a lion cub, and so on. Classic Arabic, especially, is so precise that it is difficult to distort its desired meaning.[75]

Even before the revelations of the Quran were sent down to Prophet Mohammed, he was known as "Al-Ameen," meaning "The Trustworthy." The pagan Arabs, though idolaters, considered the "word given" to be sacrosanct. Once a man gave his word, in most cases, he would rather die than break it. To tell a lie was a sign of weakness and unworthy of a man's dignity. So, even Mohammed's fiercest critics and enemies never accused him of being a liar. Indeed, such was the trust of the pagan Arabs in Mohammed that they would often leave their financial wealth with him for safe keeping.

The combination of the richness of the Arabic language and the fierce independence of the Arab people (demonstrated in their resistance to the influences of power, thought, and culture of

---

75 https://www.economist.com/blogs/johnson/2011/05/arabic_poetry; https://www.sciencedirect.com/science/article/pii/S187704281300152; George Nehmeh Saad, *Transitivity, Causation and Passivization: A Semantic–Syntactic Study of the Verb in Classical Arabic* (London: Kegan Paul International, 1982)

dominant Persian and Roman empires) could help explain why one of them (Mohammed) may have been chosen to receive God's final message to mankind, the Holy Quran (which Muslims believe to be the last testament from God), revealed in Arabic. The beauty of the message so overwhelming—and the prose, grammar and syntax of the Quran so precise and rich—the poetic style so unearthly—the finest poets and wordsmiths instantly knew they would never be able to match even one verse of the Book. It sounded poetic but was not poetry. In fact, the Quran cast a challenge: produce one verse like it if you can! (Unfortunately, the rhythm and beauty tend to be lost with English and other translations. Despite this little setback, the Quran still provides important lessons and instructions, and translations are available in all major languages spoken in the world. Try listening to the Quran being recited by different reciters in Arabic on the internet. It sounds quite unearthly.)

Slowly, Islam took root in the Arabian Peninsula and began to extend its influence. Once faith had entered into the hearts, Muslims were now ready and morally equipped—and this despite being vastly outnumbered and with fewer resources—to take on the powerful armies of the Roman and the Persian empires.

While Prophet Mohammed had been laying the foundations of a monotheistic civilization in the Arabian Peninsula—for example, through directives for the humane treatment of prisoners of war and the proper treatment of animals under their care—the abuse of power was all too evident in other parts of the world. For example, the Roman Empire of the time was hosting gory gladiatorial contests, pitting men against animals, the spectators clamoring for more blood and newer ways of entertainment through cruelty. One such estimate reveals that 2,000 people and almost 9,000 wild animals died in the space of 100 days within one coliseum. It is estimated that in the 390 years of this practice, more than 400,000 people and 1,000,000 animals died in the Roman Colosseum. This death toll included thousands of exotic animals, such as leopards, lions, elephants, and bears. It is believed that the demand for animals for such gladiatorial entertainments was so great that it may have contributed to the extinction of certain species in some areas.[76]

While Prophet Mohammed was preaching that widows had the societal right to be cared for by the whole community, and that people were equal before God except in relation to piety and good works, widows and the poor in other parts of the world were being segregated into inferior social classes and considered a burden on society; mistreated, maligned, and often ostracized. For example, in the Indian subcontinent, social stratification was a permanent feature of society, with a person either born into the nobility or into the socially and economically inferior "untouchable" (*dalit*) caste.[77] Indian society also required widows to practice *sati*, the horrific tradition of being burned *alive* on the funeral pyres of their husbands.[78]

While on the one hand leaders in other parts of the world continued to exploit women for sexual gratification or as by treating wives as little more than "glorified" domestic servants, Prophet Mohammed on the other hand was leading by example on the domestic responsibilities of a spouse– (except for two women, the rest of those he married were widows, a captive from enemy combatants, and divorcees; and having taken them in marriage, these women were

---

76 https://www.romewise.com/facts-about-the-roman-colosseum.html; http://listverse.com/2014/01/15/10-cruel-and-unusual-facts-about-animals-in-the-roman-colosseum/; S. P. Scott, *The Civil Law, Including The Twelve Tables, The Institutes of Gaius, The Rules of Ulpian, The Opinions of Paulus, The Enactments of Justinian, and The Constitutions of Leo* (n.p.p.: Central Trust Company, 1932);https://www.theatlantic.com/science/archive/2016/03/exotic-animals-ancient-rome/475704/; https://timesofindia.indiatimes.com/city/kanpur/Dalit-tortured-forced-to-eat-human-excreta/articleshow/42926546.cms

77 https://www.bbc.com/news/world-asia-india-18394914; https://www.encyclopedia.com/literature-and-arts/classical-literature-mythology-and-folklore/folklore-and-mythology/sati

78 https://www.indiatoday.in/education-today/gk-current-affairs/story/sati-pratha-facts-275586-2015-12-04; https://en.wikipedia.org/wiki/Usama_ibn_Zayd#cite_note-2

thus given an honorable status) by continuing to do domestic chores to help his wives while leading a burgeoning government with its ever-increasing demands.

Prophet Mohammed also adopted, liberated, and raised slaves to positions envied even by nobles, such as giving military leadership to the son of a former slave. The slave in question, Zaid, was freed and then adopted by Prophet Mohammed as a son. Zaid's son, Usamma ibn Zaid, 17 years old, would lead a military expedition, commanding veteran and experienced warriors.[79]

Prophet Mohammed ennobled former slaves, such as Bilal ibn Rabah, who had been subjected to torture by his former master for converting to the worship of One God, ready to die for his new belief.[80] When a close friend of Prophet Mohammed, called Abubakar, became aware of Bilal's suffering, he offered to buy the slave. Despite the slave's owner seeking an exorbitant price, Abubakar bought Bilal and then immediately set him free. Bilal became Prophet Mohammed's confidante, consulted for his wisdom, and was given the envied status of the first *Muadhin* in Islam, one who is given the honor of calling the people to assemble for prayers or crucial meetings.

While Prophet Mohammed chose people for positions of leadership based on merit, thus teaching his people not to exclude others from positions of responsibility because of their previous status or former servitude, the serfs in Russia were slaves in all but name, made to work pitilessly by their masters, with no prospect of ever owning land. The underclass in other parts o f Europe, such as Anglo-Saxon or Norman England, were not faring any better than their counterparts in Tsarist Russia, China or India.[81]

79 Muhammad Husayn Haykal, *The Life of Muhammad* (Cairo: n.p., 1935)

80 David A. E. Pelteret, *Slavery in Early Mediaeval England: From the Reign of Alfred until the Twelfth Century* (Martlesham, U.K.: Boydell & Brewer, 2001)

81 https://en.wikipedia.org/wiki/Serfdom; https://ilmfeed.com/8-rules-of-engagement-taught-by-the-prophet-muhammad/

I am reminded of a quote by Joseph Campbell, the American professor and writer: *"The black moment is the moment when the real message of transformation is going to come. At the darkest moment comes the light."* The Earth was once again to witness the light of true freedom and justice many years after Moses and Jesus— this time in the person of Mohammed (peace be upon them all).

## Islam's stance on justice

Prophet Mohammed embodied the Quranic injunction that *"The good deed and the evil deed are not alike. Repel the evil deed with one which is better, then lo! He, between whom and thee there was enmity [will become] as though he was a bosom friend"* (Quran 41:34).

Prophet Mohammed's moral stance, even in times of war, won him devoted friends among his enemies and strengthened the commitment of his followers to his mission of goodness and mercy. The result? Islam spread like wildfire from Arabia deep into the Indian subcontinent, into Central Asia, China, Africa, and Spain; areas of the Balkans; and soon the capital of the Byzantine Empire, Constantinople.

Islam blended into the fabric of different nations and cultures, adapting to the variety of circumstances it encountered. Islam was on the march: monotheistic worshipers from a tiny speck on the planet, deep in Arabia, were forging ahead, unstoppable, seeking to relieve people from subjugation to earthly masters and mortal kings, revealing to them the freedom and awe of the Ever-Living Ultimate Master of the heavens and Earth.

The Persian and the Roman empires, the greatest and most powerful empires of the time, having experienced internal conflict and endemic corruption, would soon fall to the armies of Islam. The Muslim armies were characterized by a firm discipline and great mercy almost unheard of at that time.

As noted earlier, Prophet Mohammed would often pardon those who had fought bitterly against him, he also enforced strict rules to his fighters: no desecration or destruction of places of worship; no harassment of monks or those people engaged in ritual worship; no destruction of fruit-bearing trees, palm trees, cultivated fields, crops, or vegetation; no killing ocattle, sheep, and camels except for food; no killing of the vulnerable—children, women, the sick, and the elderly [82] Prophet Mohammed insisted that these rules be adhered to by Muslims, even if the enemy had perpetrated such acts. His injunction to be merciful to prisoners of war was carried out with such diligence by many of his companions that prisoners would sometimes eat better than their Muslims captors.[83] *Tell me now: Is Islam truly that bad?*

Recent history has seen blacks suffer discrimination, segregation, and violent oppression in many parts of the world, yet if you walk into any mosque in any part of the world today, you will be reminded of the legacy established by Prophet Mohammed 1,400 years ago: *"All mankind is from Adam and Eve, an Arab has no superiority over a non-Arab nor a non-Arab has any superiority over an Arab; also a white has no superiority over black nor a black has any superiority over a white except by piety and good action."*

As you open the door and step inside a mosque in Texas, Russia, China, or Malaysia, you will most likely step onto a carpet ("You are most welcome and kindly place your shoes here. As you know, people assume the position of prostration by placing their foreheads on the ground as part of the ritual prayer, and the ground or carpet needs to be clean") and hear some melodious verses being recited from the Quran. You might become conscious of something:

---

82 https://medium.com/law-and-policy/islam-and-international-humanitarian-law-an-overview-78d2df80712f; https://reliefweb.int/report/world/islamic-law-and-rules-war; http://www.thenewhumanitarian.org/analysis/2014/04/24/islamic-law-and-rules-war; https://sunnahonline.com/library/history-of-islam/287-story-of-the-prisoners-of-the-battle-of-badr-the

83 https://en.wikipedia.org/wiki/Huli_people

whites standing shoulder to shoulder with blacks, browns, and others of color—an absence of distinction or separation between the races gathered together. Chinese, Japanese, Russians, English, and German Muslims present themselves in uniform rows before One God without the rancor that divides nations and races. Rich and poor alike bow down to the Lord, who, in His wisdom, has distributed wealth with the responsibility that it must be accounted for on the Day of Judgment (the poor, accordingly, answering fewer questions for a smaller amount of wealth received. The rich, who think thy are the favored of God on earth will have another think coming in the hereafter when they have to account for how they earned and how they spent each iota of extra wealth on that True Day of Justice). In the Mosque, the king and the subject standing side by side without difference as they prostrate themselves before the King of kings.

It is well known in Islamic history that when people came for an audience with Prophet Mohammed, and he happened to be in a gathering, they could not tell who Mohammed was until they made specific inquiries. Prophet Mohammed had no airs about him, he was one with the people, blending well with the masses. He did not criticize but counselled gently, was empathetic, smiled easily, and took pleasure in the achievements of his companions. He paid special attention to the poor, as was Jesus.

The elitist strata created by the new-model tyrannical leaders in the Muslim world are alien to Islam. Many such despots have acquired this authority in order to subdue the masses, courtesy of the Western power, a modern manifestation of the colonialism of the past. Some present day "Muslims" who cheat, lie, sell narcotics, and commit various other crimes are Muslims only in name. They do not embody the true teachings of Islam. If you want to have a true taste of Islam, travel and interact with Muslims in small villages. They, fortunately, often remain untainted by materialism, greed, and dishonesty apparent in multitudes from the big cities.

## Beauty in difference (and not beauty-indifference).

Humanity has much in common and those differences that exist should be appreciated rather than frowned upon. There are those among us who have an intolerance of differences. I think a great way to overcome bigotry is to travel to culturally different places on Earth.

I have been fortunate to travel widely, and I notice in my children the ability to look at differences with awe rather than derision. We are all different, and it should not be a cause for dissension. In fact, variations in skin color; cultural differences; difference in language, foods, clothing, facial features, hairstyles, and adornments simply add to the beauty of humanity.

We are all uniquely beautiful, if we have the humility to see it: the short pygmies of the Congo Basin and the tall Maasai of the African steppes; the Mongoloid races of Asia; the fair colored people of the Caucasus and of other parts of Europe; and the Semitic tribes of the Middle East. We have amazing cultures out there and we are losing them rapidly: the semi-nomadic proud Kazakhs of the mountains with their ancient tradition of hunting with eagles; the fearless Huli warriors of Papua New Guinea, with their ornate headdresses and their faces painted with vivid yellow clay and red ochre to attract the females; the whistling bird-language means of communication in the rugged hilly terrains of the people of the Black Sea mountains of Turkey;[84] the clicking language of the Xhoza, Zulu, Sotho, and Mbukushu peoples of Africa. Even the names of these people and tribes evoke awe.

Unfortunately, we are increasingly and universally becoming a pixel-image, movie-look-desiring, Hollywood-type monoculture.

Sad, really.

---

84  https://www.thetimes.co.uk/article/turkish-whistling-language-recognised-by-unesco-h3ln7n7bf; https://www.britannica.com/topic/Khoisan-languages

## Animal and Environmental Rights in Islam

To the old order in the Arabian Peninsula who were resistant to change, Prophet Mohammed's challenge had gone quite far already—including advocacy of the rights of women, slaves, and the poor—and now he was advocating on behalf of animals to ruffle more feathers on established powers. Imagine the collective headache the chiefs and enemies of Prophet Mohammed must have had as he preached that all creatures had rights and that no person could not deny them those rights. They must have sat in their tents in the heat of the Arabian desert holding their pounding heads, without any Paracetamol, looking at sheep and camels, wondering "what next?!" This noble man had a mandate from God he was determined to fulfill; entrenched cultural norms of thousands of years were certainly not going to deter him on his mission.

A short span of 23 years of prophetic mission to convert intolerant savages to a moral community advocating for human and animal rights—and then the inspired followers avowing to spread his message to the four corners of the world—must require a man of real grit and substance with a unique ability to trigger change. It must certainly be a unique character that would make the companions of Prophet Mohammed try and emulate their leader and strive to live up to his standards long after he had passed away—a character that still engenders awe and love for him in billions of people to this day.

Prophet Mohammed's teachings on our obligations towards all animals—vertebrate or invertebrate—are of such magnitude that it could easily form the substance for countless doctoral dissertations. We will not go there for too long—my cat is looking at me accusingly since it is past her dinner time.

Many of us will relate to animals we commonly find in our midst. The two most common animals are cats and dogs. There may be others, but those are less common. There are about 70–80 million dogs and about 74–96 million cats owned as pets in the U.S. alone (source: APPA and AVMA). That is a lot of pets! We seem to love cats and dogs, so it is a shock to discover that approximately 6.5 million of these animals end up in animal shelters in the U.S. every year. We like to think that we are good to animals, but many of us can also be fickle. About half of these beautiful creatures are euthanized due to lack of space and the availability of people to adopt them. Suddenly, we are not even close to matching the loyalty of the dogs we own. Or at least many of us are not.

Check out the Yulin Festival on the internet, or ask your humane society about it. Do not gag when they explain it to you. It is a festival in China where sometimes dogs are beaten to death, or skinned alive, before being eaten. I am not making this up. Next look up "Dog Fights" and you will not need to gag this time since the defeated dog has already gagged on its own blood in its final moments. This practice continues in parts of India, Japan, Russia, and many other countries.

Cruelty to cats is often even more extreme. These clean animals, which make excellent pets, are often treated miserably when things in the homes go wrong, or when the human has had one too many. One is reminded of Marty Rubin's observation that "*The mark of the coward is that he attacks the vulnerable.*"

Some of the Ahadith (the teachings, sayings, or practices of Prophet Mohammed) in this twenty-first-century age of awareness of animal rights may not look so profound to some of us, but once we reflect that these directives were given about 1,400 years ago, as noted earlier, they become breathtaking in their depth and were indeed revolutionary for their own time—some are even *extraordinary* for this age of much-touted progress. When Prophet Mohammed related the following sayings, or practiced them in everyday life by way of example, the message was not lost on his people. It carried great moral significance in an age when even humans were denied basic rights in many parts of the world.

One of the closest companions of Prophet Mohammed was Abu Hurairah, who reported the following:

*Allah's Apostle said, "While a man was walking on a road, he became very thirsty. Then he came across a well, got down into it, drank the water, and then came out. Meanwhile he saw a dog panting and licking mud because of excessive thirst. The man said to himself, "this dog is suffering from the same state of thirst I did." So, he went down the well [again] and filled his shoe with water, held it to the mouth of the dog and watered the dog. Allah thanked him for that deed and forgave him [his sins]. The people asked, "O Allah's Apostle! Is there a reward for us in serving the animals?" He replied, "[Yes.] There is a reward for serving any animate being [living thing]."*[85]

In fact, the name Abu Hurairah is a nickname meaning "father of the kitten," as he used to be very kind to cats and often kept a kitten in his sleeve.

Environmental awareness was an important characteristic of Prophet Mohammed. The growth of vegetation and ecological interdependence was given the highest priority in Islamic society. This is illustrated in what the Prophet had to say about planting a seedling: *"There is none amongst the believers who plants a tree, or sows a seed, and then a bird, or a person, or an animal eats thereof, but it is regarded as having given a charitable gift"* and *"If the Final Hour [doomsday] comes while you have a palm-cutting in your hands and it is possible to plant it before the Hour comes, you should plant it."*[86]

If you ever visit Istanbul in Turkey, you will be surprised to see animals treated with love and compassion by its inhabitants. One

85  http://www.quranexplorer.com/hadithebook/english/hadith/
bukhari/008.073.038.html

86  https://sunnah.com/bukhari/78/40; https://sunnah.com/bukhari/41

time we were vacationing in Turkey, wanting to take in the history of the place. In this great metropolis, I tried to feed cats and dogs with morsels I had saved from the meals we had in restaurants, but they would often simply sniff at the food and walk away. I remarked to my family tagging along with me, "They are so spoilt. Look at the dog, it sniffed at the left-over meat I put down for it, and simply walked away!" Maybe it was the chef's cooking he was objecting to, making me pause and think about having that stuff in my belly. Of course, I knew the food was good, and my worry, unfounded. The fact was that the animals were well fed and lived contented lives—even the strays.

The whole community looked after them, sharing the responsibility. People would open their doors for them to shelter inside when it was pouring rain. The imam would let the animals into the mosque and feed them when it was cold. This was Islam in action.

I remembered that while vacationing in Morocco a few years earlier, we would often find bedraggled cats and dogs on the streets, thin and starving. We saw emaciated donkeys being whipped to carry loads they could scarcely lift and often left to stand in the searing heat while the owner was probably inside his house having a meal and then a possibly a nap. We have observed, as we drove by much later in the hot afternoon sun to find the poor donkey, in the same spot, his head now bowed down with fatigue, still waiting.

We also saw tourists enjoying a donkey ride in the city of Fez in Morocco, laughing at some inside joke, oblivious of the scrawny animal struggling to pull the heavy-laden cart while being whipped by its owner to go faster. These resident Muslims were living apathetic lives in clear contradiction to the counsel of their Prophet.

This is the same Fez which boasts the oldest continuously running library in the world, founded by a woman named Fatima al-Fihri in the ninth century![87] What a disgrace to a country for not

---

87 https://www.theguardian.com/cities/2016/sep/19/books-world-oldest-library-fez-morocco

enacting strict laws to penalize obvious cruelty! Prophet Mohammed's instructions to his followers could not have been clearer: *to treat all animals with kindness, to accord respect, and to show empathy.* Sadly, while people in one Muslim country honor Prophet Mohammed's instruction to be gentle with animals, the people of another Muslim country have, to my dismay, abandoned Prophet Mohammed's teachings.

The protection of an animal in our care is a serious responsibility, and one must ensure that the necessities of life are provided for the animal. One particular Hadith illustrates the scale of that responsibility:

> *Abd-Allaah ibn Umar, one of the companions of the Prophet relates that the Messenger of Allah said: "A woman was punished for a cat which she imprisoned until it died, and she entered Hell because of that. She did not feed it or give it water when she imprisoned it, and she did not leave it free to eat of the vermin of the earth."*[88]

Causing emotional distress to an animal is also forbidden in Islam, and if we reflect that these directives were established by Prophet Mohammed 1,400 years ago, they are quite revolutionary. One of Prophet Mohammed's companions by the name of Abdullah ibn Mas'ud relates an incident that occurred when they were returning from a military expedition: "During the Prophet's absence, we saw a bird with its two chicks; we took them [to stroke them]. The mother bird was circling above us in the air, beating its wings in distress. When Prophet Muhammad returned, he asked, 'Who has hurt the feelings of this bird by taking its chicks? Return the chicks back to

---

88 https://sunnah.com/bukhari/59/124

her.' He ordered his companions to return the chicks back into the nest."[89]

In his book *Muhammad: Prophet, and Statesman*, William Montgomery Watt remarked on Prophet Mohammed's remarkable kindness to animals given the social context of his times.[90] He cites an instance where Prophet Mohammed, while travelling with his army to Mecca in 630 CE, posted a sentry to divert the army away from a female dog which was feeding her newborn babies, so that the animals would not be disturbed. Prophet Mohammed counseled that *"Those who are merciful will be shown mercy by the Most Merciful. Be merciful to those on the earth and the one in the heavens will have mercy upon you."*[91]

In our mutual desire to coexist peacefully and cooperatively with each other while taking care of the Earth, its species, and the environment, we need to have the courage to change our preconceptions and to learn about one another and our environment. Let us remember the words of George Bernard Shaw, the famous Irish playwright and political activist: *"Those who cannot change their minds cannot change anything."*

Conscious of the context in which Prophet Mohammed operated (more than a thousand years ago)—when animals were often subject to maltreatment and abuse, and environmental rights were not even subjects for discussion—I would argue that he was the *first* politico-religious animal rights activist and environmental activist. I have enough evidence to prove my point, but this would mean having to digress, make historical comparisons, and consider

---

89 https://rasoulallah.net/en/articles/article/24351; https://abuaminaelias.com/dailyhadithonline/2012/08/29/hadith-on-animals-the-prophet-admonishes-his-companions-for-mistreating-a-sparrow-and-some-ants/

90 William Montgomery Watt, *Muhammad: Prophet and Statesman* (Oxford: Oxford University Press, 1961)

91 https://abuaminaelias.com/dailyhadithonline/2010/11/16/show-mercy-those-on-earth/

other notable historical figures—but what would all this accomplish in the end? Would it bring us together to tackle the immediate challenges facing all of us, with many species at risk of extinction and vast environmental changes underway?

Since Muslims and non-Muslims are culpable in causing global climate change (let us not pretend it is only the West), both parties must cooperate to solve the problem they have jointly created. The Quran does not make an exception by stating that only those people who are not engaged in addressing climate change will be affected, but that all of mankind will be affected, the whole caboodle. The Quran makes a remarkable prediction: *"Corruption doth appear on land and sea because of [the evil] which men's hands have done, that He may make them taste a part of that which they have done, in order that they may return"* (Quran 30:41).

We need to clamber up to a common platform, this *common Earth platform*, and recognize that since we are all in this together, it is imperative that we work together.

## The Maasai and the Zulu. Dolphins too

Human rights, animal rights, and environmental rights are in themselves such noble causes that political, religious, and ethnic differences must not get in the way of dealing with them. Ego, argument, and rancor need to be put aside to allow us to engage with each other in achieving our objective.

We honor all those who are, and have been, engaged in this endeavor, be they Muslim or non-Muslim. We stand on the shoulders of these giants who taught us to "do good." It is not a mere cliché; we must persevere and remain steadfast in pursuing the truth, using wisdom, scientific data, and education.

When enough numbers have been attracted to this cause, a tipping point will be reached, overwhelming the ignorant. We are now starting to more actively condemn violence against women, our mothers. The Quran states that *"All righteously believing male or female will be granted a blessed happy life and will receive their due reward and more"* (Quran 16:97), and that *"Their Lord answered their prayers saying, 'I do not neglect anyone's labor whether the laborer be male or female. You are all related to one another"* (Quran 3:195).

Women deserve honor—and protection from those who dare to oppress them. We also need to condemn violence against the Earth, our mother: "Mother Earth," as many cultures call it. An apt name for the planet that sustains us, nourishes us, gives us life. We do not need to subdue the Earth and subjugate it, as we have so thoughtlessly been doing. Most ancient cultures, such as the Native Americans, the Inuit, the aboriginals of Australia and New Zealand, the Zulu, or the Maasai invoke blessings from Mother Earth—and Islam accords the highest respect to mothers. God commanded that mothers should be honored and respected: *"to lower the wing of humility to mothers"* (Quran 17:24).

For those few who have already decided to remain ignorant and are set in their ways, refusing to change their minds about their environmental obligations or their wasteful lifestyles, despite scientific, historical, and moral exhortation, the Quran says, "Show forgiveness, enjoin what is right, and turn away from the ignorant" (Quran 7:199). The ignorant, however, shall not weaken our resolve. We cannot afford to lose the moral high ground and we need to hear each other out. We would again be wise to take a lesson from George Bernard Shaw, *"If you have an apple and I have an apple and we exchange these apples then you and I will still each have one apple. But if you have an idea and I have an idea and we exchange these ideas, then each of us will have two ideas."*

We face derision, ridicule, intolerance, animosity by the corporate greedy, and the obliviousness of the distracted. The latter might find entertaining the poor dolphin performing an act in some Gulf state aquarium, or some water-park in China, unaware that this poor dolphin was, as a baby, _snatched_ away from its loving mother in Taiji, Japan, and that the mother's spine was _severed_ so she would drown.[92] If dolphins could talk, they would probably ask if this was how humans reward dolphins for protecting them from shark attacks.[93]

What do you think we should do?

Sit back and let selfish people decimate wildlife?

Raise our hands in defeat and go home? I guess not. You and I are going to plan strategies. We are going to act. We are going to speak out against injustice to animals. We need some motivation. And you, the noble you, is going to take the lead. I will happily follow one who is not afraid to speak out.

The first thing to do is to turn the page, an _act_ that will tell us what other _activists_ do.

92  https://www.independent.co.uk/news/world/asia/dolphin-hunting-japan-baby-dolphins-hunt-fishing-taiji-sea-shepherd-cove-guardians-a8585356.html; https://www.dolphinproject.com/take-action/save-japan-dolphins/https://www.theguardian.com/science/2004/nov/24/internationalnews

93  https://www.dailymail.co.uk/news/article-2611777/Dolphins-scare-shark-British-swimmers-8-hour-challenge.html

CHAPTER 7

# ACTIVISM AND MARTHA

*"The greatness of a nation and its moral progress can be judged
by the way its animals are treated."*

—Mahatma Gandhi

*"I care not for a man's religion
whose dog and cat are not the better for it."*

—Abraham Lincoln

A tin of sardines. A can of tomatoes. Canned lion hunt. What did
you imagine? A canned-lion hunt is not a tin one opens to eat some
canned meat from an animal that a lion killed to give someone some
sort of gory kick. It refers to the rearing of baby lion cubs to maturity
solely for the purpose of allowing some spoilt, cash-loaded, bored
individual addicted to guns and quoting the Second Amendment in a
country not his own—or a slippery oil sheikh who stole millions from
his people by selling crude—to kill a lion in an enclosed "canned"
space for some crude gory satisfaction. This happens to this day in
South Africa if one has the money he no longer needs to empathize

with the poor and the wretched. I only wish these guys would settle for a kick in the seat of their pants to satiate a "kick longing"—preferably bending down and facing homewards.

Animals to be used, abused, and killed. And we have been doing it for so long that some who will read the book will carry on with life with little change. And then there are some who, to limit or stop abuse will act. *Activism*.

Activists want to make a difference. They are people who send forth ripples of change. They do not always worry about big changes—small changes are fine, too—the ripple effect they create is like the proverbial pebble thrown into a pond. It will catch others, and soon the whole pond will be alive with dynamic shift. When confronted with pessimists as they go about saving the life of a small squirrel injured by a cat whose owner allowed it to roam free and thus harm indigenous species, a turtle whose shell is broken by a speeding vehicle, or an animal injured by a bullet, they respond calmly, sometimes with a smile, as they see the healed animal released back into the wild, *"I may not make a difference to the whole world, but I did make a world of difference to that one."*

If people opted to shoot only with a camera, and not a gun, the life of an amazing animal would be preserved, giving joy to thousands of people as they witness the living creature again and again, prancing, running, giving birth, fending for its young, hunting, competing, and trying to eke out a living in this wonderful circle of life. We could study how beautifully the animal fits into its habitat, how other animals interact with it, how the cycle of life ebbs and flows like the pulse of the heart. We could continue learning how the creatures synchronize with each other, and how together they grace our Earth. Each life form, be it plant or animal, supports and interacts with the other in a myriad of dazzling ways.

*Dead*, the animal simply collects dust on someone's wall. Probably killed in the prime of life; now pathetically lifeless, motionless, with artificial eyes staring into space, or its body parts used in crude medicine.

*Alive*, this single amazing animal would have continued to provide tourist dollars for a poor nation. The momentary adrenalin rush experienced by one selfish individual as he pulls the trigger comes at the expense of the countless poor who would otherwise have benefited from foreign visitors who want to witness this wildlife in its natural environment. Wildlife safaris bring much needed foreign currency into poor countries, thereby helping sustain the lives of those who work in the tourism industry or in associated activities that spring from it, such as food production or transportation. This income from abroad might help a sick mother to buy medicine and provide porridge for a starving child; it can enable girls to get an education and escape the downward spiral that often leads to involvement in prostitution; and it can help fund the provision of safe drinking water to save millions of lives.

We must be wary of being dazzled by the dollar bill or the euro note, which promise a quick reward but ultimately exact a high price. Having been born next door to the Serengeti, which has the greatest number of lions in the world, millions of wildebeest, hundreds of thousands of zebras, and many other endangered animals—with numbers declining rapidly—I have a particular sense of what we stand to lose. As a young boy, I remember hippos emerging from the water just 500 yards or so from our front door, on the shores of Lake Victoria. Monkeys, snakes, bats, and many other small animals were regular visitors to our property. Almost all the animals that frequented that part of the wild near our home are now gone. Animals enrich our lives, and without them, it is truly a lonely world.

As a little tyke, I once had a cheeky monkey strategically place itself on a branch of a mango tree above me and pee, catching me unawares, and forcing me to take a bath—which was not something a young boy wanted to do in the middle of the day. I had previously climbed that same tree to shoo away a troop of Vervet monkeys that I felt were "stealing" from the family orchard. While the others scuttled away making loud noises of annoyance, this one must have come back to exact its revenge. It had positioned itself directly above me and calculated with an impressive degree of precision the trajectory of the yellow liquid.

To the monkey, the mangoes were *his*, and having gained a bit more wisdom, I can easily appreciate that since monkeys were there before humans—he had more right to the land than I had. Even if I waved the title deeds to the property in his face, he would not give a monkey's hoot, and would probably leave a wet yellow stain on the paper and scamper off into the woods. Within a few years, with urbanization exacting its toll, the hippos were gone from the area. The monkeys disappeared soon after.

We now have screens to peer at, and we giggle at animated animal cartoons. And we also have people who boast that they killed the biggest elephants and harvested the biggest tusks. As a result, selective genes that determine size may have vanished and the collective knowledge that elephants pass on to their progenies to help them survive and form communal relationships may have also disappeared—because we wanted ivory keys for our piano to play soulful music of bygone days when the Earth was pulsating with exotic life forms in abundance.

We also have humans who brag about killing the biggest lion. The majestic king of the jungle no longer marks its domain with the low guttural growl that grows to a deafening crescendo, holding us enthralled by its awesome power. The lion's head is now hung with a rusty nail on someone's wall, quiet, glassy-eyed, and collecting dust.

We have a duty to educate one another about our common earthly heritage: land, air, water, forests, animals, and the whole interwoven biomass.

People across the world should cherish not only their own homelands, but also other countries such as some poor nations in Africa, which some people view as places to exploit because of their poverty. Money, greed, and ignorance enable exploitation in many countries to go unchecked if the world does not monitor the goings-on. Often, it is the animals taking the brunt: Tanzania had previously banned rich Emirati Arabs coming in by the plane-load to kill wildlife, which included some nasty ones running them down with their vehicles.[94] Is the ban still in effect? No, because, as of this writing, they have quietly been granted permission to come again to these animal reserves—some politicians in Tanzania likely dazzled by oil dollars on offer.

This is not just Africa's loss—everyone loses from this death and destruction. We share the same planet—*and it's the only one we've got.*

## Activism can get us results. Remember Blackfish?

We are quickly losing important habitats, and the species that depend on them, because some of us believe that the few that are trying to tackle this issue—such as PETA (like them or not, they have indeed brought in important legislative changes), WWF, Greenpeace, and Friends of the Earth—are enough for all of us. This is like believing that these few organizations can collect or stop the 8 million metric tons of plastic that enter our oceans every year, or replace the 90 percent of all the big fish we have already lost in our oceans, or replant the 18 million acres of forest we destroy every year.[95] It is just not possible for a handful of organizations to meet those targets.

94 https://corpwatch.org/article/serengeti-under-threat-uae-big-game-hunting-company; https://www.washingtonpost.com/world/africa/tanzania-gives-hunting-concession-to-a-firm-despite-shocking-video-of-animal-abuse/2016/06/29/b315a6cc-3d4e-11e6-9e16-4cf01a41decb_story.html?utm_term=.8138cc0a6167

95 https://oceanconservancy.org/trash-free-seas/plastics-in-the-ocean/; J. R. Jambeck et al., "Plastic Waste Inputs from Land into the Ocean," *Science* 347, no. 6223 (13 February 2015): 768–71, doi:10.1126/science.1260352; https://www.nationalgeographic.com/endoftheline/ ; https://www.livescience.com/27692-deforestation.html

We all need to pitch in, volunteer, and raise our individual voices. Our collective voices must rise to a crescendo that will blow the socks off our politicians who have been busy catching up on their forty winks.

There are many animal rights advocates, humane societies and environmental organizations that fight and advocate for animal rights, sometimes at a cost to individuals involved. These are noble institutions representing the best of humanity. Join them. There is ample goodness in you. Here are a few examples to show you what we are capable of.

When enough of us spoke out, even a household name like Ringling Brothers had to take heed. In May 2017, Ringling Bros. and Barnum and Bailey Circus announced an end to their tours.[96]

Cockfighting became illegal in 50 U.S. states when we spoke out.[97]

In 2009, the European Union began to phase in a ban on the testing of cosmetics on animals.[98] Apparently, many of us decided we didn't need to look pretty if it was at the expense of animals undergoing agony. Also, in 2009, the EU banned the import and sale of seal products (with exceptions granted for the Inuit).[99]

In 2013, the widely-viewed documentary *Blackfish* initiated a public outcry against the use of animals for our entertainment.[100]

Time is running out—very quickly! Unless a concerted effort is made to curtail such destruction, we will all lose out. The criticism

96 https://www.nytimes.com/2017/01/14/us/ringling-bros-and-barnum-bailey-circus-closing-may.html

97 http://www.ncsl.org/research/agriculture-and-rural-development/cockfighting-laws.aspx.

98 https://ec.europa.eu/growth/sectors/cosmetics/animal-testing_en

99 https://www.ifaw.org/united-states/node/2204

100 http://www.independent.co.uk/voices/the-biggest-animal-rights-victories-of-2015-and-the-fights-that-will-continue-into-the-new-year-a6790491.html

of honest research by scientists who have challenged the status quo serves only to put us further back in this race against time.

We will not be able to reverse the centuries of destruction quickly enough unless we severely curtail our wasteful lifestyle. We cannot indefinitely pretend that the beginning of worldwide famine, wars, disease, anarchy, and rapid depletion of the resources for basic survival has not already begun.

*We either respond willingly now or it will be forced upon us whether we like it or not.* And if some rich bourgeois elitists think otherwise, they better think again. When anarchy-caller comes calling en masse, the castles of the rich built upon exploitation will crumble faster than cookies. Prophet Mohammed warned his companions of the danger that can arise due to a lack of vigilance. The gist of the message or Hadith is as follows:

> *... there are people on a ship. There are two decks, one above the other. Those on the lower deck do not want to bother asking those on the upper deck constantly for water. So, they decide to get the water with greater ease by making a hole in the bottom of the ship. Unless the ones on the upper deck stop those on the lower deck from doing so, all of them will perish. Stopping the ones on the lower deck from pursuing such an idea would save all of them.*[101]

The same kind of scenario applies to us on this *Earth-ship*. Unless the wise among us stop the few greedy, unscrupulous, and foolish ones among us, we shall all pay a high price by letting them dictate our lives through clever arguments and promises. (Wisdom, unlike education, is a special blessing given to those with humility. It cannot

---

101 Bukhari, Book 1, Hadith 187

be taught. It is not the exclusive possession of those who possess fantastic degrees and libraries full of books.) Though the greedy and unscrupulous will complain that we are preventing "progress," they fail to appreciate that in the end they and their own progenies will also be saved by those of us who advocate that we treat the ship as *one ship*; sinking this Earth-ship benefits no one.

*Together we ride this beautiful earth-ship, and duty dictates that we take from earth that which is sufficient for our needs—and no more. treat this earth with wisdom, and its inhabitants with compassion and kindness, and it will keep us healthy, happy, and alive.*

Since we are on the topic of ships, the Bible too offers a snippet of wisdom for the sanctimonious human. We read that Prophet Noah loaded his ship with different animals in preparation for the coming flood. Why mention animals at this critical juncture when human life was at stake and humans were going to go "glug-glug?" Why not focus on the loading of humans, since many of us consider ourselves so much more important than all other life on the planet? Let's perk this up a bit:

One of the old timers supervising the loading of passengers on Noah's Ark may have been heard saying, "*These other conceited human folks have just arrived after mocking us for building this ark. They are late. They want to come on board. But we don't have enough space. Now, who wants to volunteer to step off the ship? How about you, giraffe? No? You want to stay and look into the distance with your long neck so we don't hit any rocks and ground the ship? Okay, you stay. How about you, chicken? Oh! You want to lay eggs for us? Organic ones, at that? Okay, you stay. What about you, elephant-size elephant, you take too much space. No? You want to stay and stabilize the boat? Okay, you stay too. Cast off. I hope these humans can swim.*"

## And then there were none. Poor Martha

Well, almost none. Once, there were millions of bison on the Canadian prairies. The settlers had no qualms about gunning a few hundred here, a few hundred there, posing with piles of carcasses and thinking how strong, adventurous, and courageous they were. I bet these people hardly gave a thought (or maybe they did) about how their actions might affect the livelihoods of countless indigenous North American men, women, and children who had survived for thousands of years with these magnificent animals, existing in a delicate balance with the land and animals, making use of all parts of the animal including the pelts for moccasins and tepees.

And then there *really* were none. No need for the human to pull out the felonious hand and start counting the guilty fingers, for there really were none that one could count. To explain what I mean, I need to take you into a bit of history, pull out some parchments from an old chest, and hand you an interesting fact. There once were billions of passenger pigeons in North America, one of the most numerous bird types on the planet. There once were so many such pigeons that when they took flight, the sun's rays would be blocked and darkness would momentarily descend over the landscape.

Merely pointing a gun at the sky with closed eyes, humming off-tune *"Two Little Dickie Birds"* and pulling the trigger could easily have brought down not two but perhaps half a dozen passenger pigeons. Pigeon stew could be served up for the family and leftovers for the dogs—which they would all ignore having been fed on the same mush for the previous fortnight.

Within a few decades, we killed so many passenger pigeons, and our reckless presence affected them in so many other ways, that they were completely wiped out. From billions to extinction—within decades! The last surviving passenger pigeon, called Martha, a 29-year-old lonely soul, died in Cincinnati Zoo in 1914.[102] *And so we are left with zero passenger pigeons, zilch, a big 0, and it's-not-hiding-under-the-rug kind of zero.* If there was one hiding under the rug, another trigger-happy culprit would probably want to flush it out.

Indigenous peoples across the world—be it in Australia, New Zealand, Canada, or the polar regions—have lived in such harmony with nature that we often find little trace of their existence: "from earth to earth" in a very real sense, leaving behind few environmental footprints.

When my family goes to great lengths to advocate on behalf of animals, especially wildlife, we are often asked a certain question, framed in different ways: *"Why exert yourselves so much to try to save this animal [referring perhaps to an elephant, a porcupine, a chipmunk, a beaver, or one of a hundred different creatures]? It doesn't serve any useful function. It is eventually going to die anyway!"* Such a question is going to get my wife going.

My wife's reply usually takes the form of a rhetorical question, presented in a deliberate manner that would leave no doubt where her loyalties lie: *"What purpose do humans serve on this Earth, then? We are also going to die eventually. The Earth was in a better state of balance before we started invading its pristine regions. In fact, the only species that often does not fit naturally into a habitat is the human one. Introduce a human, and chaos often results. The only thing that matters to a human, much of the time, is how the environmental space can be subjugated or tamed and then exploited for the sole benefit of our self-centered species. While humans can and will let us know when their comforts are upset, animals are unable to express the hardship they experience at the hands of some humans. I think I will speak for the animals."*

Should we only care if something gives us a tangible and recognizable benefit? The Earth belongs to every species: you and

---

102 http://cincinnatizoo.org/news-releases/cincinnati-zoo-remembers-martha-the-worlds-last-passenger-pigeon/

I and, unfortunately for my wife, that cricket making that atrocious racket that kept my spouse awake the whole night.

### The circle of life. Yes, it includes racoons and chipmunks.

The native people of North America believe in the circle of life and our dependence on natural gifts bestowed upon us by Mother Earth. Native cultures in Australia and aboriginals in many parts of the world also acknowledge this view of the interdependent nature of life. It makes absolute sense. Every habitat and species form individual cogs in this wheel or circle of life and each unit plays an integral part in keeping the whole system of life on Earth functioning optimally.

In verse 67:4 of the Quran:

> *Then look again and yet again [and however often you do so, with whatever instruments to your sight], your sight will fall back to you dazzled [by the splendor of God's creation], and awed and weakened [being unable to discern any flaw].*

There are many things we can do even at the grassroots level. For example, my family invited Ronald Orenstein—a zoologist, lawyer, and wildlife conservationist, and the author of *Ivory, Horn and Blood*—to give a presentation at the Science North interactive museum in Sudbury, which was filled to capacity for the event.[103] My wife paid for the venue and we had local coffee places agree to deliver free coffee and donuts. Volunteers joined to make it a success. The full-house attendance is an indication of how we have grown as a society and that many of us are eager to learn more about our responsibility to the planet.

---

103  R. I. Orenstein, *Ivory, Horn and Blood: Behind the Elephant and Rhinoceros Poaching Crisis* (Richmond Hill, Ontario: Firefly Books, 2013)

Organizations and individuals can come together and host such events, and although this inevitably involves sacrifice in terms of money, time, and effort, the rewards can be far reaching, like the proverbial pebble in the pond. The ripples can motivate others to get involved and produce their own ripples. One positive can be transformed into a multitude of positive actions: what more can you ask?

I currently live in Sudbury, a thriving mining town, which a few decades ago resembled a moonscape-type landscape, what with millions of tons of toxic sulfur dioxide pollution spewing into the air from its smelters, destroying all greenery and turning the land into a black monstrosity for miles around. Astronauts had a field experience akin to the surface of the moon, with its treeless barren rocky mineral-rich terrain.

Today, thanks to ambitious community-led regreening conservation efforts where millions of trees were planted in and around Sudbury, and have since taken to self-regeneration, the area resembles a green paradise, with beautifully restored lakes and rivers and wild animals that are free to forage close to the city (some venturing right up to my house—one bear climbing the crab apple tree in my front yard, to the great consternation of one of my neighbors). Racoons, chipmunks, squirrels, wild ducks, and a myriad of birds have established themselves around my own "habitat," or are regular visitors.

In 2015, Stats Canada considered Sudbury to be the happiest city in Canada. I think they may have taken my house into account after looking at the unkept and wild backyard space with its array of busy creatures who live contented lives.

## A Green Story

We all love a good story. If the story has a natural earthy tone to it, —incorporating the beauty and intelligence made into its creation—

then the better it is for it. So, let's have a story that gives vigor to a wealthy character called Igor who is rolling in the dough and is eager to continue making a bigger pie for himself.

Mike is a 6 foot 4 inches-tall male built like a wrestler who in his youth would have been found occupying the ideological high horse seat, touting "development and progress by taming the land." Now in his mid-forties, he has grown wiser, able to accept other ideas, and willing to change his opinion if some other argument made more sense, especially when it came to the environment. Today he is physically sitting high on the horse, in contrast to the metaphorical one he had once ridden during his former "humans-are-better-than-animals" days. He is holidaying in a pristine part of Africa.

Jacob, the editor for the local newspaper, is a short distance away. He is walking in the meadows and is admiring wild flowers. He stops suddenly and peers at a man approaching on a horse. He recognizes him as one of his former classmates in Canada where they both hail from. He quickly goes over to meet the rider. "Hi, Mike. Remember me?"

Mike does remember Jacob and is quite happy to see him; they are graduates from the same university where they attended botany class as part of their studies. They share anecdotes on their youth and catch up on what has happened in their lives. Jacob queries about Mike's sister, a passionate animal rights and environmental rights activist.

"Oh, Nancy? She lives here. She eventually persuaded her American husband to make the move because she wanted to live somewhere that was still largely pristine. She thinks she will make her husband start caring for the environment. She is patiently persevering hoping to change him. Personally, I don't think there is hope that man will change. Her husband is a rich chap who is now proposing to stand for election here, as town mayor. His name is Igor. They live at the edge of the forest in that big house with the green fence."

"I believe it is the same person I am about to meet," says Jacob. "I am going there right now to interview him for our paper. His name is Igor as well. It must be the same person."

"I wonder if you'll hit it off with him. His values are different from Nancy's. All he cares about is money. I am sure Nancy will be happy to see you".

"I would certainly like to see how she is doing. I am glad she moved here. In this small part of Africa, we have established a formula for governance that allows people to live comfortably with minimal impact on the natural habitat. Even cutting down one tree or draining a wetland requires official approval. The committee that makes such decisions is made up of environmentalists with degrees in engineering, biology, veterinary, social sciences, and related subjects. They are committed to caring for the environment as their top priority. Did you not own a lot of land back home, Mike?"

Mike recounts how his forebears owned thousands of acres of land back home, a land dotted with lakes full of fish in his native land and which at one time had teemed with wildlife. He informs Jacob that with new technology that could extract oil from tar-sands, his father sold the land to mega-corporations. The land was no longer habitable, with the runoff of toxic chemicals into the soil and the waters changing the landscape catastrophically. When he moved his family to the nearby city to escape the ravages inflicted on his former home, life became very hectic. He loathed having to endure the super-highways, concrete jungles, smog, the constant clamor for wealth, selfishness, and greed.

"I find it stressful living in the city, Jacob. Our idea of paradise is that it is green with trees in the summer, birds chirping or singing in the trees with their beautiful melody, pristine lakes to fish or take a swim in, fresh air to breathe, and animals in the forests. Yet, we are busy destroying the very paradise we all yearn for. We run to the city and then look at glossy pictures in tourist magazines of paradises that are quite similar places to what we had a short while ago. We are a queer bunch, we humans." He takes a bottle from a bag tied to the horse and walks to a nearby stream. He fills the container from the clear flowing water, walks back to where Jacob is waiting, and takes a swig. Jacob asks Mike if he would like to see some of the amazing things that are around them, knowing Mike's natural curiosity. Mike smiles, pleased to have someone who shares his admiration for nature.

"Look at this here, Mike," says Jacob, pointing.

"Ah," Mike responds, "is that the fungus that gave us penicillin? If we culture it in a Petri dish we may know for sure. Is that the Beladora from which we get atropine?"

"Notice this one, Mike?" Jacob is pointing at something on the ground.

"Is that ugly slug the kind we use to help clean our hard-to-heal wounds? Here is something that should interest doctors. I think this looks like the Madagascar periwinkle that is being studied for its two anti-cancer activity components. Aha! A worm. Better watch where I place my foot as I don't want to harm it. Its forebears could very well be responsible for much of the organic material breakdown that allowed the Earth's fertility to continue unabated for millions of years, giving us all these wonderful trees and shrubs. Look, a beetle. Better not touch it. Who knows how important its contribution may be to the finely balanced ecosystem?"

Mike points at an ant and they both peer at the little creature carrying a leaf possibly 20 times its body weight. While they have been looking at the ground, Jacob has noticed Mike's boots. "Those are real nice shiny boots you're wearing. They *are* big!"

"They are size 14; I can't find my size here, so I bought these steel-toed ones."

They both straighten up. "Gotta go," says Mike. "My wife is waiting for me. She told me to bring something for dinner. Wait till I surprise her with this fine fish I caught upstream. Give me your phone number. I'll call you later. You must come to our cottage for dinner tonight"

Mike is about to leave, but then he notices someone a little distance away jumping up and down. "What's with that fella?" he asks.

"Oh, that. He is the local joker who thinks environmentalists are cuckoo. He curses them and spites them whenever he gets a chance. He is stomping on some poor creature on the ground that was probably minding its own business. He likely saw me and is trying to mock me by killing an innocent creature. We have people like that in every society. I was talking about greenhouse gas in one of my presentations, and this guy was shouting that there is no such thing, since he hasn't seen a gas that is green. He thinks he is clever. Could I ask you a favor, Mike?"

"Go ahead" says the large man, muscles rippling under the T-shirt as he holds the horse's reins.

"When this joker bends down to see if the creature that he has been stomping on is dead, would you mind doing the honors with your nice boots?" Mike instantly understands the meaning.

Jacob parts company with Mike, as the hulking man goes to leave his boot's trade mark on the seat of the joker's pants. It is not long before Jacob hears a loud yelp in the distance. "Good for you, Mike. You scored a hit!" He chuckles.

The man Jacob is about to meet is a candidate for the upcoming mayoral race, a race in which protection of the environment was dominating the political sphere. He was a new man, a rich man bristling with some novel ideas. Voting for the mayor was next day.

Many different faiths made up the community in this large remote and pristine part of Africa. They were people from all colors, cultures and backgrounds. What they had in common was the conviction that simplicity in living was good and wholesome.

They ate good organic food, bartered a fair bit (to the despair of bankers), drank clean water and enjoyed all that nature had to offer. They were generally content and worked hard. They did not desire the creature comforts of city-dwellers. Families were intact for the most part; divorces were low, and children helped the parents and played happily outside without fear of being abducted by crazies.

Jacob clambers up the steps to shake the hand of this man, this new billionaire in the community who wanted to become a candidate for the mayor's office. "Hi, Igor. Thank you for seeing me." says Jacob, shaking hands and taking the proffered leather-covered chair, sinking into the soft seat.

"As you know, Igor, I work for the local paper here and we also have some volunteers who supply us with local tidbits. I heard you want to stand as a candidate for the mayor's office. Would you like me to put something in the paper about your political platform?"

"Certainly," replies Igor. "Have some caviar and pour yourself a drink while we talk. There is shark-fin soup in that container and roasted turtle eggs in that bowl if you feel peckish. All this hype about protecting the Earth and whatnots is regressive, and you know it."

"Do I?" asks Jacob, a little curtly, hoping the man might recognize that not all humans are apt to think as he does. But Igor was not about to be put off.

"Yes, you do," says Igor, more emphatically, lighting a cigar and drawing in deeply with a contented smile on his face, releasing a jet of smoke slowly into the air. "Look, I want to change the way we do things around here. I want to set up a paper and pulp industry right here in this beautiful country that will provide jobs for the locals. We have an abundance of mature trees, and this craziness that trees capture carbon dioxide and release oxygen for us is pure bull. Even if it was true and we do need trees, the Amazon is big enough; it can do the job for us. The locals—queer language they speak, eh? I could hardly make out what they were saying when I visited their village with their chief—sounded enthusiastic about the prospect. Hundreds gathered in a large area and heard me speak."

"What did you tell them?"

"I told them we can clear vast tracts of land and set up golf courses," says Igor. "I told them we could teach them how to golf. Of course, I would have to charge them a small fee for golf lessons. If some of the runoff from the pesticides from our finely manicured golf courses and our factories end up in our waters, so what? They'll spoil only a few of the many rivers and lakes we have here—we can afford to lose a few, eh? Make sure you write that down."

"Some people say—and I think they are right, —that it is defies logic that we put insecticides and pesticides in our lawns that eventually end up in our lakes and rivers, and then we go about drinking that stuff "

Igor shrugs his shoulders, dismissing the argument. He points to someone in the distance, shoveling some stuff for the cows penned in a small enclosure. "That is my wife." He points to a woman in overalls. "I am the brains around here and she is the brawn. We make a fine team, so long as she does what I tell her. I do not like her taking the cows out of the barn because I love this beautiful huge lawn here and want to keep it free from cow dung. I am a clean guy, y'know! The cows do not know that grain and mush made of animal and vegetable waste is better for them. They grow faster and fatter. Cows never learn. Leave them outside for only a little while and they go for grass. Nancy insists that animals should be let out and should be free to forage, but I will not let her."

"I know your wife. Nancy used to be the local rabble-rouser at our university in Canada. I must go speak to her."

"Go ahead. I will still be here."

Jacob goes over to speak to Nancy. She has become gaunt, the normal fiery sparkle in her eyes faded. Igor, relaxing on the porch and enjoying his cigar, sees her listening attentively to Jacob. She laughs. She is clearly amused at something Jacob has told her. What Igor does not know is that Jacob was telling her about her brother's size 14 steel-toe boots and the novel uses they can be put to.

After a brief chat, Jacob returns to the porch and takes a seat. "Igor, why don't you allow your animals to forage, to enjoy space outdoors, along with the sun and the air?"

"Let them out? No. See that barn there? There are chickens in that barn. If animals stay inside barns, the lawn is kept free from muck" says Igor, pointing to a huge windowless building, wanting to emphasize who was the boss around here. "I am in the business of growing chickens for food and harvesting their eggs. I do not run entertainment complexes for animals."

"I read somewhere that cramped, windowless, dark, and musty places can make animals sick. They are more prone to diseases. You land will get free organic fertilizer if you let them out."

"All our animals eat food containing antibiotics so they do not get sick in confined spaces. I know how to look after their health." He thinks the reporter must be ignorant of current progressive practices. "I do not want chicken crap all over the place. We can always buy fertilizers to feed the grass if ever we needed natural fertilizers. It is faster, cleaner, and more efficient." Igor feels a sense of superiority due to the reporter's obvious lack of knowledge on these matters. Jacob senses the haughtiness, and decides to pursue the matter more tactfully.

"Mmm. Do you mind if I told you a little bit about antibiotics?" asks Jacob.

"Go ahead. I can take a little criticism," Igor replies confidently.

"Widespread use of antibiotics in animal farms is causing growing antibiotic resistance in bacteria and other infectious organisms, you know. If I were to lay a bet, I am sure you or your family members *have* taken antibiotics. We need antibiotics to help treat infections and we need them for prophylaxis for more complicated surgical interventions like knee surgery, heart surgery, kidney transplants, and during hospitalizations if physicians feel they are needed. Recently, MDR bacteria have been able to breach the newer last-line-of-defense antibiotics such as Colistin."

"What is this MDR?"

"It is an acronym for multi-drug resistant bacteria. There is ongoing research to try to isolate antibiotics from soil bacteria, called Malacidins, but it is still in the early stages and we have no way of knowing if it is going to be widely available.[104] Then there is an antibiotic called Carbapenem, after which we are in deep trouble, hmm ... maybe I should stop there as this story may not have a happy ending."[105]

"I can afford to go to the best hospitals if I get sick," Igor retorts. "I don't worry about it. If the locals have more money, they too will be able to afford to get sick more often and go to better hospitals. They too can afford to buy medicines and filters to keep nasty antibiotic-resistant bacteria—things that you seem to worry unnecessarily about—out of their drinking water. Let us talk about the election. I plan to create jobs for these people. Please write that down."

Nancy, having finished her work, joins the two men. She listens attentively, wincing at some of her husband's proposals, but does not interrupt the conversation. Igor is domineering, and would not hesitate to insult her if she offered her opinion.

"Go on," says Jacob, quickly jotting down the pertinent points on a small pad.

"Excellent. We have quite a bit of wildlife here. We can open up hunting retreats and advertise widely for hunters and tourists to come. In a few years we will have so much money, we will be able to buy and import more wild game to replace depleting stocks," asserts Igor with a greedy gleam in his eyes. "There is a demand for elephant tusks in places like China and Vietnam. If others see us making money by charging high fees for an elephant shoot, they too will want to join in and the movement will spread, making money for all concerned. We may even be able to overturn the CITES moratoriums on elephant culling. You know what CITES is now, don't you?"

"Actually, I know about it but I do not know what the letters stand for," Jacob replies.

---

104  https://www.nature.com/articles/d41586-018-01931-4

105  https://www.scientificamerican.com/article/dangerous-new-antibiotic-resistant-bacteria-reach-u-s/

"It stands for the Convention on International Trade in Endangered Species. Endangered, indeed! The only endangered thing right now, my friend, is the right to enjoy ourselves."

The reporter interrupts. Jacob feels duty-bound to state some facts. "Rhino and Forest Elephants are endangered and some are on the verge of extinction. Do you really think it's a good idea to keep on killing them for their horns and tusks? The local aesthetician told me that the Rhino horn is composed of agglutinated keratin similar to toenails. Some people in the East use it in some folk medicine. Keratin has no healing properties." The reporter continues, "And we have plastics now that are so much better than ivory for the purpose of carving ..."

"Sshh. Not so loud, my friend. You will destroy the ivory and horn trade if you keep talking loudly. I have an idea. Why don't we ask aestheticians everywhere to ship us toenails? We will compress them into rhino horn shapes and ship them to those who want to buy rhino horns for medicine. They won't know the difference since keratin is keratin. They can use it to make soup if they want. And I have another idea. We can market it as sweet and sour rhino horn soup with a dash of soy sauce. The keratin will come from toenails, not rhinos. How do you like my idea?"

"I don't know what to say," Jacob replies, unamused. He is awed by the man's astute business brain. "You are quite sharp when it comes to business. Does your mind always work like that?"

"Yes. But let's talk about this place for now. I am promising jobs. With jobs comes money. Even if all of our waters get polluted over the next 30 or 40 years as a result of the innovations I have outlined, we can easily buy bottled water with the wealth we will have generated. Impressed?"

"I am not sure what to say." Jacob is wary of saying what he truly feels in order to prevent the interview ending prematurely. He therefore has to exercise some restraint. "Anything else?"

"Yes, there is. Now for my brilliant idea. You are one of the very few I share this with. You know by now that I am a shrewd businessman. I have assembled a team of scientists and we are going to change the world using my idea. It has never been tried before, and if it has, it must have failed because we don't hear of it. We have designed a prototype of what we call a '$CO_2$-reducer.' It will reduce the level of carbon-dioxide in the atmosphere. Since the world is becoming obsessed that we are producing too much $CO_2$, I plan to capitalize on their fears. Different governments like the U.S., Canada, Germany, and other European countries will buy into this idea. I may even win the Nobel Prize! My team will make billions! I plan to become the richest man on the planet!"

"Sounds interesting," Jacob responds warily, but Igor has perked his interest. "Tell me more about this idea."

"This contraption will use very little fossil fuel to operate, but will make use of some solar power. As sunlight is a free source of energy, the overall costs of operating the machine will be kept relatively low. Though the machine will potentially occupy a large area of land, that too will be minimized by placing the solar panels one above the other, capturing the sunlight more efficiently. Furthermore, parts of the machine will be made of biodegradable materials since there is a lot of hype about biodegradation. This invention will not only capture $CO_2$ from the atmosphere, but will do another amazing and spectacular thing—are you ready?"

"Yes," replies Jacob, eager to hear what the man has to say.

"It will capture $CO_2$ and ... produce oxygen!"

"Oh!" Jacob exclaims, barely able to suppress a chuckle. "Igor, you know we already have such machines, if 'machine' is the word I am looking for. These machines capture sunlight, convert carbon dioxide into oxygen, and grow upright to minimize land occupied. They are also 100 percent biodegradable, and have small beautiful green panels to capture sunlight. Not only do they produce oxygen—

they produce many types of amazing fruits! And these machines don't need millions of dollars to construct or maintain."

"Impossible. There are no such machines. What are these machines called?" Igor's eyes narrow. "Has someone stolen my prototype design?"

"No one has stolen your design, don't worry. These machines are called—now wait for it, Igor—they are called *trees! Isn't this the most ingenious of designs by the Ultimate Designer? They sprout beautiful leaves loaded with chlorophyll to capture sunlight to power their own selves. They produce food and seeds that make replicas of themselves so that they often self-propagate, beautify the landscape, and allow many animals and birds to live on them and eat the fruits they produce. These trees have utilized solar power for millions of years before mankind even started thinking about it as a free source of energy. Even to this day, they continue to capture and utilize energy from sunlight and provide us with fuel for our fires, helping sustain humankind for millennia. Amazing, isn't it? And yet humans are busy chopping them down and clearing vast tracts of forests hardly aware of their true value."*

Igor scratches his head, not liking this reporter one bit. But Igor, being Igor, is not to be outdone. He did not become rich by giving up when he faced a challenge. He is resilient, and he will not be knocked off-course by imbecile reporters like this one. Of course, he could simply dismiss the type of information Jacob had presented as "fake news"—just like a politician he knew in the States did regularly. Igor had crushed many mortals and had bankrupted many in his ambition to amass wealth. Many of his acquaintances were still wringing their hands in despair at having had the misfortune of having met him. They—and their lawyers as well—were still scratching their heads trying to figure out how Igor had outmaneuvered them.

"Jacob," Igor resumes, "you are naïve. You don't know the greed that some people are capable of. They are not like me. They have no scruples. They will keep on chopping down trees and then come running to me to fix things. I can wait. But regardless, my plan for this area will proceed. I will clear the trees, make golf courses, and establish hunting retreats. I think the indigenous locals are behind me on this one."

"Go on," says Jacob. "I am writing it down. Were the locals impressed? What did they say?"

"Aah, now you are talking. Every time I made a proposal, they smiled—their excitement and enthusiasm palpable. They were slapping each other on the back and laughing happily. I felt sorry for them. They must have been very deprived of material comforts. You should have seen them punching the air with their fists and shouting '*Nyoka mbaya!*'"

"Oh! Did they?"

"Yes! '*Nyoka mbaya!*' '*Nyoka mbaya!*' Smiling and shouting '*Nyoka mbaya!*' Be sure to put that in your paper." Igor was eager to go on, but Jacob was looking at the setting sun, and got up to leave as it was getting late.

"I think I better go now. It is late and I need to get this interview written up and ready for the early morning edition of the paper," Jacob explains, politely excusing himself.

"Wait, I will walk you down to the gate."

"Very well, then. And thank you for the information," says Jacob.

Together they walk down to the gate, with Nancy in tow. Unfortunately, Igor, still excited by his own plans for the future, fails to look down as he is walking and nearly steps on a snake camouflaged in the undergrowth. The snake rears its head to strike, but Igor manages to step out of its reach. The snake slithers into the undergrowth and disappears. "Aah! Bad, bad, nasty snake!" Igor yells. "All snakes should be killed! All of them, without exception, and in whatever form they come!"

"Oh. Do you know what the natives call a bad snake? They call it Nyoka mbaya" Jacob says this hesitatingly, waiting for the reaction, aware of the man's temper.

"What?" Igor exclaims. "They w ere s aying 'b ad s nake'? H ow dare they call me a snake when I am offering to improve their lives!"

"The snake you nearly stepped on was *disguised* well," Jacob responds. "The natives, however, saw through *your guise.* They may have seen that your real aim is to make money—for you—and were probably not willing to sacrifice something that is more permanent and wholesome for that which is fleeting. They called you as they saw you. It's called honesty."

Igor seethes. "If I am not elected as mayor, I will leave these philistines to rot in their primitive ways. If I am not elected, I will go home—and won't waste any time about doing it. What's the fastest way back to America from here?"

Nancy, who has been growing more and more exasperated listening to her husband's ideas, could no longer contain herself. "Igor, I thought you would change coming here. You haven't. The q uickest way to get back to your corporate office is to assume a ninety-degree posture and a size 14 steel-toe boot! I have just the person to help you on the journey!"

Jacob turns to look at Igor's wife and notes the indignant, defiant sparkle in her flashing eyes. She seems to have had about enough.

Igor scratches his head. The r eference t o a s teel-toe b oot d id not make any sense. Nancy's outburst did not make sense. Natives wanting to stay "uncivilized" did not make sense. The reporter must be crazy. They were all going crazy. It seemed he was the only one with some sense. Yes, he would leave. He would go back to his sensible corporate brothers who advocated *consumerism* to support economies. He would tell the people what they were missing by not having him lead them into the glorious future. "Jacob, tell the philistines that if they don't elect me as their mayor, I will go away and not help them cut trees and without even saying goodbye. I will not give them the benefit of my wonderful ideas."

And so, it was; the paper came out the next day. It reported that Igor had left the area. Jacob's paper, which he was holding at breakfast, fluttered in the air. This sudden gust of air was unusual. The natives must have gotten hold of the paper, he figured. The air must be a collective *sigh* of relief.

*And We furnished the land out with orchards of date-palms and vines and gave vent to affluence of flowing springs, that they may enjoy the fruits of this [artistry]: It was not their hands that made this: will they not then give thanks?* (Quran 36:35)

*He is the One who creates for you, from the green trees, fuel which you burn for light.* (Quran 36: 80) [Photosynthesis: Noun. The process by which green plants use sunlight to synthesize foods from carbon dioxide and water. Photosynthesis in plants generally involves the green pigment chlorophyll and generates oxygen as a byproduct.]

*And it is He, Who produces gardens, with trellises and without, and date-palms, and crops with produce of all kinds, and olives and pomegranates, similar [in kind] and different [in variety]: Eat from their fruit in their season, but give the dues [in charity] that are proper on the day that the harvest is gathered. But do not waste by the way of excess: Verily, Allah does not love the wasteful.* (Quran 6:141)

*O men! Call to mind the grace of Allah unto you! Is there a creator, other than Allah, to give you sustenance from heaven or earth? There is no god but He: how then are ye deluded away from the Truth?* (Quran 35:3)

## Activism by education. The polar bear and the beaver.

A Canadian senator wanted the official symbol of Canada, the beaver, to be replaced by the polar bear.[106] According to her, the beaver is "a bucked-toothed rodent, a dentally-defective rat, a toothy tyrant and a nineteenth century has-been that wreaks havoc on its environment."

This "havoc," if one were to reflect, may have come in the form of waterways, rivers, streams, and ponds as a result of the genius of the "buck-tooth rodent," as it builds dams to create water pathways that have, over the course of centuries, enabled trees and wildlife to thrive in many places across the Canadian landscape, enriching the environment and kick-starting habitats that Canadians can enjoy today.

I am not criticizing the senator and she is certainly entitled to her opinion, but the remedy for humans who are often too quick to judge and make short-sighted comments is to study indigenous communities who live close to the land and to read about each individual species from the many resources that are so readily available in this information age.

Whenever you stumble upon nature's beauty on your travels and the absolute wonder takes your breath away, thank the myriad of insects, worms, plants, and animals that made you gasp at the miracle, for a miracle it surely is. It needed a harmonious and multifaceted arrangement, each playing an important role, to accomplish the

---

106 https://www.cbc.ca/news/canada/north/canada-urged-to-swap-beaver-emblem-for-bear-1.1024431

magnificent overall effect. We need to linger long enough to reflect on the amazing qualities of *all* species.

If we have so much time on our hands that, instead of marveling at the wonders of nature, we now start arguing about which of these iconic Canadian animals should be our national symbol, simply to satisfy a current whim, then we need to step back and reflect. Th e animal, or the owl if you wish, cares not a hoot who (or hoo) is made the national symbol as they all play a part in creating the Canada we love. Any animal, if we study it with humility, has the ability to delight us and take *our* breath away, while some callous people in their cavalier attitude kill and take *its* breath away.

The Bible, the Quran, and the Torah all relate the story of Adam and Eve and their fall from grace after breaking God's command. They were sent from a heavenly paradise to spend time on Earth. Yet God, in His infinite mercy, still gave both Adam and Eve—and therefore all of us—a beautiful earthly paradise to inhabit. We, as viceroys, must safeguard, and not harm, what we have been given. Though humans have power over much of living creation, it behooves us to accord justice to those subservient to our power and ingenuity. This is a sacred trust from God, a trust we shall be required to account for.

*He has made subservient to you [humans] whatsoever is in the heavens and in the earth.* (Quran 45:13)

*And when thy Lord said unto the angels: Lo! I am about to place a viceroy in the earth, they said: Wilt thou place therein one who will do harm therein and will shed blood, while we, we hymn Thy praise and sanctify Thee? He said: Surely I know that which ye know not.* (Quran 2:30)

*It is He who has appointed you viceroys in the earth, and has raised some of you in rank above others, that He may try you in what He has given you. Surely thy Lord is swift in retribution; and surely He is Oft-Forgiving, Most-Compassionate.*
(Quran 6:165)

Short-sighted human behavior, such as trying to change the natural order of things on this planet, can often be followed by desperate attempts to undo such embarrassing handiwork (think Australia and rabbits, or bees and nicotinoids).

Is humanity, then, clever? *Maybe, but do not quote me on it.* And wise? Hmm. Are we wise in how we interact with this Earth? Think of the tar sands in Canada, palm oil and deforestation, overfishing and bottom trawling, and ozone layer destruction. Look around and draw your own conclusions.

Sudden disasters, like the oil spill from tankers, or the Shell oil release in the Gulf of Mexico, make headlines, but much worse is our inaction when we see environmental protections being chipped away by our politicians. We must confront our ambivalence and act to establish environmental standards so that we can continue to enjoy what the Earth is willing to keep providing. We need to curtail insidious pollution, such as the damage caused by tar sands, with its toxic residue spillage into our most precious of resources: our air and waters. We need to minimize deforestation and aid the planet's natural carbon-sink. We need to limit fossil-fuel-guzzling machines like the ones sitting in our driveways, and reward efforts towards renewable resources.

Despite his infinite ingenuity, the Homo sapiens (Latin: "wise man"; believe me, that *is* the definition—I am not making it up) is too short-sighted to think of the mess his grandchildren will be inheriting. His progenies will spend more wealth and resources, not to mention the health costs, to clean up the planet for the paltry sum he may have amassed from his reckless ventures. Can we force powerful corporations, whose main agenda is to make money and then more money, to put brakes on their greed and confront the consequences beyond the buck?

Stop-gap and premature legislation without educating the masses first, such as the implementation of a carbon tax, is seen as punitive. We should seek to motivate and educate, adding some honey to sweeten the medicine, so that change comes from within and people become willing participants. Education can be the honey. As Abraham Lincoln said, "*a drop of honey gathers more flies than a gallon of gall.*"

Governments need to spend millions on education first: the payoff will be acceptance of change and an end to wasteful behavior. The positive knock-on effect will be greater public understanding and an appreciation of the difficult choices governments face when asking us to tighten our belts. The previous budget in Canada (like all budgets everywhere), should have committed millions to this type of education. It would have been a win-win. A win for the government, and a win for the environment and our future.

Sometimes, however, the public needs to take a firm stance if government is unwilling to do so. Consider the Standing Rock episode on the North Dakota plains.[107] Kudos to those who made a stand. The resident population, many of them indigenous people, did not want an oil pipeline built across their waters and land, fearing an environmental catastrophe if a spillage were to occur. Even army veterans, many of whom would normally support established authority, took up the fight.

As this was happening, I recalled an earlier episode when I, a non-native, was selected from a large spectator crowd to take part in the annual pow-wow dance ritual on Manitoulin Island in Ontario. In the mid-1990s, I often visited First Nation communities such the

---

107  https://www.theguardian.com/environment/2018/sep/20/keystone-pipeline-protest-activism-crackdown-standing-rock

Wahnapitae First Nation, the Mchigeeng, and the Wikwemikong in the course of my professional practice, where I had the benefit of learning from the elders about the challenges these communities face.

My family looked on, amused and delighted, wondering how I would fare, as I warily joined the circle with many others who had been selected to take part in the pow-wow. I aimed to do my best to show support for the ancient culture. One by one, others who were less adept at the ritual dance were pulled from the circle and returned to their seats. At the end, I was the only one left from the non-natives, still performing the classic foot rhythm. I had won. They gave me a monetary prize (which I returned to be reused on another occasion).

This gesture from the indigenous people on whose land I had done the traditional dance should be a powerful reminder to us all: though they had welcomed immigrants in the U.S. and Canada, they were rewarded by being marginalized from mainstream society and sequestered into reserves—and this was *their* land. Yet they were still ready to reach out with goodwill—and I for one was determined to show *solidarity* with their causes. We must recognize the indigenous people's generosity and accord them respect for their grace. How many of us would show such goodwill after what the colonizers did, if we were in their shoes, their moccasins?

I was elated when I heard that the U.S. Army Corps of Engineers had given up the fight at the Standing Rock. The protesters had won. Bravo! But wait. Didn't the new U.S. president want to allow such pipelines to be built? I guess some people never tire of ruffling feathers. The indigenous people should not even have to ask any government for concessions. They should have full control of what happens to their land. *This is their land.* We need to belt up and accept that.

Then there is all this talk in the U S about allowing or not allowing people to migrate to, essentially, the indigenous peoples' land. The politicians who are not indigenous behave as if their forefathers did not immigrate to this, what was to them also, *a foreign land*. If immigrants should go back where they came from, guess *who* in the White House should be packing their bags? But before they buy one-way tickets, they would do well to learn about Sherlock Holmes, ostriches, and Aladdin's lamp in the next chapter.

They too deserve a snigger before they board the plane.

# CHAPTER 8

# POVERTY, GREED, AND ALADDIN'S LAMP

*"Compassion for animals is intimately connected with goodness of character; and it may be confidently asserted that he who is cruel to animals cannot be a good man."*

—ARTHUR SCHOPENHAUER

Prophet Mohammed was an amazing communicator. He had a profound effect on people with whom he came in contact. One could write books on Prophet Mohammed's communication skills, and there are indeed many books that offer insights into his character (listed at the end of this book), and skill in conveying a message. Certainly, students should not limit themselves to sources on the internet, or indeed to books by Muslims only. Objective and honest historians—books by the same historian dealing with other subjects in an academically impartial manner would give you an idea of the author's scholarship—are available widely.

Prophet Mohammed often communicated the same message three times—in quick succession—so that his audience remembered the detail. He would often *ask a question* in order to keep his audience's attention and prime them for the message he was about to deliver.

He was also adept at drawing *analogies* to everyday life and people's experiences to make his teachings easy to understand, while leaving no room for ambiguity. He placed great emphasis on directly *facing* the person he was speaking to, and would often grasp the person's hand to emphasize what he was saying and to show how much he valued that person's attention and how important the person was to him.

He was as ready to *listen* as he was to speak, conscious not to interrupt the other person. He listened attentively and engaged with the speaker fully. He had that rare ability to make others feel *special,* and he would look for the best quality in them, emphasizing the *positive.* All those who met him would think they were the most beloved to him; such was his concern, attention, and empathy. He would always *put the interests of others first,* to the extent that his companions would be hesitant to admire anything he had, since he would be so quick to give it to them.

He would go hungry in times of scarcity, so that his companions and family could eat. When he was annoyed by someone's act of disobedience to God's commandments, he would not reprimand them with harsh words—his displeasure was apparent from his facial expression, and that was enough to make them feel sad or humbled. Such disapproval would deeply hurt his companions simply because they loved him so much.

He would *not* show favor to family over those who were not related to him, but practiced the injunction of the Quran:

> *o ye who believe! Be ye staunch in justice, witnesses for Allah, even though it be against yourselves or [your] parents or [your] kindred, whether [the case be of] a rich man or a poor man, for Allah is nearer unto both [them than ye are]. So, follow*

*not passion lest ye lapse [from truth] and if ye
lapse or fall away, then lo! Allah is ever-informed of
what ye do.* (Quran 4:135)

There was to be no differential treatment of rich and poor, a standard
that his close companions sought successfully to uphold after the
Prophet had passed away.

Prophet Mohammed said, *"Whosoever begins the day having
family security and good health and possesses provisions for the day, it is
as though he possesses the whole world."*[108] He preferred to be with the
poor and the weak, and it was their rights that he particularly sought
to protect. He gave no thought for his personal comfort,
content to sleep on a mat of palm fiber and wear patched clothes,
and he would even mend his own footwear. If he was presented with
expensive clothing, he would quickly give it away to someone needy.
He did not desire worldly goods or rewards, but remained focused on
his Lord and the welfare of his people. Even in times of plenty, he
would continue to live as he did in times of scarcity.

He purposefully kept his teachings clear and simple for any
lay person to understand—and yet the teachings had profound *depth*
of meaning for astute scholars who could draw many lessons from
within the messages. *The messages were to the point, using few words, and
repeated in order to give emphasis.* His life, words and example left
indelible marks for generations that followed.

His companions remarked that Prophet Mohammed never ate
his fill, but prioritized others so they would have enough to eat; he
loved and honored the poor. What gifts or grants he received were
always passed to others without delay. Even in times of plenty, his
simple dwelling would only have the basic necessities such as a straw
mat and a small jug for water.

---

108  https://sunnah.com/riyadussaliheen/1/511

When Prophet Mohammed died, even though wealth was pouring into the State he had founded, he was still surrounded by these modest possessions—the water jar, the straw mat, and so on—having given away most of his wealth during his lifetime. His companions had often expressed concern for the way he subjected himself to such a frugal existence.

Prophet Mohammed's followers knew he was sincere. Convinced of his sincerity, honesty, and resolute determination, his followers were therefore quite receptive to his concern for the welfare of all creatures, and ready to inculcate the directives in their own lives—for did not God affirm Prophet Mohammed's mission, *"We have not sent thee, O Prophet Mohammed, but as a mercy unto all creatures"* (Quran 21:107).

In *Muhammad and Muhammadanism* (London, 1874), the Reverend Bosworth Smith said of the Prophet:

> *Head of the State as well as the Church, he was Caesar and Pope in one; but he was Pope without the Pope's pretensions, and Caesar without the legions of Caesar, without a standing army, without a bodyguard, without a police force, without a fixed revenue. If ever a man ruled by a right divine, it was Muhammad, for he had all the powers without their supports. He cared not for the dressings of power. The simplicity of his private life was in keeping with his public life.*[109]

A present-day leader or politician could learn something from the life of Prophet Mohammed on ways and methods on how to motivate the public to stick with him on his "goodly" agenda (that he is so good at marketing on the podium to win your vote) if he were to

109 https://www.worldcat.org/title/Prophet Mohammed-and-Prophet Mohammedanism/oclc/697579725

study this great man. But that is not going to happen because the key ingredient is lacking: sincerity. Their words are empty. Time and again the public tires of selfish politicians and replaces them once they have the opportunity to do so. It is a familiar pattern: we no longer vote the leaders *in*, but rather vote them *out*. The next guy comes in, and the last one with a recently acquired pot-belly and a Swiss account goes out. We will soon need to replace the revolving door.

Can you imagine a politician enduring hunger so you could eat? Can you imagine a politician sleeping on a bare mat so that he would be reminded of the fleeting pleasures of this world that amount to nothing in the end of mortal life on Earth, and that the duty was to strive and serve others? If you were lucky, the politician would leave you a little piece of meat stuck on a bone if you came knocking at the door when a famine was imminent. If the famine was already raging—and though he may have a fridge full of goodies he had kept hoarded to wolf down when you were not looking—he would come chasing for the bone thinking he had been overly charitable.

*With such generous politicians in our midst, even wolves would make better role models.*

## The first four caliphs after Prophet Mohammed

Abu Bakr Sideeq, the first caliph to assume leadership of the Muslim state when Prophet Mohammed passed away, wanted to carry on trading in the local market to support his family while leading the state. At least, that was his hope—but it was not to be.

Reluctantly, he was persuaded by the arguments of his companions this was not feasible on top of the burden of leading the growing empire, which had to be his top priority. So, he accepted a salary from the treasury and focused on his role as caliph.

However, over time he reduced what was in any case quite a modest salary, on the basis that the original amount was more than he required. When he was on his death bed, he instructed that his possessions be sold to *replace* the salary he had withdrawn from the treasury during his tenure. He had indeed learnt well from his Prophet.

Umar ibn al-Khattab, who became the second caliph of the Islamic Empire, related the following story:

> *I went to the Prophet and saw that he was lying on a mat of the leaves of the date-palm, and there was no bedding between him and the mat, and the texture of the mat had left deep marks on his body, and under his head was placed a leather pillow stuffed with the bark of the date-tree. on seeing this, I said, "My Master! Pray to Allah to grant prosperity to your followers. He has bestowed riches upon the people of Rome and Persia even though they are not believers." [Prophet Mohammed replied], "O son of Khattab! Do you also think like that? They are the people who have been deprived of the blessings of the Hereafter [owing to their ungodly ways], and hence, the comforts [Allah wanted to confer upon them] have been granted to them in this world."*[110]

Umar had accepted leadership of the state very reluctantly, keenly aware of the burden of having to account for his rule on the Day of Judgment. Nonetheless, the empire continued to grow under his leadership, providing security and care for the poor and the powerless under its just authority. Like Prophet Mohammed, Umar lived a life of austerity, residing in a simple mud house that did not even have doors, ever accessible to help people without putting up barriers to complaints.

---

110 http://quranhealing.weebly.com/hadith-of-the-day

Umar was very conscious of his duty to be a fair ruler, having learnt the qualities of justice from Prophet Mohammed, his friend and mentor. In his first speech as caliph, Umar pledged, "*o people I swear by God that there is no man among you as powerful as he who is helpless until I restore his rights to him, and there is no man amongst you as helpless as he who is powerful until I relieve him of what he had usurped from its rightful owner.*"[111] His approach to leadership was further illustrated in the comment that, "*The most beloved of people to me is he that points out my flaws to me.*"[112]

By this stage, the Persian Empire had fallen to the armies of Islam, while the Roman Empire was on the verge of collapse. Both Syria and Egypt were under the rule of Islam. Any wealth accumulated from these conquests was distributed back to now subject peoples in the form of state provision. Umar meanwhile continued a frugal life, wearing patched clothes and eating only enough to stave off hunger. Once, two travelers presented Umar with a gift of sweet-dish sent by his governor in Azerbaijan. He asked the bearers of the gift if people under the governor's authority were also easily able to partake of such sweets. When informed in the negative, Umar declined to eat it, and *commanded the governor to partake of only such foods as could also be affordable by the lay.*

Umar strengthened the role of the *Bait-Ul-Maal*, the equivalent of a modern state treasury department. The poor, the needy, the orphans, the widows, the wayfarer—anyone who required help received a subsistence from the treasury, which was the central depository not just for money but also for food and other items that could be used to help those in need. He established a kind of child welfare system, possibly the first such system in the world, whereby a stipend was paid to a mother as soon as a child was weaned.

111  http://www.ediscoverislam.com/about-islam/islamic-law-and-legal-systems/

112  https://kalamullah.com/Books/Umar-Ibn-Al-khattab-Volume-2.pdf

Umar practiced a policy of being open and available to anyone who had a grievance, and could be approached directly or through an intermediary. But he was also proactive in seeking to address the needs of his people, aware of his responsibility as the caliph, often roaming the streets of Medina at night, incognito, to see if anyone was in need.

One night, when Umar was on his usual round, he saw a distant fire in the desert. When he reached the place, he found a woman stirring a pot in the company of some children. The children were crying, and he asked permission to come closer. When he asked why the children were crying, he was told that they were hungry and that there was no food. He asked what was in the pot, and was told it was water, which she was stirring in the hope that the children would tire and go to sleep.

Unaware that she was addressing the caliph, the woman lamented, "Allah will judge between Umar and myself, on the Day of Judgment, for neglecting me in my distress." Umar started to weep, and asked how the caliph would know of her distress. The w oman replied that as, caliph he was duty-bound to be kept abreast about the affairs of the people under his rule.

Umar quickly hurried back to the *Bait-Ul-Maal*, loaded food into a sack, and hoisted it over his shoulder. One of his companions insisted that he should help him carry the sack, but Umar adamantly refused: "What! Will you carry my load on the Day of Judgment? I must carry this bag, for it is I who would be questioned [in the hereafter] about this woman."

When the food was finally prepared and given to the children, the grateful woman expressed her gratitude: "May Allah reward you for your kindness. In fact, you deserve to take the place of caliph instead of Umar." Umar consoled her and said, "When you come to see the caliph, you will find *me* there."

There is an interesting story of this God-fearing caliph. When Jerusalem was conquered during his reign, the city's leaders insisted that they would only hand over the keys of the city over to the caliph—and no one else. So, Umar made the arduous journey with one guide/servant and a camel. They took turns riding on the camel during the journey. As they approached the outskirts of Jerusalem, it was the guide's turn to ride but he argued that Umar continue to ride since they would very soon meet the receiving delegation. Umar declined, insisting that it was only fair that the guide have his turn on the camel, and so they proceeded, with the guide on camelback and Umar walking. When they were met by the delegation, a gracious welcome was extended to the rider, while the guide/servant was also acknowledged—until it was pointed out to them that Umar was the one *on foot* and leading the camel! Umar's humility greatly impressed both Muslims and non-Muslims. Furthermore, while Umar was being shown around the city, they happened to be near a church when the time for prayer arrived. The church leader invited Umar to pray inside the church, but the caliph politely declined to do so, explaining that he would rather pray outside near the entrance in case Muslims in the future sought to honor him by building a mosque where he had prayed. Umar's first thought was to protect this church—and in so doing he showed remarkable foresight, for, much later, a mosque was indeed built on or near where he had prayed! It is today called Masjid Umar, situated very close to the *Church of the Holy Sepulchre*.

At the end of his life, stabbed by an enemy with a poisoned dagger, in pain, and conscious that the wound was mortal, Umar still managed to leave a last testament for his successor:

> Treat all people equally and do not be influenced by any person who deserves punishment, and take no notice of any person's censure provided you have pronounced a just sentence. Never allow your preference or partiality for any person to influence

> your judgment in the affairs of the people whom
> God has entrusted to our authority.[113]

Four of the closest companions of the Prophet—who had been taught directly by him—became the first four caliphs, in succession: Abu Bakr Sideeq, Umar ibn al-Khattab, Uthman ibn Affan, and Ali ibn Abi Talib.[114] They ensured that the legacy of Prophet Mohammed was preserved.

So that now we know that authentic Islam has much good to offer, let us first look at the Muslims leaders of today, so that we can make a distinction between them and the Muslim leaders of the past. The leaders of the past left a legacy that was like water to a parched nation.

"And what of the leaders in Muslim countries now?" one may ask.

"Nothing like water to a parched earth. The oil-covered and slippery leaders in Muslim-majority countries of today are as different as water and oil," would be a fair reply from someone looking at them with disgust. "*They do not mix.*"

## Autocrats and Sherlock Holmes

The leaders of today, both in Muslim and non-Muslim countries, say such heart-wrenching and passionate words of generosity that the less resilient, including you and me, empty our pockets and tear sacs—and as we do so, their well-paid lawyers and accountants are hard at work

---

113  http://www.ediscoverislam.com/islamic-law-and-legal-systems/the-greatness-of-islamic-justice

114  Ali M. Sallabi, *Abu Bakr as-Siddeeq: His Life and Times* (n.p.p.: International Islamic Publishing House–IIPH, 2013); Ali Muhammad as-Sallabi, *Umar Ibn Al-khattab: His Life and Times* (n.p.p.: International Islamic Publishing House, 2007); Ali M. Sallabi, *Uthman Ibn Affan: His Life and Times* (n.p.p.: International Islamic Publishing House–IIPH, 2014); Ali M. Sallabi, *Ali Ibn Abi Talib* (n.p.p.: International Islamic Publishing House, 2010)

to protect their "investments" and off-shore accounts while wringing their dirty hands with glee. The leader—I will let you consider one, any one, that sets your teeth on edge—will possibly bemoan and wipe those hard-to-produce tears with that handkerchief (with a freshly-cut onion hidden in it) that he only owns two private jets to take him to his own few golf courses in sunny, exotic places (did I hear someone say, "Sunny places for shady people"?). We yet provide him with a retinue of bodyguards at every stage of his travels, funded by our taxpayer dollars, so that he can emerge safely to retire and write books about generosity.

Not to be outdone by many leaders in non-Muslim countries, the present leaders of some Muslim-majority countries, male despots under religious façade, win the race well ahead of their contemporaries in non-Muslim countries, with their copious apparel flailing in the wind like the mast of a sail-ship as they cross the finishing line. They heed not the counsel of their Prophet who warned them not to show garments with pride and make ostentatious display of wealth, as they will be hot-branded in the hereafter with the riches they accumulate.

These despotic chaps go about their thieving "businesses" because the public cannot build up enough courage to heed the call of their Prophet who said that the best jihad is to speak against a tyrant's oppression. *Tariq ibn Shihab said "A man asked the Messenger of Allah, peace and blessings be upon him, 'What is the best jihad?' the Prophet said, 'A word of truth in front of a tyrannical ruler.'"*[115]

These twenty-first-century model tyrants in Muslim countries may even get a bonus cup from the event organizers for cleaning the race-track with apparel that trail on the ground to clean the dust, to be shared with the tailor for stitching expensive behemoths with gold frills that can trail but not trip the owner (as explained earlier,

115  https://abuaminaelias.com/dailyhadithonline/2013/01/29/hadith-on-jihad-the-most-virtuous-jihad-is-to-speak-truth-in-front-of-an-oppressive-ruler/

the Prophet forbade one to trail his clothes on the ground out of arrogance).[116]

With the recent purge of Saudi princely "highnesses" following allegations of the embezzlement of billions, some of whom were incarcerated in an expensive hotel (by the way, it is improper in Islam to demarcate social classes into the "high" and "low." I believe that the clever public, while stifling a snigger, may mean the euphoric opiod-use "high" when addressing these aristocrats as "your highness." Gulf princes and their cronies have also been caught with evidence of drug mischief in some reports.[117] One has to wonder if the bulbous expensive apparel functions as clever conduits to carry things across the border. How they can purloin vast amounts of their citizen's wealth with such treachery is a shame to the world, especially the duped Muslim populace.

These pilferers fly through the finishing line carrying sacks of their country's treasury with such cunning speed that even the normally astute Sherlock Holmes, sitting as a spectator watching the race with his friend Watson, would probably exclaim, "Did you see the person cross the finishing line, Watson?" To which Watson, knowing that his astute friend would then supply information on the minutest detail about the party in question, would simply reply, "No, Holmes, I did not see much at all. Only dust when the person crossed the finishing line." At which point Holmes, for the first time in his career would be found scratching his head: "Neither did I, Watson. Neither did I!"

Much of the oil wealth of the Gulf States and Middle East countries is used by the ruling autocrats to buy armaments to keep the public in check, using Muslims to kill Muslims, so that their royal

---

116  https://islamqa.info/en/answers/762/ruling-on-wearing-one146s-clothes-below-one146s-ankles

117  https://www.cnn.com/2015/10/27/middleeast/lebanon-saudi-prince-drugs/index.html

and privileged dynasties can maintain their dictatorial rule within these families, preventing their replacement by wiser leaders and having their chicanery revealed.

Speaking of these potty despots, one must understand that "kingship" and "aristocracy" are *alien* concepts to Islam, imposed upon the Muslim world by its colonizers. Some of the Western colonizers may have gone, but these oil sheikhs continue with the legacy of colonization, wanting to keep it intact.

As a Bedouin in the desert would say as he watches the new oil sheikh boarding a private plane to go to Las Vegas to gamble only a small bit (like the *Titanic*); "*If there be oil, efendi, my friendi, I bet you there be da colonizers by da dozen. take one out, and another da take da place. Dis time it be our own people.*"

Actually, even the richer Bedouins now have refined English accents, having accepted the legacy of colonization within their bosoms. Rather he would say, "*My man, Smithers—I know that is not your confounded name—but it sounds more English. You see that oligarch boarding yonder aircraft? The toff with his smart attire and cultivated English accent has a briefcase full of greenbacks to distribute to deserving casino personages. What ho! I know 'What ho' sounds ridiculous in this particular context, but it does sound more english, so I anticipate using it with greater frequency, forsooth, and perchance. Righto, my man, Smithers?*"

Money corrupts and makes the head spin, and more money makes the head spin faster, and also do cartwheels, especially in casinos. Prophet Mohammed predicted correctly when he stated, "*Verily, every nation has a trial, and the trial of my nation is wealth.*"[118] In Islam, the leader is chosen by consensus among wise elders, whose selection is based on a person's lead qualities, including piety, wisdom, tact, and an ability to do justice even if it be against oneself.

---

118 https://abuaminaelias.com/dailyhadithonline/2012/08/15/hadith-on-wealth-the-trial-of-the-muslim-nation-is-its-extravagant-wealth/

*Harvard Law School,* one of the most prestigious law schools in the world has posted a verse from the Quran (Verse 4:135) at the entrance of its faculty library, affirming one of the greatest statements made on justice for all time, *"O ye who believe! Stand out firmly for justice, as witnesses to Allah, even as against yourselves, or your parents, or your kin, and whether it be (against) rich or poor: for Allah can best protect both. Follow not the lusts (of your hearts), lest you swerve, and if you distort (justice) or decline to do justice, verily Allah is well-acquainted with all that ye do".* The Arab autocrats would do well posting this verse on their opulent castles and handing pamphlets of this verse to their favored kindred. *Maybe the chap in the White House should get a copy too?*

This reminds me to of the recent ethnic cleansing in Myanmar, classified by the U.N. as a crime against humanity.[119] While rich Arab states are fighting each other for power and wealth, members of their faith are being subjected to the worst atrocities imaginable. *Who came to the rescue? Mostly, non-Muslims.* No wonder I live in the West.

We often find that when atrocities occur in different parts of the world, it is *non-Muslims* who intervene first. Think of Germany accepting scores of refugees from the war in Syria. Non-Muslim countries were the first to make a stand when it came to helping the vulnerable in Bosnia, Rwanda, and Yemen—they were not prepared to turn a blind eye to the injustices that were being perpetrated. The public outcry in non-Muslim countries rose to a crescendo upon seeing the devastating famine in Yemen. The famine was man-made: very rich Muslim neighbors using weapons against the region's *poorest* Muslim brethren, killing and injuring thousands of civilians, often bombing marketplaces where thin, starving people were going to buy food with their meager earnings or rummaging in the garbage to find edible throwaways.

119  https://www.nytimes.com/2017/09/11/world/asia/myanmar-rohingya-ethnic-cleansing.html

## The copycat phenomenon

Autocrats in Muslim countries no longer need colonizing Western powers to bend their arms in order to have them do their bidding. The colonizers have left, but their legacy remains—they are out of sight but not out of mind. The colonial mindset is entrenched in these despots who now hold sway and who seek to increase their power and prestige, trying to outdo their cousins in other neighboring Middle Eastern countries: "You've got a tall building; I will get a *taller* one. You have a dozen political prisoners who were demanding accountability—I will get myself a *thousand* prisoners."

Nepotism, flagrant violations of human rights, and extravagant squandering of these countries' resources is so rampant that it has become the norm. These autocrats cannot tolerate any criticism: *"Did you say you are hungry? Don't you see I can no longer rent a whole hotel when I go to Vegas? I now have to rent only one floor. Don't you see I am suffering too? If you do not shut up, I will call the head chopper."*

The following scenarios, believe it or not, are not entirely hypothetical. I imagine the following conversation occurring in the desert among a few friends who arrive in limousines and BMWs (camels are sitting idle, chewing cud). Wannabe A, a favored prince who jumped the queue, opens the conversation:

WANNABE A: Despite trying to rein in overspending, one of my cousins bought a dinghy and a hut. Here we are trying to reduce our dependence on our oil wealth, and he is getting a dinghy. We are all facing austerity while he is buying stuff. The people are complaining of hunger; they say they now have to pay taxes. But my cousins are the worst. They complain they are not able to throw away a ton of food after eating a few morsels. They say they only get half a ton allocated to them every lunch, so their garbage cans remain empty—unfulfilled, you might say.

**WANNABE B:** We should not have started bombing the poor starving Yemenis, you know. With every expensive bomb, a few thousand more of our own country folks go hungry.

**WANNABE A:** Now we have to impose taxes for the first time. These thousands of princes ... Are there thousands now? ... I lost count ... Anyway, all these dozens upon dozens of princes and princesses have to be fed. When we say there shall be no million-dollar handouts, they yell that it is unfair. They will not belt up! They are getting spoilt. They borrow money from the banks but do not pay it back. Many bank managers are in the jail because they demanded repayment.

**WANNABE B:** These princes need to belt up.

**WANNABE A:** Belt up? Literal or metaphorical?

**WANNABE B:** Does it matter?

**WANNABE A:** I guess not. I will take the literal meaning.

A month passes, and the friends are again sitting in the desert. Camels are nowhere to be found. They are redundant because of lack of work.

**WANNABE A:** Efendi, my friendi, last month after cutting rations, some princes started to cry out that we were being unfair, and would not belt up. I found a way to belt my cousins up. The austerity measures imposed on the people and the princes are working well, but we need better results. The princes have started to lose weight and are now having to tighten their belts. My belt factory is going full swing as it is the only one in operation in the country. The government was told to issue only one license for a belt factory, and of course, I got the license. I am imposing more austerity measures, so I can sell more belts. I put a couple of cousin princes in a classy hotel with a one-way pass: in. They are so ungrateful. I went to meet them yesterday. You know what they said? They said, "It's a jail." So, I asked them, "How can a hotel be a jail?"

**WANNABE B:** And what did they say?

**WANNABE A:** They said, "Hotel or no hotel. We can't go out. That is what makes it a jail!" I pointed a finger at the crowd outside who said they wanted to go to jail too. The commoners had heard that nowadays one can go to a hotel instead of a jail. Many were committing petty crimes so they could be sent to a hotel. Before I left, I told the crowd about the new cinema that opened up today and tickets have just gone on sale. They all ran to get tickets. So, we are free from their ruckus. I ordered the guards at the hotel to feed my cousins only with hummus and falafel.

**WANNABE B:** They will lose more weight.

**WANNABE A:** That is the idea. I visited the hotel again yesterday and they had started to thin down. I told them I was having a "Sale" on belts and they have placed some orders. I told the guards no more falafel for the next few months. Only hummus. I can sell more belts to them when their pants slip down once again. My belts are a special design for these princes—each belt has only one hole, so it can only be tightened once. If the cousin loses weight, he has to buy a new belt.

**WANNABE B:** Clever. Any new projects coming up?

**WANNABE A:** "Yes. Some friends and I have decided to set up some magic clubs. The magic clubs will be located in foreign countries inside our embassies. People go into these clubs—especially reporters we don't like—and they simply disappear into thin air. To make sure no government complains about these disappearances, we have placed large orders for armaments with them. Whether they like it or not, it should keep them quiet.

**Wannabe B:** You must be tired working so hard. You need to relax.

**Wannabe A:** I will. It has been hard work doing all this. I have already rewarded myself. I bought a big yacht costing only a few hundred million dollars and a chateau in France costing about the same. I got them real cheap as you can see. These country folks do not understand austerity like I do.

## Opera house in the desert

One country even built a fancy opera house in the desert (I am not making this up), probably because, as one chap said, "If someone has an opera house, we should have one too." I imagine the following conversation taking place as the desert chap with a huge turban (that could have dressed a hundred destitute folks in a poor nation) gets off his camel, dragging his long thobe across the hot sand.

**Desert Chap:** Did you bring my pince-nez?

**Servant:** But master, you don't need one as your eyes are perfect.

**Desert Chap:** Nonsense. How can I fit in and look less conspicuous if I do not have a pince-nez? Did you bring the Italian fellow, so he can translate when the Italian lady yodels?

**Servant:** No, sir. He said he cannot abide this confounded heat. And by the way, it is not yodeling. The venue hosts a soprano singer. She does not yodel.

DESERT CHAP: Fine, fine. No need to be so peeved about a little bit of inaccuracy. Bring that portable air conditioner that is tied to the camel. I wonder if it is working because it did nothing to reduce the temperature while we were coming here. I kept it running full blast, but I am still sweating. They must have sold us a dud. Bring it anyway, as we want people to know that we too like it as cold as it is in the Alps—wherever that is. If they like it cold, we like it colder. And while you are at it, bring my cowboy hat and the lasso that got tangled up with the camel—and bring my ski boots, too. I want to show the chaps inside we are very modern. I hope you can translate everything into Arabic, because, as you know, I don't know a word of Italian!

## Wooden dhow and ostriches

Then someone had an idea to build one of the largest wooden dhows in the world somewhere close to the desert. (Again, I am not making this up. It is there, believe me.) You may hear someone sensible in a non-Muslim country sending a general email asking, "Oh! So, when is the launch date?"

If the person is lucky, someone from the desert may send him an email replying, "I don't know. We wanted the dhow to look something like the originals we used when pearl diving. We do not have a pearl industry anymore. The pearl divers ran away into the desert to look for oil. It was just as well, because some rich sheikhs had eaten up most of the oysters. The rest of the oysters looked very lonely and could not find mates, so we buried them under millions of tons of desert sand that we poured into the ocean to create man-made islands called the Palm Islands. They can be seen from outer space. So now we don't have any pearls. The camels were looking for their desert sand but since we poured it into the ocean, we had to teach them to swim so they can still go to see what happened to their desert sand. Some camels did not want to swim, so we sent those ones to outer space so they could see it from there."

The sensible person from the non-Muslim country may ask a second sensible question: "For the big wooden dhow, won't you need very big oars?"

"As for the oars for the dhow, yes, we made very big ones," the desert fellow replies, typing on the keyboard. "We could not find a man big enough to use the huge oars—though it is not because we didn't try. We had made a big oar, but the big English chap we imported developed a strained shoulder when he tried to lift it. He is now trying to sue us, so we keep sending him to a court where trials are conducted in Arabic."

"Was he successful in suing you guys?" asks the sensible person from the West.

"No," types the desert fellow. "It has been two years now, and he is giving up and going back home because he can't understand Arabic and the lawyers and the judges that we cleverly assign him do not speak English. Let us not talk about law. Let us talk about dhows. We like doing things big, so we just thought that by spending huge sums while the poor starve, we could show the world that we have a gargantuan wooden dhow. The fiberglass ones are too cheap and we had money lying around collecting desert dust. I doubt the dhow is meant for any flood like Noah's flood because I do not think it could float carrying animals such as an ostrich. *It is hard to get ostriches in the desert. We looked everywhere for one. Darned things must have buried their heads in the desert sand and so, obviously, we could not see them.*"

"Any big projects happening in your countries?" The sensible person is typing way, happy that ostriches could not be found.

"Yes. You know we like to impress people by making big things and tall things. We do this even when we see Muslims starving in different countries. No, this is not a tall tale. It's true," types the fellow from the desert. "We have the tallest building in the world. The poor Japanese and Koreans are trying to make cell phones smaller, but we are smarter and we will show the world that we have the biggest cell phones in the world. I had someone make me the biggest cell phone in the world, but the camel refused to carry it. So now I am trying to bring elephants and camels together in one pen and see if I can get a baby, I plan to call an *Ele-Camel* that can grow big enough to carry the cell phone. I wish I could see your face right now showing your surprise and amazement."

"Wow! I do not know what to say." The sensible person is chuckling at the other end. "Any other amazing projects?"

"Oh! Yes," replies the person in the desert, squinting at the computer screen. "Have you been to our Art and Civilization Museum called the Louvre as in Paris? I guess we did not have any civilization till it was discovered by mere chance in the Louvre by one of us while walking in France wearing very dark sunglasses. He probably stumbled, his glasses fell off, and he suddenly saw light. Now we in the Gulf are civilized too. We paid a little over U.S.$500 million just for the use of the name. The poor in different parts of the world must put down their bowls of thin soup just to think about the terrific bargain we had made. You must admit we are clever, for we did not buy the Louvre name for keeps. We *leased* it. We wanted to confuse the camels when they come to see if they can spot the Louvre name a few years from now. It will be gone, just like a *mirage* in the desert! We have been chasing mirages for so long; we thought we should create the biggest mirage of them all! See how clever we are? *What a bargain, right, effendi, to get civilized?*"

## Aladdin's lamp

Islam advocates that the public must obey the leader unless the leader strays from the principles of Islam. These principles are contained within the Quran and the do's and don'ts taught by the Prophet during his lifetime. The problem is that the masses do not read about Islam from these sources, but rely, as most people do, on emotional rhetoric coming from people who claim to be "scholars" of religion. The lay also want to get their daily news from WhatsApp and Facebook. The autocrats in Muslim-majority countries, knowing this predilection of the lay, assemble sheiks and "scholars" of Islam and either cajole, coerce, or bribe them to give "fatwa" (Arabic for Islamic justification) to justify their actions.

True scholars of Islam and Muslims would do well to heed their Prophet Mohammed who told them that the biggest "jihad" (now that we know what jihad means—it means to "strive"—in case someone skipped Chapter 5) is to speak up or correct the tyrant when he does wrong, such as using a nation's army to subdue its own citizens.

These autocrats try to impress people in the West, who only snigger at their antics. They flaunt around like the "Emperor in his new clothes," wearing expensive regalia but oblivious that they are actually attired in the "naked" truth of tyranny that others can see clearly. They are a disgrace to their noble predecessors who awed people by their simplicity, their fortitude in maintaining justice in times of difficulty, and for their intellect, wisdom, and generosity. They wore rags, but the raiment of respect from the public more than made up for the patches on their clothes.

What would I wish for if a genie appeared while I was rubbing Aladdin's rusty lamp, which, if I was so lucky, I had found thrown out from the house of an Arab authoritarian (as he had acquired new gold ones with labels saying "made from parts coming from the U.S., U.K., China, Germany, Japan, but definitely not the Middle East")?

After recovering from the shock of my life seeing a genie emerging from the lamp, I would wish that these autocrats get a copy of this book so they would know how ridiculous they look flaunting around like copycats. Maybe then they would know that the free oil they have been given by God was to be used to serve humanity, not kill the poorer members of the human race. Maybe the autocrats would appreciate the beautiful and merciful legacy of Prophet Mohammed from which they can take lessons. Maybe then the autocrats would donate large sums to help animal orphanages. Maybe then they would build hospitals in poor countries. Maybe then they would *not* give large sums to those hawkish warmongers who enrich themselves producing lethal weapons that cause widespread anarchy, death, and mayhem in the guise of "democracy" in other nations, and in their own countries.

The genie, I am certain, would be happy to carry out the order. If you see him on the way, please wish him *"Godspeed."*

## Operation Decisive Storm

Maybe I am wrong about copycats. They are not *all* copycats. I agree that the condemnation of the horrors in Myanmar by Arab autocrats was feeble, considering the extensive reports of women being raped, men subjected to torture and death, and children being burned alive. They kept pretty silent, while the leaders from the West expressed outrage at these obscenities. No leader in the Arab world really matched up to the stand taken by their Western equivalents against the Myanmar regime. No copycat attitude this time. So, I was wrong.

But I can safely say that the copycats did come up with a unique name for the military operation against poor Yemenis—truly original and clever, a "never been used before" title that was their very own. They called it "Operation Decisive Storm." I guess Bush's

"Desert Storm" mustn't have registered when they picked that one. But maybe it was "decisive"?

"Decisive" my foot—or rather, "the sandal-wearing foot bogged down in the desert sand"—for the chaps are still waging a campaign that began in 1995.

The following Hadith sums up the matter perfectly. *Abu Hurairah (one of the closest companions of Prophet Mohammed) reported that whilst the Prophet, Allah bless him and grant him peace, was talking, a Bedouin came to him and asked, "When will the hour [doomsday] come to pass?" He replied: "Wait for the hour when trust will be destroyed." He asked, how it would be destroyed, and he said: "Wait for the hour [doomsday] when the rule will be entrusted to those who don't deserve it."*[120]

The Apostle had clearly prophesized that prior to Judgment Day, the barefooted and poor shepherds of the desert would vie with each other in constructing tall buildings and boast about them.[121] Imagine the starving Bedouins with tattered clothes listening to the prophesy while scanning the miles of desert sand which cold not even support basic agriculture. Guess what? The tallest building in the world at present is in Dubai, with neighboring Gulf countries trying to outdo it.[122]

I have a friend in the United Arab Emirates who owns high-rises. On one of our trips, my family and I were invited to spend some time in one of his opulent properties on the fringes of the desert. One day he informed us that his father was coming to visit the family. Where was he coming from? The desert—he is a Bedouin who preferred to stay in the desert. So, the son owns high-rises while the father follows a traditional Bedouin lifestyle. One generation

---

120  https://sunnah.com/bukhari/3/1

121  https://sunnah.com/urn/1250640

122  https://en.wikipedia.org/wiki/List_of_tallest_buildings

separates them—but what a contrast! Prophet Mohammed's prophesy came true—*it nearly took my breath away.*

## Ultra-right and neo-fascists

Unlike the Western colonialists who subjugated native populations and generally kept themselves apart and avoided too much intermingling with the locals while stealing their resources (think Australia, Africa, North America, New Zealand, and Canada), Muslims generally interacted with a local population and became one with them.

You can easily see the evidence of close intermingling in East Africa where a whole new language developed, known as Swahili, from a mixture of Bantu and Arabic, spoken by millions of people. You can see this in Indonesia, with the largest Muslim population of any country in the world; or the Caucasus region of Russia and Bosnia with people with blue eyes and skin the whitest of white going to prayer at their mosques and reciting Arabic in prayer; or the Uyghurs of Xinjiang in China with a unique cuisine that is both Chinese and Middle Eastern.

Muslims generally—yes, there are certainly exceptions— engaged with local peoples, appreciating the differences in culture and race, becoming one with them like an interwoven colorful fabric, enriching one another.

What is the problem with appreciating differences? The ultra-right or fascist-right in Europe want to barricade themselves inside a monoculture against what they describe as the "Islamization of Europe." But this fear-rhetoric is not based on historical fact—it is as unfounded as the "flat Earth" belief.

Let an intolerant ultra-right chap give a sad neo-fascist (who is planning to commit suicide by falling off the flat Earth when he reaches the end simply because he can no longer tolerate "others" coming to his country) a picnic basket with some cheese and bread and some water. Let them both shed farewell tears, and then the neo-fascist can embark on his flat-Earth journey. Imagine the shock when the neo-fascist does a full circle (through different countries and their colored peoples) and arrives back where he started.

The neo-chap now sees the ultra-chap saying a sad eulogy for the loss of someone who shared his intolerant values, and comes up from behind and pats the ultra-chap on the shoulder. The ultra-chap jumps with fright.

ULTRA-CHAP: What! You did not fall off? You are alive and well and put on some weight! You look nicely browned with a tan. You have grown a nice beard. You look happy and you are more cheerful. What happened?

NEO-CHAP: I was welcomed every place I went. Colored people fed me and shared their meager meals without hesitation. We in the West have done some nasty things to them by devaluing their currencies and buying precious resources at throw-away prices. It is not fair. No wonder they want to come to our countries now. It is actually our doing. I have decided to become a *neo-afro-indo-multi-chap*!

The ebb-and-flow of history, with peoples and nations dominant at one time and vulnerable at others, is well known. No civilization remains dominant forever, and we must understand that if our generation is to thrive then we need to alter course before our illusory infallible ship, like the unsinkable *Titanic*, starts to disappear beneath the waves. Like teeth, civilizations eventually crumble. We do not want to go down into the depths with them: hook, line, sinker, and false dentures. We must learn to resist the arrogant and greedy before they bring this whole façade down with them, us included. As Hammond Innes has cautioned, *"He who lets the sea lull him into a sense of security is in very grave danger."*

## New slavery

How about the subject of slavery? It was abolished, right? You do not find the slave in tattered clothes, polishing shoes, and blowing colorful bubbles for the little kids as your neighbor goes out with his missus to play croquet now, do you?

Unfortunately, slavery is far more extensive now (sorry to burst that bubble), if you care to know. It is simply *distance* that now separates the "Master" (superpower developed nations) from the "Slave" (underdeveloped nations).

God, In His Infinite Wisdom, allocated different resources to different geographical areas of this Earth, so that we can mutually exchange goods and services. The powerful have no right to steal the resources of others in different guises that they have become so adept at conjuring up through word play. Take for example the subjugation of the natives of South Africa, the Americas, Australia, or the establishment of puppet regimes in oil rich countries.

We artificially manipulate the currencies of different countries so that we can buy, say, coffee for our lattes, or cocoa for our smooth chocolates, trading pennies for these resources, keeping the poor in abject destitution and quickly crushing any opposition with brute force and deception in case they try to mount a more robust resistance. It is robbery, plain and simple.

We say we hate slavery while sipping coffee and munching on chocolate, not realizing that we are participants in a slave trade, keeping it intact and thriving—the only difference being the physical distance that separates master and slave. We must make a stand on what is a moral issue and demand that our institutions act in an ethical manner in our dealings with those over whom we have power.

If the poor are exploited by our corporations, we must be willing to take these corporations to task and require them to be transparent in their business deals, explaining the "small print" to those with whom they trade, so they are treated fairly.

The Prophet of Islam instructed traders to conduct themselves with honesty, to neither cheat nor hoard goods or artificially increase the price of such goods. As Prophet Mohammed said, "Verily, the traders will be raised on the Day of Resurrection with the wicked except for those who fear Allah, behave righteously, and are truthful."[123]

Those countries that have taken a lead and allowed the poor to immigrate (such as Germany), according dignity to these unfortunate people, will in the long run, and despite hiccups, experience greater growth, prosperity, and strength through diversity. I am certain of that. What guarantees such an outcome? The key is dignity.

Any person, whether a resident of France, the U.K., the U.S., Canada, Germany, or any state, when accorded dignity will be loyal to that country. It is not magic. *I am a Canadian citizen. I love my country and am loyal to my country. I also love Africa, my continent of origin.* I advocate on behalf of the poor in both places. I love and advocate for the protection of their natural resources and their wildlife, too. Both places have treated me and my forebears with dignity. And I advocate for *all* people on earth and their animals.

To protect and advocate for the weak and the vulnerable being is our common duty. It is not a complicated science. Can we also welcome Muslims? Are they really tolerant? Let us see.

Walk into any mosque today and you will find the rich, the poor, the black and the white all standing shoulder-to-shoulder praying to the One God. Islam is not opposed to cultural diversity (so long as that cultural diversity is not in direct conflict with its moral teachings). One can retain all the essentials of a distinctive way of life and mold into Islam with ease. When Malcolm X visited Mecca for Hajj, he was surprised at how people, seemingly different, blended with one another into a universal brotherhood:

---

123 https://abuaminaelias.com/dailyhadithonline/2014/02/05/hadith-on-trade-merchants-will-be-resurrected-with-the-wicked-unless-they-fear-allah/

*Never have I witnessed such sincere hospitality and overwhelming spirit of true brotherhood as is practiced by people of all colors and races here in this ancient Holy Land, the home of Abraham, Muhammad and all the other Prophets of the Holy Scriptures. For the past week, I have been utterly speechless and spellbound by the graciousness I see displayed all around me by people of all colors ... There were tens of thousands of pilgrims, from all over the world. They were of all colors, from blue-eyed blondes to black-skinned Africans. But we were all participating in the same ritual, displaying a spirit of unity and brotherhood that my experiences in America had led me to believe never could exist between the white and non-white ... During the past eleven days here in the Muslim world, I have eaten from the same plate, drunk from the same glass, and slept on the same rug —while praying to the same God—with fellow Muslims, whose eyes were the bluest of blue, whose hair was the blondest of blond, and whose skin was the whitest of white. And in the words and in the deeds of the white Muslims, I felt the same sincerity that I felt among the black African Muslims of Nigeria, Sudan and Ghana.*[124]

It has never been any different since the time of Prophet Mohammed, in any mosque and in any part of the world. Walk into a hospital or a company and, if prayer time is due, you will often find physicians, police officers, or the CEOs of corporations praying behind the local cleaner or doctor, if he happens to be more knowledgeable in

---

124  Malcolm X, *The Autobiography of Malcolm X* (New York: Grove Press, 1964).

Islam and knows more verses from the Quran. It is knowledge of the Quran—and not status, wealth, or race—that determines who will lead the prayer.

We now see environmental crises occurring all over the world. Air pollution is an increasing problem in many parts of the industrial world, a problem that threatens to engulf us all at its current rate of acceleration. The Earth is a global village. When one country in one part of the world pollutes the air, it eventually spreads and soon enough a person who had kept himself hidden in a remote part of Iceland is breathing it in.

When smog in France from fossil fuel burning saturated the air in 2016, Paris suffered the worst air pollution in a decade.[125] They began to ban the use of cars in the city center on certain days to overcome the crisis. A BBC report of May 2018 states that "According to a study carried out in 2016 by France's national health agency, air pollution is responsible for 48,000 deaths a year across France."[126]

The *China Morning Post* reports that 1 million people are dying from air pollution per year and costing the economy 267 billion Yuan per year.[127] A report by the WHO has warned that "Air pollution is especially dangerous for children, and accounts for nearly one in 10 deaths among children under five around the globe."[128]

A tipping point, such as a nuclear disaster, a meteorite strike, a major volcanic eruption, or major fires in the Amazon or the Congo could easily cause worldwide catastrophe: "Then watch for the day

125 https://www.independent.co.uk/news/world/europe/paris-pollution-increase-air-smog-france-capital-car-limits-fossil-fuels-weather-a7500426.html

126 https://www.bbc.com/news/business-43925712

127 https://www.scmp.com/news/china/science/article/2166542/air-pollution-killing-1-million-people-and-costing-chinese

128 https://phys.org/news/2018-10-air-pollution-children-year.html;
https://www.who.int/airpollution/en/

when the sky will bring a kind of smoke, plainly visible, smothering the people. This will be a terrible penalty. [ They will say] "Our Lord, remove the penalty from us, for we really do believe" (Quran 44:10–12).

Despite these warnings, there will always be the naysayers who won't accept the evidence: oblivious to any ominous signs as they continue to live as if the rest of us are making *much ado about nothing.*" They keep themselves busy playing games, or going for joy rides on speedboats, saying, *"the little ducklings following the mother should have been quicker."* They go hunting to decimate the last remaining wildlife in *vulnerable* areas. They shrug their shoulders when you tell them about the damage that we collectively cause in producing and throwing away tons of plastics into the oceans. They are the "*want*" generation.

They want fine mahogany furniture and soft tissue paper to wipe what they must wipe.

They want expensive fine wooden coffins and to be embalmed with such materials that, even when they die, they refuse to give back to the Earth the organic materials which they greedily took in life: stingy to nature, even in death, caring little about the circle of life.

They want finely manicured lawns which must be kept free from insects and weeds by spraying toxic chemicals which will then seep into their drinking water, and then drink that same water. They are ever heedless of every warning.

*They?* Think again.

God is aware of those who dispute, despite warnings and lessons: "We have given various examples in this Quran for people to learn a lesson, but the human being is the most contentious creature" (Quran 18:54).

At this point, some authors would draw a conclusion, or an impact statement of sorts. They may use a few words, carefully considered, that would motivate the reader towards an objective. Some would ask a question that would cause introspection or reflection. I guess I have already begun that process.

I ask that we be true to ourselves and not encumber ourselves with prejudice, bigotry, and intolerance. There is much good that is hidden like pearls within all of us, without exception: we just need to pry open the shells.

Sometimes all we need is a slight nudge or a reminder to take stock of where we are headed and we may still be able to shine with remarkable beauty. We are a single humanity, and this fact alone should be enough to unite our divided hearts. Our busy lives have made us oblivious to each other and the world around us. Like sheep rushing headlong en masse to a precipitous cliff, we are being pulled in a direction often not of our choosing. We should veer a little bit (if I say left or right, I may sound political) to the side, or stop and try to go back—back to the beauty of nature that *was* ours.

Living busy lives, many of us do not reflect deeply enough on the true wealth in our midst. Humans are an odd bunch; we find something that exists in plentiful numbers and then we damage it— say, pristine waters or healthy forests— or kill it —say, the bison or rhinos—and then scramble to save the remaining vestiges before the destruction is absolute.

Prophet Mohammed was a *pragmatist*. He knew the balanced approach to global environmentalism; one cannot negate global human rights and animal rights when promulgating for the environment as they are all inherently tied together. His legacy are lessons for us. You cannot have environmental rights without human rights, and if you want to test this theory, simply bring an environmental rights advocate, a human rights advocate, and an animal rights advocate into the same room and sit them at the conference table. Let the environmentalist speak. Soon you will hear some loud banging at the table: it is the human rights guy demanding equal attention. Wait a bit more, and soon there is more banging. You will not have to draw lots to see who the third chap is.

There is a tendency for humans to move from one event to another and blow it out of proportion in relation to others, and then relegate it to the back pages soon after. There was the "me-too" movement not long ago that dominated the headlines for some time because we recognized that the protection of the vulnerable—though the powerful thought they would remain untouchable—deserved attention. The me-too movement must get *consistent* attention.

Environmental abuse and human rights abuse anywhere is abuse everywhere. Environmental abuse, for example, the increase in deforestation in Brazil is human rights abuse (and animal rights abuse) everywhere. This is because the earths lungs provide oxygen not only to Brazil but provides oxygen to us all, including *Bolsonaro*, unless he wants to breathe something other than oxygen. Kudos to *Leonardo DiCaprio* and *Greta Thunberg* for bringing the spotlight on the Amazon forest.

Let us step back for a moment and take stock of our obligations towards all life and towards the Earth. The plunder and ravage we inflict upon the Earth and the environment are not sustainable. Mahatma Gandhi said, *"Earth provides enough to satisfy every man's needs, but not every man's greed."*

Once we were richer, much environmentally richer, if you think about the pristine state the Earth was in a few centuries ago. We have been steadily losing true environmental wealth. We are not only physically poorer, we are also emotionally discontent. Most of us have enough food for the next day, but did you know that there are 795 million people on the planet who suffer from chronic hunger, according to the United Nations World Food Program?[129]

---

129 https://www.latimes.com/world/la-fg-global-world-hunger-day-20170528-story.html

As Prophet Mohammed stated, *"If the son of Adam had a valley full of gold, he would want to have two valleys. Nothing fills his mouth but the dust of the grave, yet God will relent to whoever repents to Him."* [130]

The world has its poor wishing, envying, or striving to get what the rich have—and the rich constantly clamoring for more. Prophet Mohammed spoke the truth when he said, *"Riches are not from an abundance of worldly goods but from a contented mind."* [131]

We were rich with pristine waters; clean air; good soil enriched by organic nutrients; unadulterated food; a mostly vegetarian diet to sustain healthy living; and an active lifestyle that did not involve the car.

"Rich living" does not mean materially-endowed lives—as many of us now appreciate. We now realize the value of forest bathing, known in Japanese as *"Shinrin-Yoku."* We now know that plants release phytoncides that have significant h ealth b enefits fo r those who walk or spend time in forests, once again demonstrating how intimately we are connected to nature. Evidence-based scientific studies conducted to produce "before" and "after" measurements of forest bathing showed a significant reduction in pulse rate and in the scores for depression, fatigue, anxiety, and confusion; and a marked increase in the score for vigor. Those who engaged in forest bathing also had a marked decrease in the levels of the stress hormone cortisol with an increase in "happy hormones" and immune cells.[132] We now also have a better understanding of the benefits of drinking pure water, of eating organic foods (unadulterated by pesticides and

130 https://abuaminaelias.com/dailyhadithonline/2011/05/21/valley-gold-still-wants-more/.

131 https://sunnah.com/muslim/12/157

132 http://time.com/5259602/japanese-forest-bathing/; https://www.ncbi.nlm.nih.gov/pubmed/27493670; Qing Li, *Forest Bathing: How Trees Can Help You Find Health and Happiness* (New York: Viking, 2018)

hormones), of eating more vegetables to sustain a healthy gut, and of walking and daily exercise.

We are trying to circle back, but even as we make the attempt, our minds are bombarded with images on screens to forever make us discontent. We need to accept that not all of us will have what others may have (though nobody will have all that they desire): maybe a melodious voice; maybe a strong physique; skin that looks young and hair that is thick and shining; or that cheerful positive attitude to life we occasionally witness someone experiencing (who may well have little in terms of material wealth). *No one wins all the gold medals at the Olympic Games.*

Again, Prophet Mohammed provides a prescription for this pervasive discontent. If we see someone possessing greater wealth or beauty, we should consider those who have fewer of those attributes we might desire.[133]

We need to learn to be grateful for the things we have, and put aside envy of those who have more. Contentment and true wealth lie in the contentment of the heart. You and I probably have many things others do not have: eyes that can still see; ears that can still detect sound; legs that have not been amputated.

We are "naturally" rich, but due to discontent and the clamor for more, we are increasingly becoming emotionally poor and dissatisfied wrecks: humanity unhappy with itself. Dissatisfaction appears to be clinging to us like huge hungry leeches that drain us of the wholesome blood of contentment. Many seem or are made to think that the solution is to ravage the Earth and quickly extract its entire lifeblood which was meant to sustain us for millions of years.

Our politicians say they are here to serve us. "Water, is it? And so, they shall have it," pointing to fluorescent greenish-blue waters with the last bloated fish floating upside down in the toxic mixture. "There, your grandchildren can quench their thirst from

---

133 https://sunnah.com/muslim/55/12

that water there. Who said we steal waters from the mouth of babies?" They are busy appeasing the masses for votes, and then the masses are voting to keep them in. *As if the politicians have the power to wave magic wands on our behalf that will reverse all the damage done to the environment, wands that can force nature to keep providing, for greed, forever.*

If one is already standing in green paradise, and a blind politician is pointing at the desert, promising, *"greener grass up ahead,"* does one have to close one's eyes to mimic the politician and rush headlong? You would think the answer to any sane mind would be obvious.

**You would be wrong.**


## The Earth

If the Earth could speak, it would still try to reason, "You extract drops of dirty oil from Tar Sands in Utah and Alberta—literally the most damaging industrial practice to the environment, ever—while polluting fresh water, good land, and clean air on a massive scale. The oil will be burnt, the good land and pristine waters will be lost, and more pollutants will spew into the air. You are creating an inhabitable desert."

"What? What desert? If that is true, it's still a bit far," you would hear the nonchalant quip, ignoring the symbolism, looking at the toxic pond with toxic spillage from industrial waste: a wet desert.

The Earth persists, for the sake of its inhabitants, "You cut down large swathes of old forests in the Amazon, Congo, and Indonesia. You want palm oil, hardwood furniture, and ultra-soft tissue paper to wipe what you must wipe. You want plastics galore. You know this type of extravagant and ultra-soft lifestyle is unsustainable. You need to think of sustainable and renewable resources."

"We are not worried. We do not need to increase investment in renewable sources of energy at the moment. We can wait a bit more, can't we? Oil is much cheaper and more convenient," the nonchalant person states, and then, as an afterthought, he poses a brilliant question. "Is there some source of air or water that comes from space, or is the air or water we have, finite?"

The Earth ignores the question, for the answer should have been obvious. "The UN predicts that one million species will become extinct within a few decades.[134] Do you really have time to think about all this before you make drastic changes in the way you live?"

A few decades pass.

The nonchalant person is no longer shrugging his shoulders when he hears of environmental disasters that are spreading and approaching ever closer. Politicians have gone into hiding. The aftermath of nuclear disaster has made the air toxic. He thinks back to when he used to say politicians were smart enough not to engage in nuclear war and that deterrence by amassing more weapons was enough. He should never have trusted them. There is universal food shortage. Most low-lying cities are under water. There are many forest fires and the air thick with smoke. Disease is widespread. Civilization, as he knew it, is convulsing in the throes of death in the aftermath of carnage. All this because he was too busy mocking.

He was busy mocking environmentalists because he thought they were merely alarmists who had too much time on their hands. For too long he thought these were temporary nightmares one always wakes up from, back to reality, back to a pristine, green, wholesome environment. Havoc happened elsewhere. This other reality of devastation has been the true new reality for years now, but it happened in other places, though it had been getting closer. Today,

---

134 https://www.cnn.com/2019/05/06/world/one-million-species-threatened-extinction-humans-scn-intl/index.html; https://www.washingtonpost.com/climate-environment/2019/05/06/one-million-species-face-extinction-un-panel-says-humans-will-suffer-result/?noredirect=on&utm_term=.6d1e49950978

some kind of an ominous feeling is in the air, and he tries to put a finger to what must be bringing it on.

Then he looks through the window and sees them approaching in the smoky haze. *His eyes open wide, his stomach cramps into a tight knot, there is an ominous shrill sound in his head, and he can hear his heart pounding, making dull thuds in his ears.* Anarchy. Starving mobs with pitchforks, machetes, and guns are pillaging the neighborhood. A month ago, it was a nearby village. They wiped the whole village out. There is a scream next door.

He has not yet heard the Earth speak, for the Earth has been quiet for some time, having been unable to change the behavior of humans. Even through the dull thuds of his heart, he is able to hear the ravaged Earth speak clearly. The Earth speaks for the last time, before it permanently stops engaging the human species in conversation.

Earth: "*Sorry, can't go back to what life used to be. The damage is irretrievable. The waters are toxic. The air you breathe is toxic. Ecosystems cannot be revived because there are toxins everywhere. Millions of species are extinct. Didn't you realize that extinction is permanent? You left all that was good, wholesome, healthy, and with ecosystems working in amazing harmony, to get here. Without food, water, and the ability to breathe, did you not think anarchy and chaos would result? Now, please enjoy what your collective hands have wrought.*"

Is there any good news in all this? Yes, fortunately, there is, if we take stock quickly enough. Sad though the state of affairs, we are optimists. We have to be. Despair is not going to overwhelm us. Despair would breed apathy, making it hard to take a step forward. We can start by using the human intellect to drastically alter our wasteful lifestyles, stop and *even reverse* the damage being inflicted on ourselves, the animals who inhabit this planet, and the environment.

How can one sum up—in one short sentence—our absolute optimism and obligation to do our utmost to care for this Earth—to never lose hope—even though things may look so bleak, so overwhelming, and *so calamitous?*

A profound sentence—*one sentence*—that sums it all up? A twenty-first-century-type statement, now that we have finally woken up and realized that we are part and parcel of the circle of life—plants, earth, air, water, animals, ourselves—the whole caboodle?

How about, *"If the Final Hour [Doomsday] comes while you have a palm-cutting in your hands and it is possible to plant it before the Hour comes, you should plant it."* That about sums it up, with astonishing clarity: our unfailing duty and our optimism for our Earth. It is a startling message.

You know who said that? It was said 1,400 years ago by an orphan from the desert. *His name was Prophet Mohammed. He was an **environmentalist par excellence, a human and animal rights activist.** And he would have ensured that your rights are protected too, no matter the faith, in any such event that those rights are being trampled or ignored. In times of starvation or deprivation, he would have starved and given the little _he_ had so that you could eat and sustain your life.* Read his life history.

Then you will  truly know.

And then you will ask yourself and those around you: what is there not to love about this great man?

# A note from the author:

Dear Reader,

It is not a mere cliche, oft-repeated: God loves you. It is absolutely true, as true as you looking at this note at this very moment. He wants heaven for you.

God benefits naught by putting people in hell. But complete justice _must_ be established, and those upon whom we did wrong _must_ be compensated.

Since God desires to forgive all our sins, we need to make amends before its too late. The Merciful Lord has given us so much from His bounties. He restricts a few things to test our faith. He often gives us respite so that we can correct our course.

The end has to come though, death is guaranteed, and it **will** come, and we better be prepared for final judgment. I sincerely hope you and I are forgiven for many of our failings on that tremendous day.

**I have a favor to ask you: Would you be so kind as to leave this book a good _review?_** It will take a minute and it will be tremendously appreciated. **Thanks so much.**

Please visit **www.aseedlingofhope.com** for more information, constructive comments, or if you have questions of a positive nature for which I promise to answer. There is information there that is truly and absolutely stunning and exciting! And there is a _freebie_ ebook there for your next enjoyment!

# INDEX

Printed in Great Britain
by Amazon